P9-DBM-231

All the Way from Yoakum

All the Way from Yoakum

The Personal Journey of a Political Insider

MARJORIE MEYER ARSHT

TEXAS A&M UNIVERSITY PRESS COLLEGE STATION

To my children, my grandchildren, and my great-grandchildren

First edition

The paper used in this book
meets the minimum requirements
of the American National Standard for Permanence
of Paper for Printed Library Materials, Z39.48-1984.
Binding materials have been chosen for durability.

LIBRARY OF CONGRESS CATALOGING-IN-PUBLICATION DATA

Arsht, Marjorie Meyer, 1914–
All the way from Yoakum : the personal journey of a political insider / Marjorie Meyer Arsht.
p. cm.
Includes index.
ISBN 1-58544-476-6 (cloth : alk. paper)
1. Arsht, Marjorie Meyer, 1914– 2. Politicians—Texas—Biography. 3. Jewish women—Texas—Biography. 4. Republican Party (Tex.)—Biography. 5. Texas—Politics and government—1951– 6. Yoakum (Tex.)—Biography. I. Title.
F391.4.A77A3 2006
976.4'063'092—dc22 2005014262

All photographs are from the author's personal collection.

Contents

Illustrations

Preface

One day in 1996, I watched my little great-granddaughters playing educational games, their heads bent over a computer. They lived in California at Vandenburg Air Force Base, where their father, my grandson Jim, was stationed. I suddenly realized they would never know what it was like to grow up in Yoakum, Texas, in the early part of the twentieth century. I had an immediate urge to tell them what life was like without television, without air-conditioning, without computers, and with only books and self-generated activities for diversion. And that there was a time in the South when no one had ever seen a live Republican. I wanted to tell them what I knew about their ancestors, realizing there were so many things I wish I had asked my own grandmothers. And so I began this venture.

Along the way, it evolved, of course, into a chronicle of broader scope. It became the story of my life through the most eventful portion of the twentieth century—from 1914 through the turn of the millennium. As a result, it also became the story of a Jewish family in Texas during this time of radical transition, when the state grew from a predominantly rural landscape of small towns and small cities into the present dynamic, idiosyncratically urban environment it is today.

Throughout this period of societal change, I lived both a private and a public life. I raised a family, embroiling myself in the myriad of domestic details that were common to wives and mothers of my generation. I reacted to familial disputes, struggling for independence in a dominant family of prominent Jewish Houstonians; I strove to withstand the mercurial moods and sometimes disastrous whimsies of a mother I now understand to have been mentally ill; I survived the premature loss of a beloved daughter and two grandchildren to a rare and terrible illness; I coped with the career swings of my charming and handsome husband, as he carved out his place in the Texas oil business of the midcentury. And, late in life, I was obliged to be involved in unpleasant and contentious legal proceedings over family property.

In the midst of it all, I involved myself intensely in the affairs of my community and my country, speaking out nationally against political Zionism, working tirelessly on many levels for the fledgling Texas Republican Party through the exhilarating years when John Tower won his Senate seat and former president George H. W. Bush chaired the Harris County Republican Party and then served in Congress. I even sought public office myself, the first Jewish Republican woman to do so in Texas. Later, at the age of seventy, I witnessed firsthand the workings—and occasional abuses—of the Washington, D.C. bureaucracy from my post as an assistant in the Department of Housing and Urban Development. After ninety years, I look back on this life that has now extended into the twenty-first century, and I hope I have conveyed the sometimes heartbreaking, sometimes joyful, but always fascinating journey it has been.

A word about my approach: I have used literary license in re-creating conversations in order to describe certain situations properly. There may be some errors in dates, times, or names, for which I apologize in advance, but I have made an honest effort to describe events and characters, acknowledging that this account reflects only my point of view. Witnesses to the same scene often differ in their observations. I have changed names in only a few cases, where subject matter might be uncomfortable for the living.

All the Way from Yoakum

Chapter 1

Yoakum

On March 31, 1913, my father, Marcell Achille Meyer, thirty-two, married my mother, Myrtle Levy, in Lake Charles, Louisiana. She was twenty.

Born in Galveston, Texas, my father managed the Woodring logging camp in Sweetville, Louisiana, ten miles from Lake Charles. Sweetville was hardly a town at all, just a few buildings housing the workers and a country store. My father traveled to town on horseback and then engaged a carriage and a matched pair of prancing stallions to court the young ladies of the town. A young man with light eyes and chiseled features, he was much in demand.

My mother, with an eighteen-inch waist and ample bosom, had large dark eyes and black hair. Being the daughter of a leading merchant in Lake Charles and the niece of the celebrated couturier Henri Bendel of New York enhanced her desirability as a prospective wife, especially to a young man like my father, whose only assets were his intelligence and good looks.

According to the custom of that day, Daddy courted Mama the required nine months before asking her to marry him. Her unequivocal response was, "I will not live in or near that logging camp."

"I'll talk to Mr. Woodring," my father replied. "He has some retail lumber outlets in Texas."

Mr. Woodring accommodated them. His largest Texas lumberyard was situated in Yoakum. The trip from Lake Charles to Yoakum was their honeymoon.

In 1913, Yoakum was a busy little town where the Southern Pacific Railroad had located its repair shops. It also functioned as the center of a cotton- and corn-farming community with a population that included many German and Czech (we called them Bohemian) immigrants. Farmers came into town on Saturday to do their shopping for the week. On Sunday, abiding by the Texas blue laws, all of the stores closed, and the populace, dressed in their Sunday best, went to church. Such a rough-edged South Texas country town came as something of a shock to my mother, who was accustomed to the relaxed, genteel atmosphere of southern Louisiana. After a brief sojourn in Yoakum's St. Regis Hotel, my mother and father moved into a small white cottage on Coke Street, where, according to the custom of delivering babies at home, Dr. Thomas James brought me into this world.

My birth certificate read: "Female, born to Myrtle and Marcell Meyer in Yoakum, Texas, November 1, 1914." And it stayed that way until 1933, when I was eighteen years old and needed a name for a passport.

Yoakum today remains much as it was when my parents arrived, an unpretentious little South Texas town, located thirty-five miles south of Interstate 10 between Houston and San Antonio. Over the last half-century, the population of approximately four thousand souls has remained relatively constant. The town reflects the same measured pace of living it enjoyed throughout its past.

No Jewish house of worship has ever existed there, and only two or three Jewish families ever lived in Yoakum at one time. On the holy days of Yom Kippur and Rosh Hashanah, my father took me to Houston or San Antonio, alternating between Reform temples and orthodox synagogues. The tradition of both my parents' families, however, was distinctly Reform. When Reform Judaism was transplanted from Germany to the United States under the leadership of Isaac Mayer Wise, many of the old traditions, such as dietary laws and ritualistic circumcision, were no longer considered mandatory. Those customs, originally based on health and cleanliness considerations at a time when there was no refrigeration or medical practice as we now understand it, seemed irrelevant in the New World.

My mother rarely went with us to holy day services. Unlike my father, who had received an in-depth Jewish religious education under the tutelage of the famous Rabbi Henry Cohen of Galveston, my mother had attended a Catholic school in Lake Charles. Her parents simply considered it the area's best school. As a result, however, her understanding of Judaism and its customs was limited to the use of occasional expressions she thought were "Jewish." I always imagined these expressions were Yiddish until my mother-in-law said she'd never heard of some of them, words like "lahockalus," meaning "just to make trouble."

My mother's mother, Grandmother Lena Bendel Levy, shared this less-than-traditional practice of the religion. Born in Lafayette, Louisiana, she confined her observance of Jewish ritual to refraining from handiwork on Saturday. And she knew how to make gefilte fish. That was about it.

When I was three years old, Daddy felt it was time to move from the little house on Coke Street to a larger house, which he proceeded to build across town on Grand Avenue. Though a smart man in many ways, my father always guessed wrong in real estate. He thought Yoakum would grow to the west. It didn't. In fact, it didn't grow much at all.

Most houses of the time, including ours, had a sleeping porch whose wall of screened windows was designed to capture the southeasterly breezes drifting inland from the Gulf of Mexico. Electric fans provided the only air-conditioning. Our sleeping porch served as my parents' bedroom, with "his-and-her" closets, even then. We had no central heat, just a pot-bellied wood stove in the middle of the porch, around which everyone dressed on cold mornings during the short period we called winter. A fireplace anchored one wall of the living room, but I don't remember a fire burning in it. No one used the front entrance, although it was never locked. Everyone, including guests, entered through the kitchen door.

Most families in Yoakum then had "help," the custom in the South even for households of very modest means. At salaries of one or two dollars a week for six and a half day's labor from 7 A.M. until after supper, domestic help was affordable and considered as much a necessity as food and shelter. Almost every dwelling had servant's quarters. The term "servant" in that era was not considered derogatory. It's what the servants called themselves, a part of the language and the culture of that day.

In the cottage on Coke Street, Mama had managed with one servant, but when we moved to the larger house on Grand Avenue she needed more, and not just because the house was larger. She had frequent severe headaches and what she called "nervous spells." In retrospect, they must have been bouts of depression. I was too young then to realize that these episodes would constitute a serious lifelong condition. I was certainly unaware of the effect that condition would have upon my own life. Frequent indisposition caused her to spend a great deal of time reclining on the rattan lounge on her sleeping porch with cold compresses on her forehead. Her lethargy required constant service, and she demanded perfection. She wrote her mother: "I just cannot find any decent help. Could you locate some Louisiana girls who would come to Yoakum?" In due course, two black teenaged sisters, whom I knew only as Aggie and Oley, agreed to come to Yoakum from Louisiana if they could learn to read and write. Aggie and Oley lived in a room with a bath above the garage behind our house. Aggie was the cook, and Oley my nurse. Where Oley went, I went.

Mama employed thirteen-year-old Mildred Smolka, daughter of the janitor from Westside School, to come every afternoon after school to teach the girls their ABCs and how to add and subtract. When they had lessons, I sat at their feet on the floor, and I learned what they learned. After six months, Daddy said to my mother, "Myrtle, I have heard about a Mrs. Williford who teaches kindergarten. I think Marjorie is ready for school." Because she wasn't interested in "playtime," Mrs. Williford's kindergarten had no sandbox. She taught multiplication tables and didn't care a bit that I was only four years old or whether I understood what I memorized.

By the time I was five, Daddy called Mrs. Mollie Green, principal of Westside School, which was located directly across Grand Avenue from our house. Schoolchildren in those days began the first grade when they were seven years old, and six, if they paid tuition. "I know Marjorie is underage," Daddy said, "but she is ready for the first grade. Please give her a try." I lasted in the first grade only a few days. Mrs. Green called to say that I was disrupting the class by calling out the answers out of turn, so she was going to put me in the second grade. After a week, she called again.

"Mrs. Meyer, the second-grade teacher is beside herself. Marjorie is just so young she doesn't understand proper behavior. I think we will just have to wait a while."

Marjorie, age four, dressed by Uncle Henri Bendel.

My father didn't hesitate. "It may be unorthodox, but why don't you try her in the third grade, where she might be challenged?" And that is how I happened to enter the third grade when I was five years old.

My education continued along this unconventional path. There were no middle schools at that time. So, at eleven, after being named valedictorian of the elementary school, I progressed directly to Yoakum High School. Instead of the four-year, four-course high school program, however, I took five courses for three years and studied solid geometry and trigonometry in the two intervening summers. Yoakum's education had no frills. Electives meant home economics for girls and shop for boys. I had looked forward to taking the cooking and sewing class for high-school freshmen, but my father had other ideas. He called the superintendent, Mr. McGuffin, who was also the high school principal. "I don't want Marjorie wasting her time in that class," he said. "She can learn to cook and sew on some man's time. On my time she takes another year of Latin."

Even though he had never earned a single diploma, my father was the most educated man I ever knew. Somewhere along the way I deduced that he attempted to live through me the academic life he loved and had been unable to pursue because of his family's circumstances. He was a real intellectual without any formal certification. Mama, on the other hand, had a sophisticated education at Ward Belmont in Nashville and at a music conservatory in Washington, D.C., but she simply wasn't interested in the world of higher learning.

In addition to my formal schooling, my father insisted I learn something new every day. No novels were allowed except those assigned in school—just history books and biographies that he gave me to read after he had read them. To his delight, I graduated from Yoakum High School at fourteen as valedictorian in May of 1929. In the fall of that year, I entered Rice Institute, now Rice University, with sixteen solid credits and a secondhand typewriter.

During my childhood in Yoakum, our lives revolved around meals, and the kitchen was Mama's realm. All of the headaches, nervousness, and lassitude that plagued her during the fall and winter disappeared with the first hint of summer. She then presided over her domain with the authority of a commanding general. A superlative cook, Mama confined her efforts to creation, leaving the cleaning, peeling, chopping, and stirring to the help. I don't remember ever seeing Mama work from a recipe. She just poured in ingredients and tasted.

From June through August, smells of browning sugar and spices, lemons, and oranges wafted through the open windows. Everyone who came to our house walked under the grape arbor that led to our back door and inhaled the mouth-watering fragrances. The bunches of small, sour, hard green grapes that hung from the arbor's vine were not very good to eat uncooked, but they made the most delicious, tangy preserves.

On summer evenings when friends and neighbors gathered to share watermelon on our front lawn, Mama would carefully scrutinize each melon and save the thickest rinds for pickling. A servant would peel and cut them into one-inch squares. After soaking overnight in lime in an oval white enamelware tub to make them crisp, they were thoroughly washed. Then I would insert one whole clove into each square. I can still taste those luscious, spicy, sweet cubes in dark syrup that were so creamy and smooth on the outside and crisp as crushed ice on the inside.

By fall, the shelves of our walk-in pantry overflowed with pint-sized mason jars of that pickled watermelon rind; fig, green grape, and peach preserves; glasses of dewberry jelly and red plum jam; and homemade chowchow. Quart jars of dill pickles filled one whole shelf. Canned peaches, tomatoes, and green beans filled another. On the floor sat sturdy white crocks of sauerkraut and herring, pickling for the winter. During this process, the sauerkraut smelled like rotten eggs and old garbage, so no one dared uncover it. Mama always put a slice of bread on the lid when she cooked cabbage to absorb the odor, but nothing helped sauerkraut. Somehow, though, even without peeking, Mama always knew when her concoctions were done.

Daddy took enormous pride in Mama's culinary skills. Visitors were first taken to see Mama's pantry, and the best present my father could bestow on anyone was a jar or can from her larder. Daddy's diabetes prevented Mama from serving rich desserts except when we had company, but she made wonderful cakes, pies, and custards, which she delivered to the sick or to grieving households. One of her specialties was something she called her "1-2-3-4 cake." Since she never measured, she couldn't explain to my satisfaction which number applied to the eggs, sugar, butter, or flour. Memories of another special dish—a concoction of vanilla wafers and crushed pineapple held together by custard—still make my mouth water, although the correct proportion of ingredients also remains a mystery.

As a newly married cook, I once asked Mama how to prepare baked eggplant.

"Chop up some onions, celery, and green pepper . . ."

"How much of each?" I interrupted.

"Just use your judgment."

"*What* judgment?"

She became irritated. "If you have a big eggplant, you use *more!*"

In those days—the 1920s—the only succulent, tender beef came from Kansas, where farmers shipped their range cattle to fatten on corn, which tenderized them for the urban markets. The beef *we* had access to, however, was tough, so rare steaks or roasts were unknown. Instead, we enjoyed pot roasts, rump cuts that were cooked, as Mama used to say, "slow, slow, slow" for hours. Anything that looked even slightly pink was underdone and inedible.

We rarely ate seafood because we lived too far inland for anything other than canned, which Mama frowned on using, except for sardines. Therefore, day in and day out, we consumed a variety of foods—such as scrambled veal brains and eggs—the mention of which today makes my children cringe. We ate domestic pigeons and wild doves shot by hunters as well as lots of pork—fresh ham roasts and chops. No one had heard of cholesterol at that time, so, with no feeling of guilt, we enjoyed liver and onions, kidney stew, all kinds of smoked sausages and hams, and many fried dishes like chicken, potatoes, and green tomatoes.

In this environment, finicky eaters often encountered difficulties. My cousin Gina, for example, wouldn't touch anything she thought either had a personality or was related to some organ. Although she usually ate chicken, if she heard Mama tell the servant, "Go out and kill that big hen, the one with the purple feather," that finished it for Gina. Not a bite passed her lips. One Sunday, while Gina and her sister Pauline were visiting me, Mama brought in from the kitchen what I thought was a platter of fried chicken. Gina looked at it closely and surmised that something about the pieces seemed strange.

"Aunt Myrtle," she asked, "What's the matter with those chicken legs?"

Knowing Gina, Mama didn't want to tell her what the meat really was, so she said, "Oh, those chickens just broke their legs." That wasn't any better, however, than telling Gina that we were eating rabbit.

During the early part of the twenties, Mama's parents came to live with us. Grandmother Lena was a good cook, too, and on Sundays we always had turkey and rice dressing prepared with giblets. No other turkey has ever tasted like hers. Grandmother laid cheesecloth over the breast and basted the bird every fifteen minutes. This tactic allowed the turkey to brown without burning and kept the breast meat moist. She had a simple recipe. One cup of cold water, an apple, and lots and lots of butter. She never needed a thermometer or a pop-up button, but those turkeys were always perfectly cooked. Once in a while Grandmother prepared something special. Everyone who knew my grandmother adored her, so very often one of her admirers, returning from a trip to Houston or San Antonio, would bring her a huge white fish in a bucket filled with ice. She would steam it whole, extract all the bones, and create a marvelous amalgamation of breadcrumbs, seasonings, and the flesh of the fish, which she then stuffed into the empty fish skin. Finally, she baked what looked like the original whole fish. When it cooled, she sliced it crosswise into slabs. Stuffed fish. The true gefilte fish. The fish balls served nowadays with horseradish for Jewish families at Passover may be called gefilte fish, but they're not the real thing. It's not what we ate in Yoakum.

"Uncle Henri is coming!" Uncle Henri, my mother's uncle, had just announced a visit to Yoakum, and Mama was beside herself. Even though she seemed frantic most of the time, this was different—almost no one ever came to Yoakum in the twenties except for special occasions, like a death.

Uncle Henri Bendel, a famous New York couturier, was the most important person in my mother's family. All babies' names were first submitted to him for approval, and anyone getting married had to pay a prenuptial visit to him either in New York or Connecticut or Louisiana. His home on Long Island later became the Maritime Academy. Near Stamford, Connecticut, he owned an estate called Laurel Lake Lodge. The "lake" was only a pond, but the swans gliding on it were as elegant as the house. In Lafayette, Louisiana, his property is today a subdivision named Bendel Gardens.

Uncle Henri, who sported a tiny Charlie Chaplin moustache, was short, round, and slightly balding. If he hadn't been rich and famous, I don't suppose anyone would have noticed him. New Yorkers believed Henri Bendel to be a Frenchman, perhaps because of the spelling of his name and perhaps because he loved everything French.

His admiration for the French extended to providing ambulances for France during World War I, an act of generosity for which he was awarded the Croix de Guerre. No one seemed to know or remember that he was a Jew from Lafayette, Louisiana.

Uncle Henri was a generous man, extending gracious hospitality to all the brothers, sisters, nieces, and nephews who made regular pilgrimages to visit him. Naturally everyone received clothes for special occasions or at least material to make them. However, as is often the case, his generosity did not come entirely without strings. Although he himself remained a bachelor, it was important to him that all of the female members of the family be married. Whenever a niece seemed unable to find a husband, Uncle Henri generally made sure that eligible prospects learned that he usually gave his nieces a wedding present of five thousand dollars. That practice may not have always been followed, but there were no unwed nieces around.

Uncle Henri allegedly married when he was quite young—a woman who had a store that sold trimmings—and that is how he began his career as a renowned milliner. He is memorialized in the Broadway musical comedy *Anything Goes* with the phrase "You're a Bendel bonnet" in the Cole Porter song "You're the Tops," made famous by Ethel Merman. Everyone seemed vague about the existence of Uncle Henri's wife, saying only that she had died in childbirth. In any case, Uncle Henri wasn't lonely. Two tall, very handsome men about his age lived with him in his various residences. One or the other or both always traveled with him. I particularly liked Mr. Blish, but only Mr. Bastedo came with him on this visit to Yoakum.

Because the subject had never been mentioned, I became aware of Uncle Henri's homosexuality only when I reached adulthood. When I questioned my mother directly about this, she answered in a whisper that everyone had been so sad about it. I had never noticed any sadness, however. His companions were simply a part of our family. By the time I began to wonder how he managed his unconventional lifestyle that many years ago in the small conservative town of Lafayette, it was too late to ask. I suppose his wealth, fame, and generosity trumped any objection to his sexual preferences.

In preparation for Uncle Henri's arrival, our house bustled with excitement. We had scoured every corner. Our maid, Celia Benys, was on her knees for a week, and Oscar Washington, who also worked

Marjorie with some of her mother's aunts and uncles. Left to right: Isaac Bendel, Henri Bendel, Marjorie, Lena Bendel Levy, Louise Bendel Meyer, in Lafayette, Louisiana.

at the lumberyard, saw to it that every prism, properly cleaned in ammonia water, had been returned to its slot in the dining room chandelier, a present from Uncle Henri. And the cooking! We paid a great deal of attention to what Uncle Henri liked and didn't like. In typical Louisiana superlative, the fire under the roast had to be low, low, low, and the food had to be served hot, hot, hot. Because he was arriving at noon, Mama planned a feast—but then every meal of his day-and-a-half visit was a matter of grave concern.

Since no one had died, I never really knew why he came, but it was a memorable visit nevertheless. Just before he left, he said to Mama—and not in a stage whisper, either—"Myrtle, you have to do something about Marjorie. She is entirely too fat!" Humiliated, I cried the rest of that day.

In 1920, Mama sent a message to Miss Newsom, my third-grade teacher, inviting all twenty-five children in the class to my sixth birthday party. That day, my mother had everything arranged in the living and dining rooms, areas that under normal circumstances were never occupied. She had made a wonderful chocolate cake, and she used her second-best plates, silver, and glasses, which were reserved for such occasions or when someone beyond our immediate family came for dinner. This was the middle of three sets of china, silver, and linens, which anyone "of quality" in those days felt obliged to own, including one for very special company that was almost never used. Mama had even put out Grandmother Lena's crystal punch bowl, although she did substitute her second-best glasses for the delicate crystal cups that matched the bowl.

To her chagrin, only four children arrived—the ones from the surrounding farms—whom I didn't know very well and who had never been to my house before. Seated in chairs much too large for them, they were in an intimidating environment. Furnished with French tapestries, a richly hued Persian rug on the floor, and heavy brocade draperies at the windows, our living room must have appeared ominous. Moreover the children had nothing to do since Mama wasn't into games. They didn't stay long.

After they left, the ice cream melted, the pitcher remained full of punch, and the cake looked untouched. Mama fumed.

"And where were your best friends, Dessie and Cora?" Mama shrieked at me, her eyes flashing. Cora Hall was the daughter of Yoakum's only plumber, and Dessie Finch, the daughter of the town's barber. The three of us were virtually inseparable. Cora, a wiry, funny, happy-go-lucky little girl, and Dessie, with her sweet oval face, were excellent students. I was younger than they but in their grade. They never came inside the house much, so we played outdoors or in the schoolyard across the street. On rare occasions I went to their houses.

"I don't know," I replied. "I think Cora had a fever."

"Well, let me tell you, young lady, you aren't going to play with them any more. I don't want them here, and you can't go to their houses."

I started crying. "Dessie is having a party next Saturday."

"Well, you can't go. And that's final. There's such a thing as *principle!*"

I discovered later that most of the children hadn't come because they didn't think they had the right clothes to wear. Actually, I think they were scared of Mama. So, even though I didn't quite understand Mama's definition of "principle," I learned an important lesson on that sixth birthday.

Three years later, I heard that the Coke Street girls, the ones who attended East Side School and lived on the east side of Yoakum—the "better" side—were forming a Forty-two Club. They had decided that a certain invited group would meet every Saturday afternoon at someone's house to play Forty-Two, a domino game that could be played indoors and was usually saved for rainy days or something very special. A few girls at Westside had been invited to join, but I learned that I had been blackballed. I felt terribly hurt. Somewhere down deep, however, the lessons of that birthday party kept me from telling Mama. I remembered her idea of "principle," and even at nine years of age, I thought those girls might ask me some other time to join, but if Mama knew I had been blackballed, she wouldn't let me accept. The next year they did just that, and Mama beamed with pride.

Such restraint on my part seemed at the time to be the "better part of valor." The flip side of that coin, however, was that Mama came to think I never had any problems or heartaches. Even when those difficulties couldn't be hidden, Mama felt sanguine about them. She often said, "Marjorie is strong and tough. She'll be all right."Though she was correct, I paid a high price.

At the time I never had any hint that the blackballing episode might have occurred because I was a Jew. Although I always knew I was Jewish, I thought of it as simply another religion like being a Methodist, Baptist, Lutheran, Catholic, or Presbyterian, which all my friends were. Such considerations never interfered with growing up in that overwhelmingly Christian town. In fact, the only time I can remember the subject coming up was around this same period, when I was in the third or fourth grade.

With the entrance facing the wrong direction, Westside School occupied the center of a square block. The front steps of the school led to an open field. What population growth there was in Yoakum developed in back of the school, where we lived. The PTA mothers decided a sidewalk leading to the back entrance needed to be built so that, on rainy days, the children didn't have to walk all the way around the block to go in. My father contributed the cement for the walkway. One day I overheard a boy declare, "They're building that sidewalk so the little Jew girl won't get her feet muddy," whereupon the principal—who had overheard it, too—took him into the cloakroom and spanked him hard. This was a widespread practice in schools in those days and remained so until years later, when it was outlawed.

For a couple of reasons, I think it was possible for me to remain largely unaware then of prejudice against Jews. One is that our practice of Reform Judaism did not appear markedly different from the variations of religious practice common to Christian denominations. The other is that I often went to church services with my friends. If I were spending the night at someone's house on Saturday night, I would go to church with her and her family on Sunday morning. I frequently accompanied my friend Nina Vance, a Presbyterian, to her Wednesday night prayer meeting. (Later Nina founded and for many years directed Houston's distinguished Alley Theater.) Also, while in high school, I went to the Catholic convent for music and French lessons, often attending a Catholic mass. This diversity of religious experiences helped me develop the tolerance necessary to understand that the basis for all religions is essentially the same.

"Guess what? After all these years, I'm pregnant!" Mama, thirty-two years old, sat on the cedar chest in the butler's pantry, her back to the wall, holding the stem of the telephone in one hand and the receiver in the other. Standing in the kitchen, I heard her voice, uncharacteristically lilting and joyful, giving Lucille Alexander all of the details. Lucille, a plain-looking, middle-aged woman who lived on Coke Street, was Mama's best friend at the time. I peeked around the corner. Dressed in a yellow wool dress, Mama looked really beautiful. Her big brown eyes were sparkling, and her jet-black hair, drawn over her ears into a bun at her neck, framed her fair-skinned face. I had come home from school for lunch and couldn't wait to get back to class to tell Cora and Dessie.

That February day in 1924, when I was nine years old, I was so excited at the news that it didn't occur to me to wonder why Mama was telling someone else about such an important event before she told me. Every night afterward I sat on the back porch steps, looking at the sky and religiously reciting:

Star light, star bright,
I wish I may, I wish I might,
Have the wish I wish tonight.
Please give me a little sister.

Mama was sick all the time at first, and Daddy hovered over her constantly, as did Grandmother Lena. No one explained anything to me. I didn't know that nausea was a normal manifestation of pregnancy, so privately I worried a lot. By June, however, Mama felt better, and her stomach got larger and larger. It was layette time, and I was an excited participant in the preparations. Oh, how I wanted that little sister!

The only things bought for babies in those days were knit undershirts and Bird's-Eye diapers by the dozens. Everything else was handmade, and everything had to be ironed. After a while, Mama let me cut out all of the little dresses. She had never done that kind of sewing before. For me, however, making the baby clothes seemed like fashioning doll clothes. I liked figuring out the patterns and sewing the pieces together. After learning how to use the sewing machine, I would stitch the side seams while Mama sewed the laborious rows and rows of tiny tucks by hand. Grandmother was busy knitting blankets and crocheting booties. She also embroidered rosebuds with adorable French knots on some of the little dresses. It never occurred to anyone that the baby might be a boy.

It was summertime, and I was out of school, so I had a lot of free time. And I prayed, *Oh, God, please give me a baby sister!* By the end of that summer of 1924, Mama was miserable and spent most of her time trying to get comfortable on the rattan lounge. The baby things—the little dresses made of fine lawn, the nightgowns of printed flannel—were all ready, washed, ironed, and carefully folded. Mama stored them in tissue paper in the front bedroom closet.

On October 7, 1924, Elène was born. We pronounced it improperly, as though it were spelled "Elaine." Uncle Henri had named her for Grandmother Lena. As I mentioned earlier, he considered it his prerogative to name the babies in the family, so everyone accepted his decision.

Before noon on the day Elène was born, Mrs. Green, the principal, left her office at Westside and came to my sixth-grade class to get me. "Marjorie, your father is coming to take you to see your new little sister!" I was beside myself with excitement. It was three weeks before my tenth birthday.

Daddy had bought a large hunter-green Buick sedan, called a Brougham, which had small, fixed, glass ovals called "opera windows" located to the rear of the usual side windows. It was to be a surprise for Mama, and he was so proud. I myself thought it the most gorgeous car I had ever seen. When we got to the hospital, Daddy drove it onto the hospital grounds under the window so Mama could see it. He couldn't wait to tell her to look out the window. When she did, she asked, "Do those little windows in the back open?"

"No, they're just for visibility and decoration. Aren't they pretty?"

Mama turned away from the window. "That car will be too hot. Take it back."

Elène was a cuddly and truly beautiful baby with enormous dark eyes like Mama's and a mop of dark, curly hair. She wasn't chubby like I had been. Inasmuch as Mama was in her thirties and Daddy in his forties, she was like a toy in the house, and I couldn't wait to come home and play with her after school. But she had trouble falling asleep at night, so every evening after supper, we took a ride to lull her to sleep. And every night Mama and Daddy had a dreadful argument on the same subject.

"This is a terrible car. There is no excuse for a car to have windows that don't open."

"Goddamn it, Myrtle. I'm sick of your complaining! We're going to keep the car, and that's that! I'm tired of hearing about the damned windows. So shut up about it!"

Every night.

"Why did she kill herself?"

"Because she was going to have a baby," I whispered.

"She couldn't have a baby! She wasn't married!" My cousin Pauline's indignant voice carried across the half-empty movie theater, evoking widespread titters from the audience.

In 1923, my Houston cousins, Pauline and her sister, Gina, were visiting Yoakum as they did each summer for three weeks. Gina, thirty days older than me, was a beauty with long auburn hair, a sharp contrast to fat and freckled me. Pauline, eleven, with dark brown hair and large brown eyes, looked the way she was—sweet and nice and good. Every single day Pauline practiced the piano for a whole hour in our unbearably hot parlor. Every day she also wrote her mother and father, and each night before going to bed, she brushed her hair fifty times. She was terribly homesick.

In contrast to conscientious Pauline, Gina and I were mischievous. We often conspired to ensure that Pauline lost whatever game we played. Our chief pastime, however, was going to the picture show, proudly called the Grand Theater. It changed films three times a week, with a different matinee on Wednesday, plus a serial that preceded the main presentation. That year, the Wednesday serial featured *The Perils of Pauline,* starring Pearl White, who, at the end of each week's episode, found herself falling off a cliff, being dragged by a horse, or facing the business of a gun held by an outlaw. *The Broken Commandment,* starring Milton Sills and Doris Kenyon, prominent actors of that era, followed the serial. It was a scene from this movie that precipitated Pauline's outburst.

When the movie was over, we came home to our front-yard gazebo, where honeysuckle vines grew up the latticework sides. On two small benches that faced each other, we sat in relative privacy, still discussing the plot and its mystery. Pauline insisted that I had to be mistaken about the baby. The girl must have committed suicide for some other reason, she believed. I don't know where my knowledge came from except that my curiosity made me ask questions of older children. In those days, at least in my family, no adults ever discussed "s-e-x" with children.

The closest Mama ever came to approaching the subject of the human body was to give me a book, when I was about ten, called *Know Thyself.* Customarily, mothers gave their daughters such a book to read before they reached maturity. I am positive that the one Mama gave me was out of date, even in the 1920s, because the illustrations portrayed women with huge pompadours and wearing bustles. Although I read every word, I thought the pictures were silly. As far as I can remember, it explained everything *except* how babies are created.

That summer afternoon in 1923, when I tried to explain the facts of life to my two city cousins, Gina was all ears, not doubting me at all, but Pauline was furious. Drawing herself up to her full height, she exclaimed, "My mother and father would never do anything like that!" Nevertheless, she must have eventually come to terms with my explanation, for years later she had three children of her own.

Even for adults in the twenties, sex was a very different matter from what it is today. One evening I looked up from my homework and noticed that the door to Mama and Daddy's room was shut. Without any shame I put my ear to it and heard Daddy say, "It wouldn't have happened if that woman had stayed home where she belonged with her children instead of spending her days in the meat market." I couldn't imagine what they were discussing, but "meat market" meant the Womack family. Their daughter, Christina, a bit younger than I, had just started high school. She had a face full of freckles to match her red hair. Thinking about Christina, I suddenly realized that she had recently gained a lot of weight. I wondered, *could it be*? Indeed, so.

The next day, the school buzzed with the news that Christina Womack had given birth to a mulatto baby, and her parents hadn't even known she was pregnant. When she developed a bad stomach ache, the Womacks called the doctor, who promptly delivered a small, brown-skinned baby boy. Christina was thirteen years old. Several weeks later, a black man who worked for the Womacks was found dead in a creek bottom. In 1920s' Texas, no one investigated the death.

The Womacks, however, were straightlaced, deeply religious people who believed that people should pay for their sins. They kept that mulatto baby and Christina on their farm. When it was time for the child to enter first grade, the Womacks brought him to Westside, whereupon all the parents boycotted the school, and the poor child had to be withdrawn. Although such cases may still draw wrath and scorn in small towns, it is hard for those who grow up in urban environments to imagine that kind of cruelty and prejudice.

There were other examples both then and later. Although I didn't know about it at the time—such things weren't discussed with children—the Sullivan case was recounted in whispers. Ken Sullivan, one of Daddy's best friends, was a handsome man, tall and sinewy. He had the look of the successful rancher that he was. His wife, Molly, was a true beauty. A lithe, graceful woman, she had borne four children with no damage to her figure.

Ken was gone a lot while Molly stayed with the children. When he came home one evening without notice, he surprised Dr. Thomas James, the town's general practitioner, in flagrante delicto. Dr. James, stark naked, jumped out a window and ran for his life. Even though the culprit had fled, Ken didn't stop looking for him. When he heard that the physician was in Houston and staying at the Rice Hotel, he went there to investigate. Told by the desk clerk that there was indeed a James registered and given his room number, Ken knocked on the door and shot the man before even identifying him. It turned out to be the wrong James.

In 1920s' Texas, this was called an accidental death. For fifteen thousand dollars—a fortune in those days—paid to the widow of the unfortunate James, there wasn't even a trial. It was rumored that Yoakum's Thomas James had gone to Alaska, then a remote wilderness. No one in South Texas ever saw him again.

During high school, I was by far the youngest member of my class, and I spent the majority of my free time with friends like Nina Vance and Kathrine Browning (later Stokes), who were my age but two grades behind me. My best friend in my own class was May Miller (later Douthit), a very devout Methodist. I often went with her to church on Sunday, and afterward, in the afternoon, the Millers had a regular social for the boys and girls in May's class. This provided a primary opportunity for young people to get together.

It was at a class party, however, that I had what I think of as my first date because we agreed to meet there. The young man's name was Bergin Dunn, the son of the Methodist minister and one of my classmates. My father took me to the party and picked me up afterward. I was thirteen.

At that time in Yoakum, there were no Girl Scout troops, ballet lessons, or soccer teams. Our entertainment was fairly simple; our diversions, self-generated. We read, exchanged, and discussed books. Most of our fun centered around movies. Every Wednesday on my way home from high school, my friends and I stopped at the Grand Theater to see the week's installment of the *Perils of Pauline,* the same long-running serial that my cousins and I had watched so zealously a year or two earlier. We knew perfectly well that Pauline wasn't going to die falling off a cliff or taking a blast from a shotgun or suffocating while trapped in a burning building with no apparent exit. Nonetheless, we simply couldn't wait to find out how she would extricate herself from last week's dire situation. Our discussions were just as serious as those that followed the season-ending episode of the renowned 1980s' television drama *Dallas,* the one that posed the question "Who shot J. R.?"

One Wednesday, walking home after the movie and musing over the latest calamity to befall Pauline, I was startled out of my reverie by screeching tires. There was Mama in our old Buick Brougham, her eyes blazing, her mouth distorted as she yelled, "*Where* have you *been?"* It wasn't really a question, but she wanted an answer. On any day but Wednesday I was home promptly at three thirty in the afternoon. It was now almost six o'clock.

"I went to the picture show. Don't you remember? You gave me a nickel at lunch."

Even though she had forgotten and I hadn't misbehaved, her fury didn't dissipate. "Just get in!" she barked.

I slunk down in the corner of the front seat as far away from her as I could get. Somehow she made me feel guilty even when I was blameless. The phrases "I'm sorry" or "It was my fault" or "I apologize" or even "I forgot" never passed Mama's lips. Even "excuse me" came out as a threat. Accepting apologies was difficult enough for her; offering them was out of the question, even if it was simply because she had forgotten it was Wednesday.

This characteristic also caused her trouble with friends from time to time. Many years after my father's death, when Mama was living in Houston, she entertained frequently. She was still a good cook and plied her skill, if not with ease, at least with diligence. Several weeks after having hosted a large luncheon in her apartment, she called me, gasping, as she always did when she was furious. I held my breath and wondered, *what have I done now?* I didn't have to wait long.

"Marjorie, you won't believe it, but Irene Wolf is giving a huge party at the country club, and she didn't *invite* me!" Her breath was coming in short bursts. She seemed almost out of control.

I sighed a sigh of relief. At least someone else was the current culprit. Mama and Irene had gone to school together as girls and had recently traveled to Europe together. Although they returned not speaking to each other, they were now friends once again. It was typical of Mama that, as soon as she vented her wrath from an indignity, imagined or real, she immediately forgot the whole thing. Everyone else went along, glad for peace. While she was spewing out vilifications of Irene Wolf, I was thinking. "Mama," I said, "I don't remember seeing Irene at the luncheon you gave a few weeks ago. Did you forget to invite *her?*"

There was a pause. "Well, you know, now I'm glad I *didn't* ask her!"

During my senior year, 1928–1929, some of us—especially a classmate, Otis Scruggs, and I—were deeply involved in the presidential campaign between Al Smith and Herbert Hoover. No problem guessing who we were for. No one then living in Yoakum would have supported Hoover. That would have been a call for a justifiable tarring and feathering, which atrocity still took place, however rarely. Despite the difference in party affiliation—at that time there were no Republicans in Texas—I can see that involvement now as a forecast of things to come.

Chapter 2

Rice, the Sorbonne, and New York

September of 1929. On my first day at Rice Institute, as Rice University was then called, I was fourteen years old and newly arrived from Yoakum. I was scared to death.

"Want me to go in with you?" Mama asked from behind the wheel, fingering her marketing list.

"No. I'll call when registration is over."

Dressed in my best dark printed dress, with its snug waist and accordion-pleated skirt, I wondered briefly whether I were underdressed without a hat and gloves. As Mama drove away, I walked toward the impressive arch of what I assumed was the main building, hearing my high heels crunch as they sank into the gravel driveway. Not a soul was in sight. My heart beat a mile a minute. What if I wasn't in the right place? I passed under the arch and, with a sigh of relief, saw a sign on the left walkway that read "Registration," with an arrow pointing to a few steps leading up to a locked door, so I just stood there looking around. At least I wasn't lost.

I knew the names of the buildings from a map in the catalogue. Besides Lovett Hall, where I stood, there were only a few structures—the biology building, the chemistry building, a dormitory for boys, and Cohen House, which looked like a home. Uncle George and Aunt Esther Cohen, my father's sister, together with Uncle George's sister, Gladys, had given Cohen House to Rice Institute in honor of their mother and father, Agnes and Robert I. Cohen of Galveston. It still serves as the faculty club.

Gradually students began to arrive—the boys in coats and ties and some of the girls indeed wearing hats and gloves. At 9:00 sharp the door opened. I was first in line. To the right of the door of the registration office stood several tables. Behind the first table, a smiling, bespectacled woman with graying hair beckoned to me as I hesitated just inside the threshold. There were no computers or ID numbers in those days. Students were people. The woman introduced herself, "I'm Mary Hadley. Please fill out this form with your name, address, and telephone number." She handed me a card with the following handwritten entries: biology, English, math, French, and German (the language electives). Rice, primarily a school for engineering and architecture studies, offered liberal arts for a minority of students, mostly girls. It was done in five minutes.

"Is that all?" I asked.

"Not quite. There is an orientation meeting at 10:30 in the biology lecture hall, and, oh, yes, Mr. McCann, the registrar, wants to see you in his office over there." She pointed to a door. My heart sank. There had been a small snafu after I had received my acceptance.

As high school valedictorian, I had received a scholarship to any teacher's college in Texas, but my parents dismissed that option out of hand. My father had examined the catalogue of every school he could think of and decided that Vassar was the most difficult. He sent in my application, and I was accepted. But my grandmother, so the story goes, insisted I not go so far away from home at fourteen. In reality, she and my mother wanted to move to Houston—as they would be obliged to do if I attended Rice—and, more important, no one could afford the expense of my attending Vassar. My father was too proud to discuss the fact that Rice charged no tuition. Still dreaming, however, he told the *Yoakum Herald* that I would attend Rice for two years and then go to Vassar. Who could imagine that anyone in Houston would read a four-page newspaper from Yoakum? However, Mr. McCann read it and wrote me immediately. "Rice Institute is not interested in accepting students who do not intend to get a degree here." It took some scurrying to unruffle his feathers.

My father contacted Uncle George, who, using his not insignificant influence, told Mr. McCann that I was his niece. In addition, I wrote an appropriate letter, assuring him that I had every intention of graduating from Rice. Since we had heard nothing more after that, I assumed all was well. Now my heart was beating so fast I felt faint. But this wasn't what Samuel G. McCann had in mind.

Mr. McCann was no ordinary man. Tall and lanky, with reddish hair and skin that betrayed a once-freckled face, he leaned back in his chair when I entered, put his feet up on the desk, and smiled warmly, "Welcome to Rice Institute. Do you have any questions?"

"I don't know where the biology lecture hall is—or any of these classes."

He rose from his chair. "Come along." He took my arm and guided me out of his office and up the stairs. On the second floor, to the left of the stairwell, the library took up half of the available space. Compared to the Yoakum High School library, which consisted of a few shelves of books at the end of the study hall, Rice's library seemed huge. The bookstore occupied the remainder of the area. A long counter, relieved only by a cash register, separated the student salesperson from the stacks of books piled haphazardly everywhere.

Leaving me at the biology building, Mr. McCann said, "If you have any problems or just want to talk things over, come see me." During my four years at Rice, I did just that, as did almost every other student there. It didn't occur to me at the time how extraordinary it was for the registrar himself to give me a personal tour of the campus.

Everyone complained about Math 101, the nemesis of Rice freshmen then and for many years to come. More students, both girls and boys, were eliminated from the student body because of that course than any other. Miss Alice Dean was the instructor, and students feared her almost as much as the subject she taught. A graduate of Rice's first class, she had never married. She was the only female instructor on campus, and she was austere. No makeup, no smiles. I was scared to death of her. I had a good background in math, better than that of most of the incoming students: two years of algebra, a year of plane geometry, and a year of solid geometry and trigonometry. Nevertheless, Miss Dean's differential calculus, the subject of Math 101, was unbearable. I never really knew for sure what she was talking about.

I had several personal exchanges with Miss Dean. About four weeks into the year, *The Rice Thresher* published its first issue, including an article on the oddities of the freshman class. The newspaper listed the student with the longest name and the shortest, the student who had come the farthest distance, and naturally, the youngest student, Marjorie Meyer. I was humiliated. Shortly after its publication, I had a summons to Miss Dean's office. In a state of panic, I walked in the door. Miss Dean sat at her desk, reading the *Thresher.* "Is this person you?" she asked without looking up or even smiling.

"Yes, ma'am," I said, my eyes fixed on the floor.

She shook her head. "Too bad. A woman with a brain." I waited. "That's all," she said, dismissing me with her hand. I left her office, sighing with relief. I didn't have the vaguest idea then what she meant by her comment, but at least I hadn't yet failed Math 101.

Despite my valiant attempt to be grown-up like everyone else, those were awkward times for a fourteen-year-old from the country. In the absence of any student union or lounge, girl students would sometimes gather to socialize in the rest rooms, where an anteroom was furnished with a few chairs and a sofa, in case someone became ill. One day in the anteroom, a girl I had seen in class offered me a cigarette. I was still smarting from the publicity in the *Thresher,* so I didn't want to say "I don't smoke." Instead, with great sophistication, I said, "No, thank you, I've just eaten." I disregarded the strange look the girl gave me. I was so proud of having thought up such a good excuse on the spur of the moment that I couldn't wait to get home to tell Mama how I had handled the situation. Mama burst out laughing and rushed to the telephone to call her friends. My family paid no attention to sensitivity or the consideration of feelings, particularly concerning children. To them, children were put on earth to please parents, unlike today, when parents exist to satisfy their offspring. After I finally found out what a faux pas I had committed, I cried every time I thought of the incident.

Rice had numerous traditions, none of which were written down, and I had a hard time keeping up with them. Perhaps because of the age difference between me and the other entering students, the scuttlebutt didn't filter down to me. For example, I didn't find out until the last minute that, on the first Friday of the school semester, freshmen were to wear a string of wieners around their neck all day long. I had to rush to the grocery store before it closed. There were no 24/7 grocers in those days. And what to wear with the wieners? It was so hot I knew I'd be sick from the smell.

Another confusing tradition took place on April 1. I had driven to school only to find the gates locked. Not a soul was in sight. I panicked. I thought the world had come to an end. I ran from gate to gate until I found a gardener, who explained no classes would be held that day. I hadn't been told that Rice always declared an unofficial holiday on April Fools' Day.

My age also presented obstacles in class. George Williams taught Freshman English. No student of his ever forgot that class or him, a wonderful teacher. In the 1940s, *Time* magazine wrote an article about him and reviewed his book titled *Some of My Best Friends Are Professors,* in which he decried the system that endorsed the "publish or perish" mentality to the detriment of a professor's obligation to teach. I worried about his assignments almost as much as I fretted about Miss Dean's math. He assigned a theme to be handed in every Saturday morning, and he chose the topics. The one I remember best was "What is your philosophy of life?" I was a good student, but I was accustomed to learning theorems and vocabularies. At fourteen and fifteen, who had a philosophy of life?

In 1930, all of the young Jewish students in college and high school attended temple services on Friday evenings. After temple, our parents dropped us off at someone's home, where we picked up the rugs and danced to big-band music on the radio. Several of the boys got their family cars and took the girls home after the party. This was called dating.

The Rice boys and I had college classes on Saturday morning, whereas the other girls at these Friday night parties were still in high school. At that age, high school girls displayed a much greater interest in the boys than the other way around. The Rice boys—my classmates—would gather in a corner and talk about next day's class, and they would call me over.

"Marjorie, what answer did you get for that fourth math problem?"

It didn't take me long to discover that the girls were furious at the attention I received. My cousin Gina brought the news, and she didn't mince any words. "It's pretty tacky for you to monopolize the boys all evening talking 'school.' You aren't going to be invited again if this keeps up."

Not being invited was an intolerable prospect. The next Friday night, when Julian Frachtman called me over, I said, "Oh, come on, let's talk about school later. We're here to dance." A strategy for self-preservation.

All during my freshman year I had been going to Sunday school in preparation for confirmation, which Jewish boys and girls participated in together. In those years, no thirteen-year-old girls were Bat Mitzvah, which is a relatively modern ritual. I suppose it was established as a counterpart to the boys' Bar Mitzvah, which took place at that age and commemorated their entry into manhood. At fifteen, all boys and girls were "confirmed" in a group, symbolizing their entry into the adult Jewish community. This ritual continues today.

On Wednesday afternoons I even went to Dr. Barnston's study for extra lessons in Hebrew since I had had no such preparation in Yoakum. I'm sorry to say now that my year's cramming didn't stick. I don't even remember the alphabet.

The confirmation service took place in May on the holy day of Shevuos, the celebration of spring and new beginnings. In those days, the service was scheduled for the morning of the holy day. Nowadays, more accommodatingly, it's held on the closest Sabbath weekend. At the end of the school year, when final exam schedules were posted, I was distraught to discover that my math final fell on the same morning as confirmation. First I went with my problem to Mr. McCann. "You can take the exam in the fall," he said.

That meant a whole summer of worrying about that awful course. "Oh, please, *please,* that's my worst subject. I'll forget everything I know."

Mr. McCann sent me to see Dr. Malcolm Lovett, president of Rice, my one and only visit to the Ivory Tower, as students called his office on the top floor of Lovett Hall. "You will do just fine on the exam in the fall," said Dr. Lovett.

I was hysterical. I just couldn't wait until fall, and yet I wanted to participate in the confirmation ceremony after working so hard all year. In desperation I went to Miss Dean with my predicament. Looking up from her book this time but still not smiling, she asked, "When is the confirmation service over?"

"At noon," I murmured. A glimmer of hope. She thought for a moment, while I held my breath.

"I'll be in the library from 1:00 P.M. until late afternoon. Be there."

And I was. After the confirmation ceremony, I dashed home, changed from my fancy white dress into clothes suitable for school. In a blouse, skirt, and high heels, I rushed to the library, thinking that, as exhausted as I was from my performance in confirmation, it would be better to fail math in the spring than in the fall. Miss Dean was waiting for me as promised. Without comment, she handed me the exam. I've always wondered whether I truly earned the good grade I received or whether she was just sorry for me.

My studies at Rice took place during the early years of the Great Depression, which began with the stock market crash of 1929. In a way, my family was somewhat prepared for the economic collapse. Hard times had hit Yoakum earlier than elsewhere in the country, after the Southern Pacific railroad shop moved away and crop failures caused the banks to fail.

That was in 1927, when I was a junior in high school. One night I remember the lights at home burning way past midnight because people were talking in our front room. My father and other community leaders were trying to figure out how to salvage things. Their solution was to convert the smelly old tannery into a business that would produce quality "Western accessories." A committee of citizens, including my father, found a designer to make bridles, belts, wallets, and so on from the cattle hides farmers brought in to be cured. Those products were given the name Tex-Tan. It was a tremendously successful venture, and the business became one of the largest leather goods manufacturers in the world. Needless to say, it was by far the largest company in Yoakum.

My father's lumberyard suffered from the Depression, too, but our lives seemed relatively normal to me. A big change occurred, however, when it was decided that Mama and Grandmother Lena would move to Houston with me while I attended Rice. In order to do that, Daddy arranged to rent the Yoakum house to another family. During the week he would live in one of the apartments Mama had converted from a two-story garage behind the Yoakum house and on weekends come to Houston. Although not a word was ever spoken about it, I have wondered whether he found this separation from his family uncomfortable or disheartening. Perhaps he found the relative peace and quiet in Mama's absence a relief.

Mama rented a large house at 1630 Richmond Avenue near the Mandell Street intersection in Houston. Except for minor architectural details or slight differences in the color of the dark brick, all of the homes on the north side of the street resembled one another—similar front porches, sturdy brick columns supporting the roof, servants' quarters above two-car garages.

In a porchlike space that Mama called the music room, she put the Steinway grand piano Uncle Henri had given her when she got married. In her eyes it was a valuable possession, although I never heard her play a note on it. In the living room, Mama simply transplanted her Yoakum Louis XIV furniture, along with the heavy damask and Oriental rugs. This area opened onto a dining room, which comfortably housed Mama's mahogany dining room set. That space in turn led to the large kitchen. Between the kitchen and the music room, on the right side of the house, was a breakfast room, where we ate all our meals except when we had company.

We always had a Rice student living with us. Because there were no dormitories for girls at Rice, female students had to live with local families. The students paid Mama fifty dollars a month for their room and meals. This not only helped with our rent but also enabled Mama to save money on the side. First there was Camille Williamson from Dallas, a tall, slim girl with red hair, not carrot-colored or auburn, just plain fiery red, with freckles to match. Camille and I both had problems with fish on Friday nights, which Mama insisted on having for the two Catholic Bohemian girls from Yoakum who worked for us as domestics. On Friday afternoons, Camille and I had biology lab, where we cut up frogs. We came home with a clammy, fishy feeling on our hands and a smell of formaldehyde lingering in our nostrils. Mama was impervious to my complaints, saying that the girls' religion took precedence. Camille was silent. Like most people, she was scared of Mama.

There were no leases then, so every month Mama complained to the landlord, threatening to move. In those dark Depression times, no one who owned property wanted to lose a tenant. "Mr. Asbury, I'm just going to have to move," she would say. "The rent is too high. I have a friend who is paying half as much for a larger house." She was thus able to negotiate such an alteration in the rent that, by the end of the first year, it had been reduced from $150 a month to $75.

Our family was fortunate. Even though we never had a great deal of money, we managed to live a relatively genteel life despite the Depression. As a result, I was never personally aware of the great miseries so many endured during those bleak years in the Eastern cities where factories closed. Because we were in an agricultural community there was always something to eat, and therefore we saw no breadlines.

The sadness we experienced at the beginning of the Depression came from a more personal cause. In early December of 1929, a few months after we moved to Houston, I arrived home after classes from Rice to find my beloved Grandmother Lena in bed and very upset. She looked terrible. Her sweet face under that beautiful, silvery hair was ashen and drawn. I had never seen her without her false teeth. "Where's Mama?" I asked.

"She's gone out somewhere." Grandmother turned her head to the wall.

"Did you all have a fight?"

She didn't deny it.

"What was it about?"

She continued to stare at the wall, but I could see she was agitated. The subject of the quarrel didn't matter. It was typical of Mama to engage in a diatribe, which gave her almost orgasmic relief, and then leave the house. When she cooled off and returned, she expected everyone to have forgotten the incident just as she had. Suddenly Grandmother began to gag, and I saw blood. I rushed to telephone Dr. Moise Levy, who came quickly. In those days it was customary for doctors to make house calls. After the briefest of examinations, Grandmother was on her way to Hermann Hospital before Mama came home.

Later Mama came rushing to the hospital, wailing, "Marjorie, why didn't you wait for me?" I panicked. *Once again,* I thought, *she has forgotten what she did, and I will feel the vengeance of her wrath.* The doctor's sudden appearance, interrupting Mama's tirade, spared me.

Grandmother's condition worsened rapidly. No one mentioned cancer, which was in those days considered a disgrace. On Friday night, December 7, 1929, my dear best friend, my grandmother, died.

Mama wore the customary black of mourning for a year. In the hospital she had been the soul of the dutiful daughter. Perhaps she meant it. I was the only one who knew about the altercation just before Grandmother went to the hospital. It occurred to me, and not for the first or last time, that Mama could never acknowledge any personal error. I asked myself, *why doesn't she ever feel guilty*? In retrospect, it seems to me that this inability to acknowledge her misdeeds or register remorse might have been symptoms of her mental illness.

"Well-bred young ladies *must* speak French," my beloved and regal Grandmother Lena had often said to me as she sat at her dressing table, twisting her lovely gray hair into a topknot above her pompadour. Therefore, year after year I went to the convent in Yoakum after school for French lessons. From the nuns I learned how to conjugate French verbs, regular and irregular, in all of the tenses. Then I took four years of French at Rice, where I absorbed the works of Molière, Racine, and Zola. In all that time, however, I never heard the French language spoken by a native.

I knew I needed some conversational practice, so I planned to go to the Alliance Française in Paris the summer before I entered the Sorbonne. I truly had no idea of the challenge I would face. That I was going to the Sorbonne at all still amazed me. It seemed miraculous, although, when I graduated from Rice in June—an eighteen-year-old Phi Beta Kappa—everyone acknowledged that I should continue my education. Daddy still had visions of Vassar for a master's degree, but Mr. McCann was horrified when I confided this to him. "You can't do that," he told me. "You need to go to Europe—to the Sorbonne." I assured him he was dreaming. Undeterred, Mr. McCann called my father, then my mother, each of whom wondered whether the other would agree. Mostly Mama wanted to consult Uncle Henri because she routinely submitted all major decisions to him for adjudication. Not only did Uncle Henri, the Francophile, heartily approve, but he also offered to pay for my ship's passage. Moreover, I would travel with his nephew, Buddy Schmulen, a buyer for Bendel's who made several trips to Paris each year.

My Meyer uncles chipped in as well. Together they gave me a graduation present of one thousand dollars for my school year abroad. Aunt Esther, my father's sister, gave me a top-of-the-line

Marjorie and Buddy Schmulen on the SS Berengaria.

Oshkosh steamer trunk with its signature stripes. Everything just came together.

Buddy and I left for Europe on June 25, 1933, aboard the grand old British liner, the *Berengaria*. I was so inexperienced I didn't even realize what a treat it was to travel first class. For a teenager from Texas, the *Berengaria* was a glamorous new world. Every evening the enormous dining room filled with formally dressed guests who danced to the music of a huge orchestra.

Buddy had prepared me in advance. On the night of embarkation, just a simple dinner dress would be appropriate. Traveling clothes were in order after crossing the English Channel, when we would disembark at the French port of Cherbourg to board the boat train to Paris. On all other evenings, formal dress was called for, so I took thirteen evening dresses (most of which were cotton) in my steamer trunk. Of course, I had made many of them myself.

The first night after dinner, I entered the magnificent library to write my parents a letter. I had never seen such writing desks. Two people faced each other across a small divider that held the ship's embossed stationery. I went to one that was unoccupied on both sides. Head bent, I busied myself writing about all the exciting things that had happened that day. I told them Uncle Hyman Meyer had sent me an orchid, the first I had ever received, and Uncle Henri had sent an impressive basket of flowers. I acknowledged the telegram from my father, which said, "Remember not to talk religion or politics with strangers." Finishing my letter, I looked up to see Douglas Fairbanks Jr. sitting across from me. I thought I was dreaming.

"Good evening," he said. "Where are you going in Europe?"

I realized I had been holding my breath, so my words came out in a rush. "I'm going to the Sorbonne in Paris." He was most congenial, and I know we had a rather long conversation, but even the next day I couldn't remember a word we had exchanged.

When the *Berengaria* arrived in Paris, I took up residence at the Rockefeller House, which was inexpensive housing for American students abroad and part of the Cité Universitaire, across from the Parc Montsouris. During my first day there I learned that the residents had a policy of "showing the town," Dutch treat, to any newcomer. Of course, as a Texan, I was an oddity. Most of the students were Jews from New York City. The girls from Hunter College were attending summer school. The boys, mostly from City College of New York, were in Paris to study medicine because of a quota system used by New York professional schools that severely limited the number of Jews accepted. The evening was memorable.

Where I came from, boys paid the check even if only for a five-cent Coca-Cola. I had never heard of Dutch treat, but it proved to be the least painful of my lessons. We stopped first at the Café Select, still the most famous gay bar in the world. Many of the patrons were heavily rouged and wearing flamboyant attire. I thought it a costume party. "We don't belong here," I said. "We're not dressed properly." Howls of laughter ensued.

Then we went to a corner boîte, or nightclub, in Montmartre, where one of the boys bribed a black gigolo to dance with me. By that time, I had learned what a greenhorn I was. I tried to act nonchalant, as if I danced with black men everyday. The man was a marvelous dancer, and I didn't turn into a pumpkin, but I wondered what my father would have thought if he had seen me. I kept a pretty stiff upper lip the rest of the evening until our last stop—at a bar where the waitresses were nude. They were neither young nor pretty, and I fell apart. I excused myself, found a rest room, and lost everything I had eaten during the evening.

The New Yorkers at the Rockefeller House thought all Texans lived on ranches and used outdoor "plumbing." I was a very interesting curiosity, and they enjoyed me immensely.

After only a few weeks, I complained to my medical student friend, David Zakin from Brooklyn, that, living around so many Americans, I wasn't hearing enough French. He replied very seriously, "There's only one way to learn a foreign language, and that is in bed! I'm going to introduce you to a young Madagascan, who should be a help."

His name was Chopie, and he looked like a cherub. I had been a bit anxious when he called me to have lunch in the Parc Montsouris, but the sight of this fresh-faced, very young man erased any doubts I may have had. We had a delightful lunch. Afterward, this sweet, childlike fellow stood up and said, "Alors, mademoiselle, maintenant allons à ma chambre." My French was still halting, but it didn't take an accomplished linguist to understand that he was inviting me to his room. This was so bizarre and such a shock, considering his appearance, that I burst out laughing. At that, Chopie became furious. He turned beet red and stalked away. A few days later I moved from the Rockefeller House to a pension. Forget the Parisian way of learning a language.

Instead, I haunted French theaters and movies with notepad in hand. I refused to date Americans, even though the mores of the young French men were different from mine. I didn't have many repeat dates when they found out I was interested in their argot, not their romantic prowess.

After about two months, as I was walking down the Boulevard Raspail one day, I stopped dead in my tracks. I had passed two women talking, and I understood what they said! It was as though a light bulb had been switched on. With my solid grammatical foundation, it was smooth sailing from then on. Nevertheless, I was intensely focused. In addition to the Alliance, I attended the Institut de Phonétique. In front of a mirror I practiced, especially the French "r," the mispronunciation of which generally identifies Americans. I learned how to utter the most difficult of all French words: *rue*. When Buddy returned on one of his buying trips three months later, I couldn't believe what a terrible accent he had. I knew then I was ready for lectures at the Sorbonne. And for Strasbourg.

Before leaving Texas, I had been given strict orders to visit my paternal grandfather's relatives in Strasbourg, the capitol of Alsace-Lorraine. When my grandfather, Achille Meyer, was born in Wolfesheim, a suburb of Strasbourg, the province was German. The cemetery in Wolfesheim, where all the generations of European Meyers are buried, is a must-stop for all foreign relatives. Despite the usual misgivings of any eighteen-year-old about meeting those strange old people, I had written to them soon after my arrival in Paris and said that I would come to visit on November 1, 1933, the weekend of my nineteenth birthday.

By the end of October, I had been in France four months, and my French was better than just good. Although some of the younger cousins spoke a little English, they delighted in being able to converse with me in French. I was pretty proud myself.

I arrived on a Friday evening, and the whole large family had dinner at the home of my father's first cousin, Palmyr Dreyfus. She was a lovely, statuesque, blond woman without much, if any, makeup. None of my grandfather's siblings were alive, but their children, my father's cousins, were vociferous, agreeable, energetic, and oh, so glad to see me. Their hospitality was overwhelming. I felt ashamed of having dreaded the trip.

More observant of Jewish ritual than my family, they had prayers and candles and the "breaking of the bread" on Friday night. The dinner itself was a feast. I had never seen so much food. First there was chicken soup, then roast chicken, and, just in case anyone preferred it, they served roast beef, too. The vegetables, salads, potatoes, and breads were followed by a rich custard-filled cake. I felt stuffed, but everyone insisted on going into the city for *après dîner*. That didn't mean a drink. It meant pâté de foie gras as it is made only in Strasbourg-like pure butter-plus cheesecake and pastries of all kinds. It would have been rude not to eat.

Palmyr Meyer, my hostess that first evening, had married Mathieu Dreyfus, tall, distinguished, and elegant. Six months before I arrived, their handsome blond son, André, who was twenty-six, had married Paulette, who was nineteen—six months older than I. She was as brunette as André was blond, with a round dimpled face. A darling bride. It had been decided I would stay with the young people.

The contrast between the generations was vivid. André and Paulette's apartment was modern with modernistic furnishings, while Palmyr's home and those of the other older Meyer cousins were traditional. The stolidity of their dark heavy furniture did not detract from the personal warmth they expressed, however. I kept remembering they lived under a Germanic influence, and the guttural accent of their French was apparent even to me. The Alsatian accent is as distinct from the French of Tours or Paris as the Southern drawl is from Brooklynese.

Every minute of the weekend was planned. And planning meant food. I woke up Saturday morning to face Paulette's sideboard. I wanted just orange juice and coffee, but there I saw sausages, liverwurst, cheese, and cakes. I had to be polite. Next on the schedule was lunch with Palmyr's brother, Artur Meyer, and his wife, Francine. She was a striking brunette but quiet and retiring, while he, a tall, brash, not-at-all-handsome man, displayed a manner that reminded me of my father's brother, Arthur Meyer in Houston (whose wife, coincidentally, was named Frances).

We were barely through lunch, it seemed to me, when it was time to visit Gustave and Sarah Meyer's house for *gouté,* a ritual not to be confused with our "tea." Our hosts served rich pastries and chocolates. No one seemed obese, but Sarah was plump and Gustave stocky and heavyset, reminding me of Hyman Gustave Meyer, another of my father's brothers in Houston.

Dinner was again at Palmyr's, this time with roast duck, sweet potatoes, pastries, and the usual *après dîner* in town. It would have been rude not to participate, but I became very uncomfortable, and, not surprisingly, I was up all night, as sick as I have ever been in my life. Next morning, the day of my birthday—when really grand festivities were planned—I apologized—and consumed nothing but water all day. My relatives were gracious, but I knew they were disappointed. I just couldn't help it. I felt very much like one of the geese they fattened to make the foie gras.

We visited Wolfesheim as promised and discussed the war clouds looming over Europe. I knew trouble was brewing because clairvoyant Jews were already seeking refuge in Paris. But for me, war seemed so remote as to be almost unimaginable. We had one difference of opinion, not strong enough to call a dispute. The Meyers all insisted that the United States would simply have to enter the war, and they had no doubt that one was bound to occur. Privately, I considered it arrogant of them to think the United States had such an obligation—and highly unlikely as well—since France had never repaid the debt it owed the United States from World War I.

When the weekend was over, I left, laden with gifts and promising to return. We did correspond and keep in touch, but I didn't get back to Strasbourg for sixty-one years.

On September 1, 1939, Germany marched into Poland, and World War II was under way. That date was also the first anniversary of my marriage to Raymond Arsht. Our first thoughts, of course, were for my relatives, who were in grave danger. Aunt Esther and Uncle George moved heaven and earth to try to help them all, but without success. Very early in the war, the Germans overran Strasbourg, that charming city of joy and laughter. Poor, sturdy Gustave was shot in the street as a hostage; his wife, Sarah, and two daughters went to concentration camps. Storm troopers invaded Artur's home and shot him, Francine, and their daughter in cold blood. Their son was swimming and escaped but was later killed in a railway accident. Mathieu Dreyfus, a diabetic, died in the south of France from a lack of insulin.

We didn't know then that André and Paulette, with their infant daughter, Danielle, had been hidden by a French farm family in their barn. At the time, I felt we would never see them or Strasbourg again. Gustave's two daughters, Julienne and Marie, also survived. Aunt Esther and Uncle George located them through an American soldier, Sidney Schuman, who was sent over with a reconstruction team after the war ended. His father worked for Uncle George at Foley's. Sidney found them in Paris, although Julienne was frail and ill and soon died. Later Aunt Esther provided Marie with a dowry, and she now lives in Switzerland.

After the war, André and Paulette changed their names to Mathieu, the first name of André's father, because they felt a Jewish name like Dreyfus would always be a hindrance in France. Their prosperous boutiques all over Strasbourg before the war were gone. Nevertheless, André started over and developed a successful department store in Strasbourg called Mathieu's. That store, once so successful, no longer exists. Paulette died in March of 2003, and her daughter, Danielle, a widow, as well as Danielle's son, daughter, and their family are seriously considering emigrating to Israel. Anti-Semitism in France has become virulent once again.

I was on the Riviera before my last summer semester at the Sorbonne when I received a letter from Mama. It arrived by way of American Express, that home-away-from-home for students traveling abroad.

Dear Marjorie,

I have news for you. You must come home as soon as your school ends. Your father has been seriously ill so your Uncle Lep sent us to the Mayo Clinic in Rochester, New York. Doctors discovered he had severe neuritis from malnutrition due to his strict diet for diabetes. Mayo's prescribed insulin, a medicine he takes by shots every day so that he can eat more food. Although he is better, he is still very thin and frail.

I have been in touch with Uncle Henri and he thinks you should go to Columbia to get an advanced degree in French. He has offered to finance your stay in New York. I don't have to tell you that as much as your father wants to have you home, he is ecstatic at the thought of your getting a Master's degree.

If you leave as soon as your term is over, there will be time for you to spend a few days in New York making living arrangements and still have a week or ten days in Yoakum before you go to New York to enroll at Columbia.

Love, Mama.

I was in shock. The family back in Yoakum, my father ill, and Columbia—all a fait accompli! I was really tired of school, but no one had consulted me about what I wanted to do. After a year of being on my own and making my own decisions, I came face to face with the fact that things would be different when I returned to the United States. A myriad of emotions engulfed me. And I had another problem as well. I remembered my father's words when I left for Europe: "Don't come back with any funny accent like many people do when they go away to school. You come back speaking just the way you do now." I hadn't realized that in the year I had been gone, I'd spoken English mostly with foreigners who had learned English in Great Britain. That very day I had found myself in conversation with a midshipman from the U.S. Naval Academy whose training ship was anchored at Villefranche. I recognized his Louisiana drawl and, as I passed him on the boulevard, asked, "Sailor, what part of Louisiana do you come from?"

"Why, ma'am, I didn't know you foreigners knew anything about Lew-si-aana! But, since you asked, I'm from Monroe. Ever heyah of it?"

"I have a cousin who lives in Monroe—Dr. William Bendel. Do you know him?" I said.

"Well, bless my soul! Dr. Bill brought me into the worl'. He never told us he had foreign relatives."

"I'm no foreigner. I was born and have lived all my life in Texas. I've been in school over here."

"You're joshin' me, miss. No one from the South has an accent like yours!"

I pulled out my passport and watched his look of disbelief with my own heart sinking. My father's words rang in my ears. I didn't even laugh when the sailor bellowed, "Well, I'll be hornswoggled!" When I left him, I headed straight for the American Express office to change my reservation to an American ship. "I have to change my Reservation for the United States. It's a matter of life and death," I blurted out.

"What is the date of your prior reservation and the date you wish to leave?" asked the bored agent. She didn't even look up from the form she was examining.

"I was due to leave on the *Ile de France* on September 15, but now I have to leave on the *United States* whenever it sails after August 15," I said, my voice shaking, obviously distressed.

"Whenever it sails?" Suddenly I had the agent's attention. "I thought you said it was a matter of life and death. What's so special about the *United States?* Everyone who comes in here wants to sail on the *Ile de France* because the food is so great and the service impeccable." She waited expectantly.

Finally I gave up and blurted out, "I've lost my American accent, and I have to be around Americans so I can get it back." She had the grace not to laugh.

It was September of 1934—Indian Summer in New York. All of my sad thoughts on leaving Paris disappeared when I saw the Statue of Liberty. My cousin, Henri Bendel II, met me at the ship. He was really Uncle Henri's nephew, Benjamin Levy. After his father died when Benjamin was twelve, he had been adopted by Uncle Henri, who changed his name. Everyone still called him Little Henri, although at the time he was twenty-eight and anything but little.

Henri drove me from the dock to Laurel Lake Lodge, Uncle Henri's Connecticut estate. At the end of a long, tree-lined drive, the house rose like a French chateau. Inside, the impression continued with ornate French furniture, every piece an authentic antique. Some of the pieces were probably still upholstered in their original fabric. Certainly the satin damask covering some of the sofas was worn to shreds. I thought it pretty awful to have shabby old furniture, but I realized that whatever Uncle Henri had was expensive, so I didn't offer my opinion.

Every one of the five bedrooms, some with little sitting areas, had its own dressing room and bath, and each, its own decor. My room was swathed in a luxurious chintz. Blue and white flowered material draped the windows, papered the walls, and covered the upholstered chairs. A downy, quilted coverlet of the same material lay upon the bed. I felt like a princess.

The second day, I went into New York with Uncle Henri, who said, "You'll need some new clothes. Little Henri will take you to the Young Timers shop and help you pick out some things for the fall." Disparagingly, he added, "I despise the American *prêt-a-porter,* but with these times, customers want a cheaper, ready-to-wear line for their daughters going to college." Actually, what Uncle Henri called "cheaper" appeared pretty expensive to me. Some of the dresses cost almost a hundred dollars, and I gladly took everything that was offered: a new cloth coat, some sweaters, skirts, suits, and dresses.

Uncle Henri would have disowned me if I had worn a dress above my knees. (Women did not wear pants in those days.)

The third day I went out to the International House on Riverside Drive to make living arrangements for the fall. It was the counterpart of the Rockefeller Center, where I had first stayed in Paris. The same architect must have designed both buildings: one tower of sleeping rooms for men and one for women, joined by common facilities for eating and receiving guests. Moreover, the sleeping rooms in New York were just as cell-like as the ones in Paris, although they provided the necessities.

My fun-filled few days in New York, however, quickly made me forget how sorry I was to leave Europe. One night Uncle Henri had Little Henri take me to dinner and the theater. What a treat! We saw *Merrily We Roll Along,* starring Walter Huston. The play made a tremendous impression on me. It opened with a gathering of tuxedo-clad, middle-aged men and formally gowned women holding cocktail glasses. From their conversation one gleaned a clear picture of their cynicism, their jaded, unhappy lives and their moral corruption. As scene after scene unfolded, the characters got younger and younger. Their lives moved backward, detailing the compromises, the small cheatings, even thefts, and the cutting of corners here and there, until the play ended with a valedictory address given by the principal character at his high school graduation. A moving, passionate speech outlined his aspirations of a life dedicated to upholding moral values and to contributing meaningfully to the world he was entering.

I have often thought of the play's lessons as my own unfolded: those shattered dreams of being the best daughter, the best sister, the best daughter-in-law, the best mother, the best wife; the compromises everyone has to make along the way. In the end, most people just do the best they can—and muddle through.

Uncle Henri and I worked out a budget for my year in New York. He decided that, since I had managed my money so well in Europe, he wasn't going to give me a monthly stipend but instead would give me $500 when I entered Columbia and another $500 at midterm. I thought he was the most generous man in the world.

I registered at the university and made my living arrangements, and then it was time to go home to Yoakum. I stayed overnight in Houston, just long enough to greet my aunts, uncles, and cousins.

The little electric train that had once traveled between Houston and Yoakum no longer operated, so the next day I took the Sunset Limited, the Southern Pacific's best train. On its way to California, it made a stop at Flatonia, the closest station to Yoakum, forty miles south. After the flurry of warm greetings by Mama, Daddy, and Elène, I asked, "Did you have Oscar bring the pickup to take my steamer trunk?"

"My goodness," said Daddy, "I forgot all about that. We'll have to send for it tomorrow."

I walked quickly to the stationmaster's window and said, "I have a steamer trunk being unloaded. Here is my claim check. Will you please take care of it until tomorrow when someone will come in a proper vehicle to haul it to Yoakum?"

I saw Mama's sudden movement out of the corner of my eye and heard her say in a stage whisper, "Well! Just look at that. Taking complete charge! I'm not sure sending her to Europe was such a good idea!"

I thought, *Oh boy, I'm home.*

We arrived in Yoakum in time for dinner at noon. Mama had prepared a banquet. However, when I reached for a piece of bread, she started to shout "Stop!" but only the "st" actually sounded. She caught herself and said, "Well, I guess since it's your first meal at home, but after this . . ." Our trip from Flatonia had been spent discussing my weight:

"How could you let yourself go like this?"

"I'm surprised at the way you look."

"You're just going to have to do something about all that fat."

"Just how much do you weigh, anyway?"

"You left here with a nice figure."

Mama's comments were interjected into whatever we were discussing. I kept trying to change the subject, but somehow she never got past my appearance. Her concerns focused on various possible diets. She didn't seem to have any interest in my other activities, past or present. One day I asked her, "Mama, didn't you, some night when you were putting your head down on your pillow, ever wonder where I might be or what I might be doing in Europe or about any dangers I might be facing?" Her answer was a dry, matter-of-fact "Why, of course not."

The International House on Riverside Drive in New York City didn't just look like its counterpart in Paris. It was equally restrictive, antiseptic, and boring. So, when I happened to meet Elizabeth Jacobs from San Antonio at a party and discovered she was looking for a roommate to share an apartment, I was ready and willing. I lasted longer at the Paris dormitory than at the one in New York.

Elizabeth and I found a small suite at an old residential hotel within our combined meager budgets. Unimaginatively named the Midtown Hotel, it sat squarely at Seventy-second Street and Amsterdam at a subway stop on Manhattan's West Side. To us, the shabby apartment looked like the Waldorf-Astoria. We had two small rooms: a living room and a twin-bedded bedroom, one closet, and a bath. The sparsely furnished living room boasted a faded sofa and two chairs as well as a kind of armoire that concealed a small refrigerator below a shelf holding a two-burner electric hot plate. Two shelves above the "stove" provided space for utensils, dishes, glasses, and canned goods. It is hard now to believe the amount of entertaining we did with those dilapidated and inadequate facilities. Shortly after my cousin Pauline came to New York, we extracted from the hotel management a rickety card table and four metal folding chairs in order to accommodate our marathon bridge games. The table also served as my desk.

Pauline lived at the Barbizon Hotel for Women on Madison Avenue, a really upscale place, but men were not allowed above the lobby, so our apartment became a gathering place.

I was the only one going to school seriously. Uncle George and Aunt Esther had sent Pauline to New York for a year after she graduated from Rice. As someone always interested in the theater, she took a few drama courses at Columbia but wasn't working toward a degree.

After college, Elizabeth, in her early twenties, had made her way to New York for "broadening," as such a postgraduate experience was called. She took a few courses in drama and English literature, but most of the time she haunted Greenwich Village. She drew people to her, although no one could say that Elizabeth was a beauty. Her drawl identified her roots immediately, and her enthusiasm charmed everyone around her.

Marjorie with cousin Pauline Meyer and friend, New York, 1934

For me, Greenwich Village was a poor imitation of Paris's *Rive Gauche*—Left Bank. Instead of the ambiance of the sidewalk cafes of Montmartre, students enjoyed the sterility of Formica tables in the cafeterias. Instead of the plaintive whine of violins in the boîtes of Montparnasse, tunes came from nickelodeons.

New York in 1934 was suffering miserably from the Depression. Most students had little or no money, but there was no shortage of conversation. Discussions and arguments over art, drama, poetry, and politics raged furiously, albeit in the dingy nightclubs and the inevitable Automat rather than in more formal venues.

Waiting for Lefty, a drama by Clifford Odets, played on Broadway to rave reviews. He had come out of the cafeteria crowd and was considered an example for every aspiring artist. Once in a while he came back to his old neighborhood, to the delight of the ragtag assortment of struggling painters, poets, playwrights, writers, and students like Elizabeth and me.

Elizabeth wanted to go to the Village every night. Most of the time I had to study, but often I dragged along, primarily because I worried about her wandering around the Village alone. She was so naïve, so trusting, and so enamored of the poetry she heard and the dramatizations she saw by would-be playwrights that I felt she presented an easy mark. Elizabeth's contribution to an evening's agenda generally consisted of reading the poems of her idol, Edna St. Vincent Millay. Mine was debating politics, government, and social theories.

For the most part, the primarily Jewish group we socialized with held views that were politically left-wing, if not outright communist. At that time, New York's intelligentsia drowned in Russia worship because the Russians were opposing Hitler. Those Jews didn't admit it, but they operated under the premise that "Any enemy of my enemy is my friend." One night a wild-eyed, young, self-styled communist named Albert Weiss and I violently debated the relative merits of capitalism and socialism. As the evening drew to a close, a storm developed. He looked at Elizabeth and me and said, "I think I'd better see you girls home." I thought, *Hmm, this radical nut isn't completely bad, after all.* When we arrived at the subway stop, Albert said, "Either of you girls have any extra change?"

"I do," I said with scorn. "Here's a capitalist quarter!" The guy just needed carfare home.

Uncle Henri often invited Pauline and me to spend the weekend with him at his Connecticut estate. One weekend I had to refuse the invitation. "I'm sorry, but on Friday I'm going to Garden City."

"Garden City?" he exclaimed. "What in the world will you do in that place?"

"I'm going to visit a friend I knew in Paris who has just come home. Her family lives there."

My uncle chuckled. "Don't you know they don't allow Jews in Garden City?"

I couldn't believe it. "Are you sure? It's only a few miles from Great Neck, where Aunt Fannie and Buddy live. How could that be?"

"Well, that's the way it is. Jews live in some towns and not in others."

I couldn't wait to ask my friend Beatrice Bogart, nicknamed Beaty, about this. She and I hadn't seen each other in six months, but we had kept in touch. After warm greetings and an introduction to her gracious mother and father, I simply had to find out. "Just before I came here, I heard that no Jews were allowed in your town. Is that true?"

Beaty looked at her parents, who looked at each other. They seemed embarrassed but also a bit defensive. "We really don't know how that situation developed," Mrs. Bogart said.

Mr. Bogart quickly interjected, "I wouldn't say they aren't allowed. They just don't live here. It's truly regrettable. I suppose we just don't rock the boat. We go along with the status quo like everyone else."

Beaty injected her bit. "I had forgotten about our town. It's a far cry from the heterogeneous society Marjorie and I knew in Paris."

I felt compelled to add, "It's mighty hypocritical for people in the East to look down on the South as segregationist when they themselves have whole towns that are ghettos." Everyone agreed. We never discussed the matter again, and we all enjoyed a pleasant weekend. The Bogarts were more uncomfortable than I was.

Columbia University divided master's degree candidates into groups of three under the supervision of a thesis adviser. Dr. Spencer led my group. A tall, thin man with an unruly mop of white hair and an angular face, he reminded me of Ichabod Crane. He might have been only forty-five, but to my nineteen years, he seemed a very old man.

One of our group, an innocuous young man, had terrible colds all of the time and in that harsh New York winter missed most of our sessions. I can't even remember his name. The other member was José Ferrer, whom we knew as Joe. Born in Puerto Rico and the only son of a prominent Catholic sugar planter, he had many sisters who had spoiled him unmercifully, and I understood why: He was irresistibly charming. He wasn't much to look at—small to medium stature, with a prominent nose and large ears—but what a personality! In addition to impeccable French and Spanish, he spoke the King's English with panache. A brilliant but not a stuffy student, he was a natural comic.

Joe became a frequent visitor to our apartment at Midtown. He arrived early and stayed late. He helped me with my thesis, an analysis of the works of the French playwright Jean Giraudoux, with emphasis on his then current work, *Amphitryon 38*—when we weren't laughing. I kept telling Joe, "You ought to be on the stage!" How prescient I was. And how proud I was at the great success he came to enjoy on Broadway and in Hollywood.

More important, though, was the fact that at Columbia he saved my life—or at least my sanity. After just three sessions into the term, both Joe and I noticed that Dr. Spencer was giving me the wrong kind of attention. The professor began suggesting that I stay a bit after class so he could help me personally. When his hands began to wander under our conference table, I sought help from Joe. "What in the world am I going to do? I'd like to tell the old bastard to go to hell, but the approval of my thesis is up to him."

"Don't worry," Joe comforted me. "I'll think of a plan." And he did. In December, Professor Spencer suggested that perhaps he and I could work in the evening.

"Do you like Italian food?" he grinned, with a lecherous glint in his eye. "I know a wonderful little restaurant with good dance music."

"Oh, I eat everything." I didn't have to lie about that.

Joe had prepared me. "What's the name of this restaurant, and where is it?" I asked. Dr. Spencer fell into the trap.

"Mama Leone's," he said quickly, apparently delighted at what he took for acceptance of his invitation since I had brushed off earlier suggestions for dinner meetings. I passed the necessary information on to Joe.

I met Dr. Spencer at the restaurant, and we had just ordered when

Joe came in with a friend. Performer that he was, Joe expressed enormous surprise, "My goodness, isn't this a coincidence?" He introduced us to his friend Jim Cook. "Jim, this is Dr. Spencer, my professor from Columbia, and one of my colleagues, Marjorie Meyer. What's good here, Professor? I heard about this place, so Jim and I thought we'd try it." I didn't dare look at the professor, who hadn't uttered a sound. Joe continued, "Say, why don't we join you? There's plenty of room in this booth. What fun!" Without waiting for an answer, he sat down. I sighed a deep sigh of relief and enjoyed my dinner tremendously. Dr. Spencer fumed all evening.

Like most girls my age, I had been able to fend off my professor's ridiculous attempts at kisses or gropings. Nevertheless, I worried constantly. Once, when I just couldn't think of any excuse, I agreed to meet him again for dinner, but, with Joe's coaching, I insisted on knowing the telephone number of the restaurant. I explained that my roommate and I had promised our parents that we would always let each other know where we could be reached.

Shortly after our dinner and just one miserable dance, I was called to the telephone. It was Joe. He couldn't very well show up again personally, but he delivered what he said was an urgent message, dying laughing all the time. I returned to the table, apologized profusely, and explained that my roommate was violently ill. I absolutely had to leave. Dr. Spencer's disgust was obvious.

Chapter 3

Teaching, Marriage, and Family

Late in the summer of 1935, I received my degree from Columbia University and left New York for home without any clear objective. I did have a couple of firm resolves: I would not live in Yoakum and I didn't want to teach school. Mainly I just wanted to rest since I had been going to school one way or another for all of my twenty years.

In Yoakum, my father seemed even weaker than a year earlier. He was grayer, thinner, and more stooped. His enthusiasm at having me at home prevented my even discussing the possibility that future plans would take me away.

Ten days after I returned from New York, Daddy came home at noon, waving his arms and shouting at the top of his still vibrant voice. "I have marvelous news. Superintendent Barron called me. He found out that one of the young teachers is married, and you know that's not allowed in the Yoakum schools. He heard Marjorie was home and needs her to fill that opening."

My heart sank, but I thought, *Poor Daddy, he doesn't know that's an impossibility.* Trying not to show my glee, I said, "Daddy, I can't do that. I'm not qualified. I've never had practice teaching, which is required for certification."

He was adamant. "That's ridiculous. You have more degrees than any teacher in Yoakum."

"Maybe so," I said, trying not to show my relief, "but I'm positive that the schools will lose their accreditation if they employ uncertified teachers."

Daddy was at the telephone and back in a split second. "We're going to Austin tomorrow to see the state superintendent."

I still wasn't too worried. However, I underestimated my father.

We traveled to Austin the next day only to learn that the superintendent was attending a conference in San Antonio. Not skipping a beat, we drove on to San Antonio from Austin to get the poor man out of his meeting. I still don't quite know how Daddy did it. Furthermore, once we had the superintendent face to face, my father put on a performance worthy of Sarah Bernhardt. He pulled out my records and diplomas and began his recital.

"My daughter has been away for years now—in Europe and New York. I'm sick and old, and I want her to stay at home for a while with me. I know I can't keep her unless she has some occupation. I know she's qualified."

The man looked at my father and then at me. He didn't even glance at the records. "If I issue you a temporary teacher's certificate, will you promise to take practice teaching next summer without fail?"

I knew I had lost. But because I spent every weekend in Houston, it became obvious to my father that I would leave Yoakum at the end of the school year. In those days there were more teachers than jobs, but Uncle George knew the superintendent of the Houston schools, who found me a place at Hogg Junior High School in Houston's Heights area.

I kept my promise. I took practice teaching, and, for someone who never wanted to teach school, I found myself doing just that. In retrospect, this decision changed the direction of my life. It undermined my as yet unexpressed wish to be involved in public affairs. I had had visions of being a translator with the State Department, a course of action that would have led me far away from Texas. Why didn't I resist? I suppose I wanted to please my father. I had a long history of doing so, and besides, he was so frail. Also, I guess I instinctively tried, then and later, to avoid the controversy and strife that had been so characteristic of my family while I was growing up. It was simply easier and less stressful to go along, subsuming my own needs and desires to the demands of my elders.

Daddy wrote his sister, Esther: "Marjorie will be coming to Houston in the fall, and I expect her to live with you." It was just as unheard of for an unmarried woman to have her own apartment if she had a relative living in the same town as it was perfectly normal for one

Meyer sibling to give an ultimatum to another. Not that Aunt Esther and Uncle George Cohen were unwilling or ungracious. Childless, Uncle George loved young people from babies on up, and what he liked, Aunt Esther liked.

No young adults I know today would have accepted without protest my living arrangements with Aunt Esther and Uncle George in their enlarged cottage at 607 Kipling, although my accommodations were certainly attractive. I occupied the small but elegantly appointed guest bedroom and bath. That is, I occupied it when Aunt Esther and Uncle George didn't have guests. It was not at all unusual for me to come home from school to find that all of my possessions had been moved to Aunt Carrie's house six blocks away.

No vestige of my occupancy remained at the Cohen home. Frank Mouton, the houseman and chauffeur, did the best job he could of making the transfers. However, it took several days of searching at Aunt Carrie's or back at 607 Kipling to locate blouses that went with skirts or cosmetics that occasionally ended up in the stocking drawer. No one could have been more hospitable than Aunt Carrie, and I dearly loved her, but she never had any more notice than I did when I—and all of my belongings—suddenly occupied her sleeping porch.

There were rules in the Cohen household. I installed my own telephone and paid for it. Seven whole dollars a month out of my $175 monthly salary. However, even though I paid for the telephone, I was not allowed to answer it if we were at dinner, for no one left Aunt Esther's table unless the house was on fire. Inasmuch as I taught school all day and went out on dates most evenings, only a small window of time remained when I could receive calls. The phone would then ring and ring and ring. I finally bribed Frank, with a dollar a week, to answer it for me.

When I reported for duty at James Hogg, the office personnel thought I was a matriculating student. At twenty-one, I was short and, once again, slim. I had to show them my letter of assignment before they would usher me into the assistant principal's office.

Leslie Center and I hit it off immediately. He was very good-looking, and I didn't consider a harmless flirtation with such an attractive man damaging, even if he was married.

I soon learned that the administration arranged sections of classes on the basis of the students' tests and records from elementary school. The sections were alphabetized and changed each year, so no particular letter became associated with either the low level or the gifted students. This was a wonderful system in contrast to the subsequent homogenization of students that inevitably led to the discouragement of those who couldn't keep up and the loss of interest by those who were held back. The "dumbing down" median eventually paralyzed America's schools. Despite its efficacy, the school policy had, I thought, one defect. New teachers taught the lower sections, and the more experienced teachers taught the gifted classes. I went to the principal.

"Mr. Brandenberger," I said beseechingly, "couldn't you *please* give me a class of gifted students? There are no heights to which I couldn't take them."

A serious man with just a hint of Germanic accent reflecting his ancestry, he looked at me with some compassion and a bit of a twinkle in his eye. "Miss Meyer," he said, "the gifted classes don't need good teachers."

I taught English, math, and general science. In those days no one paid attention to a teacher's major. And certainly, during the Depression, no one needed to learn French. I was a conscientious teacher, interested in my students' learning, but it was a time of "progressive education." This program had emanated from the Department of Education of my alma mater, Columbia University. Their theory was that children should not be bored with repetition, drills, or memorization. Grammar should develop from reading enjoyable books like the Bobbsey Twins series.

I thought the whole program a disaster. Because the children couldn't construct a complete sentence with subject and predicate, beginning with a capital letter and ending with a period, I started diagramming, the way I had been taught. The kids loved it, but it was against the rules. As a result, Leslie Center would come to my room to warn me when a supervisor entered the building. I would then pass out the Bobbsey Twins books, and that day the children read stories.

One day Leslie left school for a meeting downtown. A supervisor appeared in my doorway and walked to the back of the room. I had covered the blackboard with diagrams. I thought, *The fat is in the fire. There's no avenue of retreat. Well, let's go for it.* Instead of teaching the students the new lesson I had intended, I put them through a review of what they had learned. Children love to perform, especially when they know the answers. Hands went up. Everyone wanted the floor. I had one break. The supervisor had gray hair, so I deduced that she came from the old school. When she left the room without saying a word to me, I followed her into the hall and said, "I hope you enjoyed our class."

She held her head down, not wanting to look at me, and hesitated. "Way-ul," she dragged out her words, "the students *did* seem interested."

I did the same thing in math. The students memorized multiplication tables and drilled, and I think they profited.

Throughout my life I had been what my father derogatorily called a "good timer." I went with anyone anywhere. I knew lots of young men, but I refused to be restricted to just one or "pinned." In the 1930s, those days of deep economic depression, most young people could not afford to get married. Several couples that I knew went together for years. They weren't engaged because that meant setting a wedding date with financial obligations, but their eventual marriages came as no surprise.

When I left for Europe in 1933 at eighteen, marriage was the farthest thing from my thoughts. I left several boyfriends in Houston, one of whom, Jerome Levy, a very bright young lawyer, gave me his beautiful pearl-encrusted Phi Sigma Delta fraternity pin and his picture. Another was Al H. Sakowitz, who was leaving for Cambridge University in England. Al H. was not interested in his family's fashionable clothing store and instead devoted himself to scholarship, eventually becoming a professor, first at Texas A&M University and then at the University of Texas. We saw each other often in Europe. Somewhere along the way, he changed his last name to Sackton.

The weekend of January 14, 1938, Al H. Sakowitz, then teaching at Texas A&M University in College Station, came to Yoakum with me for my father's birthday. On our return to Houston, Al H. misjudged a vehicle coming over a hill near Weimar, Texas, and, by swerving sharply, he overturned his small car. In those days without seatbelts, I flew, back first, through a closed window and landed in a ditch. Al H. walked away without a scratch. An ambulance took me to Weimar, where they cut away the new, most expensive suit I had ever owned.

It was a Christmas present from Aunt Esther. With collar and cuffs trimmed in black karakul fur, it had cost ninety-eight dollars.

The doctor just sewed up the long, deep gash in my left buttock, and, within a day, infection flared. Another ambulance then took me to Houston, where the nuns at St. Joseph's Hospital told my father that the Lord surely had something in store for me because that wound—anywhere else in my body—would have severed a limb or fatally penetrated a vital organ.

There were no antibiotics then, only sulfa powder, so the wound was reopened and, with powder applied, allowed to heal from the bottom up. After two weeks, I faced a long convalescence while the muscles and nerves reestablished connections, so I went home to Yoakum to recuperate. I wasn't able to walk, much less work, and so the accident brought my teaching at Hogg Junior High to an abrupt end. Six months later, I walked first a few steps across the room and then a mile, increasing the distance each day. When I was able to walk eight miles along the Yoakum highway, I felt ready to resume my life.

Doctor bills were not unconscionable then, as they are now. The average family could pay them. Nevertheless, after the automobile accident, I had more medical expenses than either my family or I could handle. Texas law favored insurance companies. If one willingly rode in a car and didn't demand to get out, there was no liability.

The Sakowitz family, who owned one of Houston's most fashionable clothing stores, had a great deal of money. Al H.'s father, Tobe Sakowitz, came to see me in the hospital after our accident. He came alone, and I soon knew that his visit was more than a courtesy call. He explained in his broken English that, although Al H. was not going to work in the store, he was going to share equally in any inheritance with his brother, Bernard.

I found myself remembering the question my sister, Elène, had asked me when Al H. had been in Yoakum the weekend of our car accident: "Are you going to marry him?" When I answered "Of course not!" she was shocked and said, "But think of all those furs and diamonds you could have." She was thirteen years old.

I looked at Mr. Sakowitz sitting there next to my bed and said, "I'm glad for Al H. that you cherish your children equally, but if you're suggesting that it would make a difference to me, you're wrong. Al H. is just a long-time friend."

He smiled, nodded, and left. We understood each other. I wasn't interested in being his son's wife. It never occurred to me that this might have sabotaged any chance of a big settlement from him or the insurance company. I was also too young and inexperienced to recognize a clear conflict of interest. My lawyer, Uncle Morris Meyer, was best friends with the Sakowitz family, as were all the Meyer brothers who lived in Houston. It was unthinkable for them to press a liability charge against their friends.

When Uncle Morris held out little hope of a settlement for me, I went to Uncle Leopold Meyer—whom everyone called Lep—an executive with Foley Bros., the Houston department store owned by my uncle George Cohen. As a friend of the Sakowitz family, he, too, avoided approaching Al H. or his father personally. Instead, he dealt directly with their insurance company, threatening to take away the Foley's insurance account if they didn't honor my claim. Eventually, the company gave me enough to pay the hospital expenses plus a few hundred dollars.

Any mention of strangers who meet, get engaged within two weeks, and marry two months later inevitably evokes strong reactions. The idea of a whirlwind, passionate, swept-off-your-feet romance—à la Rudolph Valentino carrying his princess off into the desert on a camel—is a customary supposition. In my case, nothing could have been farther from the truth.

Sometimes I think of the cartoon of a pitiful applicant at the desk of an interviewer who asks, "Can't you think of a better reason for wanting this job than a desire to leave home?" Of course, as a cartoon should be, this is an exaggeration of Ray's and my circumstances, but it is important to understand our mindsets when we met.

Our relationship actually began while I was still in Yoakum completing my recuperation. A letter arrived from Gertrude Cohen, who was married to Uncle George's nephew, Bobby, both friends from my childhood. She insisted that, the first weekend I planned to come to Houston, I stay with them, and incidentally, they had met this wonderful young lawyer. I remember turning to my mother, saying, "Another one of Bobby's drunken friends!"

I wrote to Gertrude, "I have to come to Houston next Friday to see Uncle Morris and finalize the insurance settlement. I'd love to stay

Raymond Arsht, West Frankfort, Illinois.

with you and Bobby for the weekend, but I have a date for every night I'll be there, so please no blind dates. I know enough people."

She met me at the train, saying, "I broke your date with Sam Miller for tonight. You have a date with Raymond Arsht." I was furious.

That night, June 13, 1938, the four of us went to a prizefight at the old coliseum. Ray was nice looking, pleasant, polite, and interesting. When he asked when he could see me again, I apologized for being busy until I went home. "Can't you stay a few days longer?" he asked.

I demurred and mumbled something, thinking, *What do I have to do in Yoakum that is so important?*

The day before I was to leave Gertrude's, Aunt Esther called and asked me to stay with her a few days while Uncle George was out of town. She didn't like being alone. I was delighted, of course, and not just to accommodate her. Now I had a valid excuse to see Raymond Arsht again.

There is one indelible image in my mind of the first night Ray brought me home while I was staying with Aunt Esther. He tipped his hat when he said goodnight. Most of the boys I knew didn't wear hats. I thought, *Hmmm.* On our third date, he kissed me goodnight. It was nice. I thought again, *Hmmm.* Even after Uncle George came home, I stayed longer.

At the end of the first week, I had a letter from my mother. "You write about all the places you are going, to Galveston, to the movies, to the Country Club. Are you just going with Bobby and Gertrude? Aren't you having any dates?" I had deliberately omitted mentioning Ray's name or the fact that I was seeing any one person regularly. I didn't want questions. I had had crushes before. Lots of them. This time was different, although at first I really didn't know why.

Before the first week was over, Sam Miller's mother called. She told me she was having a small dinner party at home for Sam before he left for his medical internship at Michael Reese Hospital in Chicago. Would I be Sam's date? Sam and I had been friends all through college, so of course I accepted.

Ray called every day, making plans for every evening. When I explained why I would be busy on Thursday evening of the next week, he seemed to understand. I had no idea that Thursday evening would change my life.

Ray was twenty-five, a graduate of the University of Arkansas School of Law who had done his undergraduate work at Washington University in St. Louis. He was not a scholar. Rather, he was a lawyer because his parents wanted him to be one. They doted on him and gave him everything they themselves had missed during the hardships of their youth. They lived their lives over, for, and through him. He never worked a day in the stores they eventually owned. Instead he spent all of his leisure time on the golf course, and his parents rejoiced in his prowess. I always thought Ray must have been born with good instincts because, with his upbringing, he could have been very spoiled.

Although his parents were not very religious, they gave him only one firm directive: "Don't marry a Christian girl." Predictably, he fell in love with Mary Arnold, a wonderful young Christian woman whom I met years later when I lived in West Frankfort, Illinois, during the war years. To Raymond's discomfort, we became fast friends.

Because Ray was a dutiful son, he knew he couldn't marry Mary; moreover, his parents didn't want him around her in West Frankfort, where they lived. Licenses to practice law in Texas and Arkansas were reciprocal, so it was natural for the Arshts to consider Texas as a new location for Ray. They first went to Corpus Christi and then Houston. Somehow Ray ended up in the law office of Morey Epstein, Uncle George's attorney. He met Bobby, who worked for Uncle George, in a courtroom during a lawsuit involving Foley Bros., and they became close friends.

There is another strange thread to our story. Cyrelle Finston was a comely young Houston woman who could not have been more unlike me in appearance or personality. Shy and retiring, she had delicate features, beautiful fair skin, and brown hair, whereas I was a sturdy brunette and anything but shy. However, for some strange reason neither of us could explain, we would invariably end up at a party wearing the same dress or the same hair ornament. More important, every boy who took me out also took her out. We laughed about it often because it seemed to happen consistently.

After I stopped seeing Jerome Levy—the boy I'd been dating most regularly but did not want to marry—I was not at all surprised that he started taking out Cyrelle. It just seemed a part of Cyrelle's and my destiny. It had never been more than a curiosity to me because none of our shared experiences mattered emotionally.

When Raymond called about 5:00 P.M. on the day of Sam's party, I thought, *Poor thing, he won't have anything to do tonight.* We chatted for a while, and then I asked, "What are you going to do this evening? Will you be with Bobby and Gertrude?" He answered innocently, "Someone made a date for me with a girl named Cyrelle. I don't remember her last name." I stifled a gasp. *With all the girls in Houston, this is just too much,* I thought. Somehow I collected myself and told him she was lovely and also a friend of mine. He said he would call me the next day and hoped I would have a good time at the party.

Instead, at Sam's house, at the gala dinner his parents had arranged, I spent a thoroughly miserable, awful evening. I kept thinking, *This is ridiculous. I've known Raymond Arsht hardly a week. Why, of all the times that Cyrelle's and my paths have crossed, is this one so different?*

The next day Gertrude called. "Ray's mother is coming for a visit to see how Ray is doing, and so we're having dinner. I told Ray not to make other plans for you." It honestly never occurred to me that there might be any ulterior motive for her visit. She was obviously a doting mother who wanted to be sure that Ray was comfortably settled in his apartment at the Plaza Hotel.

Only a few days after Ray's mother returned home, Ray and I went to a movie. On the way home, he slowed down and angled his car into a parking space on a busy street. Cars were passing, and people were walking around. I said, "What are we doing here?" Ray pulled a letter out of his pocket and gave it to me to read. It was from his mother.

"I was delighted to meet Marjorie. I have told your father all about her. She is certainly all you described and more. She is exactly the kind of girl we always hoped you would marry." To this day I can't remember just what I said or did. I think I murmured, "That's very nice," or made some other inane remark. But Ray looked at me, and I looked at him. He said, "Well, what do you say?" I think I just said, "Okay." Almost in unison, we both said, "Let's go tell Gertrude and Bobby."

The next day, fourteen days after Ray and I had met, I wrote my parents, "I'm coming home for the Fourth of July weekend and I have a surprise. I'm bringing Raymond Arsht with me. We plan to marry on September 1." I had never before mentioned his name.

After the automobile accident, it had become torture for me to ride as a passenger in a car, so I explained to Ray that I wanted to drive his car to Yoakum. He owned a four-door convertible Packard, truly the snazziest car I had ever seen. We didn't make a speedy trip. For the whole 120 miles, every half hour Ray would find a reason for us to stop. Either he wanted coffee or a Coca-Cola or he thought we'd better get more gasoline. I knew he was terribly anxious about the prospect of meeting my parents, but I didn't have any qualms. I had made up my mind.

My mother met us at the front steps of our house on Grand Avenue. She was so nervous that, when she opened her mouth, no sound came out. We sat in the normally unoccupied, always hot, living room. My father was nowhere in sight, so I went looking for him. I found him in the bathroom, washing his hands, slowly and calmly. When he saw me, he looked up and said, "Hello, baby," and kept right on washing his hands. I said, "Daddy, please stop that and come meet Ray." Despite his cool exterior, Daddy was a wreck. However, he was polite. He didn't even start asking about Ray's politics, which was atypical. Somehow everyone began to relax, and my mother regained her voice.

Mama had worked her usual kitchen magic, serving her favorite special dish. We had called it Spaghetti Tetrazzini until someone discovered that recipe called for a cream sauce, whereas ours contained tomatoes and curry. Subsequently, everyone called it Yoakum spaghetti, which I, my children, and everyone in Yoakum still serve.

Ray pleased Mama very much. He ate a lot. Maybe it was nervousness, but the food was really very good. After dinner, Mama called me into the kitchen. She whispered, "Marjorie, are you sure this boy isn't Italian? The way he ate that spaghetti and with that scar on his neck?" She was referring to the scar left by a childhood operation. I assured her that he wasn't Italian or a part of any mafia and that she had just watched too many gangster movies.

The wedding plans began at Aunt Esther's house in Houston, where my cousins Pauline and Gina had also been married. Was two months too short a time for us to make all of the necessary arrangements? Aunt Esther thought it ample, so we kept September 1, 1938, as the date.

Next came the trousseau. Aunt Esther did the usual proper things: monogrammed handkerchiefs (I still have them), monogrammed sheets and towels, engraved notes (with "Mr. and Mrs. Raymond Arsht"), and engraved calling cards. For a wedding present, Aunt Esther and Uncle George gave us twelve place settings of monogrammed sterling silver flatware and all the serving pieces that International Silver made in the Norse pattern. The Meyer uncles gave us a sterling coffee and tea service on a large tray—also monogrammed.

We invited only family to the ceremony—aunts, uncles, and cousins—sixty people in all. A week of festivities preceded the wedding, so the Arsht family, Ray's favorite cousin—Lillian Linkon—Lillian's husband, Bill, and two of Mrs. Arsht's sisters, Sarah Silverman and Minnie Stein, came early.

Aunt Esther took complete charge of the wedding, although my father—who didn't drink a drop of anything alcoholic—provided the champagne. Mama was a problem, however. Instead of appreciating Aunt Esther's generosity, Mama resented everything she or I did and became increasingly hostile as the plans proceeded. This reaction wasn't really a surprise. For decades, Mama had resented the Meyers and everything to do with them. Nonetheless, it didn't stop there. The very first thing Mama said to Ray's mother when they met was, "You know we won't contribute any money to this marriage." She didn't say "We can't afford to" or "We don't want to," even though both statements would have been true. At the time, I didn't understand that her antagonism derived from envy and jealousy, bolstered perhaps by insecurity.

Aunt Esther was an experienced hostess, of course, so the wedding went off without a hitch. I remember my friend Lorraine, Jerome's sister, helping me into my wedding dress—a simple, off-white satin sheath with a heart-shaped neckline—saying, "It is positively unladylike for you to be calm enough to button all those tiny covered buttons on your sleeves." She didn't know I was preoccupied less with the novelty and excitement of getting married than with concerns about mothers. I was afraid Mrs. Arsht, who had been tearful all week, would sob. I hate tears at weddings. And I didn't know what my mother would do since she could stir up a storm anywhere, any place, at the least provocation, or even with none at all.

Elène was my only attendant. All of our friends came to the reception. Jerome brought Cyrelle—who, this time, was definitely not wearing the same dress as mine. Sometime later, they married.

We honeymooned in Mexico. Upon our return to Houston, Aunt Esther was frowning as she met us at the railroad station.

"What's the matter?" I asked.

"Well, there was a bit of an accident."

"What kind of accident?"

"Your mother decided to come to Houston for a few days and set up your apartment. The stove wasn't connected properly. When she opened the oven door, there was a blast, and she was burned—not badly," she hastened to add as she saw the look of horror on my face.

And I *was* truly horrified, not only by the possibility that she might be hurt, but also because it had happened in my house and would

Marjorie and Raymond honeymooning in Mexico, 1938.

certainly be viewed as my fault. "Where is she?" I asked, thinking she was hospitalized.

"Oh, she went back to Yoakum. She left you a letter."

What had she been doing at the apartment? There was nothing to set up. Ray had been living there for a month before we married, and we had moved the presents from Aunt Esther's before we left. My heart pounding, I rushed into the apartment to read Mama's letter: "I came to Houston for a couple of days to do some shopping and decided to stay at your apartment. I also thought I'd fix some food for you on your return. So much for my good intentions. I would have thought you would have checked your damned stove. I expect Raymond to sue the gas company immediately." Dear God, what a welcome home.

I telephoned Mama. "Are you all right?"

"No, I'm *not* all right. My hair is singed, and my face and arms are scorched."

"Have you seen a doctor?"

"Yes, I have some salve. But I'm principally interested in suing the gas company. Raymond is a lawyer, isn't he?"

He was. He had been working in Morey Epstein's law office for six months. Ray asked Mama for her doctor's bills and for a description of her accident so that he could process the claim. Mama wanted $250 and she got it. I sighed with relief, thinking all had gone better than expected. Then the ax fell. Morey Epstein's office sent Mama a bill for $35. She was outraged, nearly hysterical.

"How dare you charge your own family! I simply cannot believe such gall!"

"But, Mama," I tried to reason, "Ray doesn't own the office. He just works there."

"It makes no difference. I had a right to expect some courtesy!"

It's hard for young people nowadays to believe or understand that, in 1938, people really did marry before they slept together. I firmly believe that such a pattern of behavior was normal, not just for me but for every girl I knew. The truth is that the Pill did not exist at the time, and an out-of-wedlock pregnancy was as deadly a fate as Hester Prynne's in *The Scarlet Letter.* More important, if you acquired a reputation of being available for sex, the conviction existed that no nice man would ever marry you. Fear was a more compelling imperative for our virtue than any moral niceties. Times are different now, but, in my opinion, change is not always progress.

Ray and I complemented each other, and, at the same time, we were very different. He rejoiced in my achievements, although he wasn't a scholar. He had a different kind of intelligence. The oil business, when it finally came his way, was a natural, and it offered him excitement. A new world was out there waiting every day, although I didn't understand the appeal that held for him. If I had been working, I might have earned only fifty dollars a week, but I would have earned it regularly. Also, I used to say—not facetiously either—that if I died during the first game of the World Series, my family would have to wait for a funeral until the deciding game concluded, even if it were the seventh.

I don't think that, when Ray and I were married, we were in love the way people are in the movies. All these years later, however, I'm not sure that the reasons Ray and I married weren't more valid and enduring than those based solely on passion. We met at the right time. We were ready for a permanent relationship. We were lucky. We liked as well as loved each other. And more important, we had no unrealistic expectations.

Also, we shared the bond of similar small-town origins. Although Yoakum was very different from West Frankfort, where Ray had grown up, the fact is that small-town living has a peculiar culture of its own. Its slow pace and relaxed, neighborly atmosphere contrast sharply with the impersonality of urban life. We recognized this quality in each other, and we were comfortable in that milieu.

When Ray and I started our married life together, I had $700, saved from teaching school and the insurance money after the medical bills from my accident had been paid. Somewhere along the way after we were engaged, I asked him what we were going to live on. "Whatever we need," he said, an answer typical of his attitude toward life. He didn't tell me he made $75 a month at the law office or that his parents intended to give us a cushion of $3,000 to draw on as needed. All I knew was that Ray had been living at the upscale Plaza Hotel and drove a Packard convertible.

The Arshts were visiting us when we first saw the duplex at 2315 Swift. I thought the monthly rent of seventy dollars extravagant, but the Arshts loved the place. Mr. Arsht insisted we have two bedrooms. At the time I didn't understand why.

After we spent three weeks getting settled and becoming used to a new living arrangement, Ray's father came to visit. Sam Arsht was a nice, quiet, genteel man with even features and silvery hair. He suffered, however, from chronic illness—stomach ulcers and high blood pressure. These required him to eat stewed prunes or Cream of Wheat every two hours. I didn't know how to cook either one. When I tried, the cereal was customarily underdone, and the prunes overcooked, both of which mistakes he called, however pleasantly, to my attention. By the end of each day I was exhausted from the stress, but Mr. Arsht, who had spent the day in his robe, perked up when Ray came home in the evening and was suddenly ready to go out on the town.

During visits and in between, Ray's parents continued to treat him as a youngster instead of as an adult. Because he was the center of their world, they selected his cars and clothes. They wanted him educated, of course, but working? Well, not very hard, at least not enough to interfere with his pleasure—or theirs. Ray was a championship-level golfer. As soon as his parents came to Houston, they arranged for him to join the Westwood Country Club, where for the rest of his life he spent many happy hours.

When they arrived by train for their visits, they expected him to meet them regardless of the time of day—and to stay home from work while they were in town. I tried as tactfully as I could to explain that I would have to take his place during the day. They would be able to see him in the evenings and on weekends.

Sam and Ida Arsht, Raymond's parents.

On that first visit, Mr. Arsht stayed for ten days. Mrs. Arsht came the weekend before he left. Every two months that pattern repeated itself. In fact, every time Mr. Arsht felt more ill than usual, he wanted to come to see the "children." Ray never understood the problem until we had married children of our own, when he recognized how, as in-laws, we viewed our roles so differently from the way his parents had treated us. They never understood the importance of boundaries.

Mrs. Arsht was a large woman, taller than her husband. Short-waisted with long legs, she was a bit ungainly. She had a slight overbite and uneven teeth, but she seemed pleasant and, at least in the beginning, went out of her way to be gracious to me. At the time I didn't realize she was so very grateful that Ray, after never dating a Jewish girl in his life, had chosen to marry one. That initial gratitude eventually wore off.

Mrs. Arsht came from a culture where all the women worked, principally in stores, and the husbands pursued whatever interested them. Put on pedestals, men were admired, revered, and served by their wives. In contrast, I was reared in an environment in which husbands worked and wives stayed home, ran their households with servants, and raised the children. Even if the wives brought little or no money to the union, they considered themselves equals in marriage. Mrs. Arsht and I therefore had different value systems.

She saw all of my wealthy relatives and the big department store where so many of them worked. From her viewpoint, that meant a solid berth and future for Ray. I fervently disagreed. I vowed that no husband of mine would fall under the unrelenting, merciless—however benevolent—tyranny of our uncles at the department store.

Pauline's and Gina's husbands both worked at Foley Bros. Pauline and Gina's father, Uncle Marcus, also worked for Foley's as its public relations officer. He was beloved in Houston. A hail-fellow-well-met man with a smile on his face and a wonderful personality, he was suited to his job. Although neither of his sons-in-law worked directly for him, the Meyer brothers stuck together, no matter the issue.

All eight of the Meyer brothers had grown up in Galveston in a poor but ambitious family. At that time, Galveston was a cultured town where very rich and important families such as the Levys, the Kempners, and the Moodys—Jews and Christians alike—mingled comfortably in high society. The Meyers looked up to those families with awe, vowing one day to occupy that kind of place in their community.

The young Meyer brothers had to work extremely hard, and they were subjected to the indignities and abuses that came to workers without influence in those early days. My father, Marcell, and the next three brothers, Leon, Marcus, and Hyman, began working very early and helped the younger brothers go to college.

Just before World War I, Uncle George Cohen, who had married their only sister, Esther, bought Foley Bros., which was then a small clothing store, and kept the name. Not long afterward, he gathered all of the Meyer brothers from their various places of employment in and out of Texas and persuaded them to become part of his establishment. Only two escaped—my father, Marcell, who owned the lumberyard in Yoakum, and Morris, an attorney who practiced law in Houston.

Back row, left to right: *Meyer brothers: Hyman, Leon, Marcell, Arthur, Morris, Leopold ("Lep"), George Cohen, Lasker, Marcus;* middle row, left to right: *Leon's wife, Sylvia; Marcell's wife, Myrtle; Grandfather Achille Meyer; George Cohen's wife, Esther (Meyer); Lasker's wife, Lucille; Marcus's wife, Carrie;* bottom row, left to right: *Elène Meyer, Marjorie, Lois Meyer, Pauline Meyer, Lasker Jr., Gina Meyer, Felix Meyer.*

Inflation raged during and after World War I. Merchandise ordered to stock Foley's shelves increased so much in retail value that, by the time it was sold, enough profit had been generated to retire the debt Uncle George incurred when he bought the store. Then, in the 1930s and 1940s—in their middle years, prosperous, and with some economic and community authority befitting the heads of large departments at Foley Bros.—the uncles treated the relatives who worked under them with the same velvet-clad iron fist under which they themselves had labored as young men. Even as successful businessmen, they still suffered from Uncle George's domination.

I loved my uncles and aunts. They were interesting, intelligent people. Nevertheless, the uncles micromanaged their nieces' and nephews' lives. They always let it be known when they disapproved of our dates or our clothes. Every one of our actions was open to critical scrutiny. They insisted on our adherence to their wishes, however capricious, regardless of our own parents' authority.

With that kind of background, I didn't want my husband or me to be under their thumb, at least not any more than my being their niece demanded. Their interference was so haphazard and therefore so insidious that I feared Ray—easy going, malleable, interested mostly in golf—would do anything they wanted because he respected them all. I couldn't abide a future tied to that kind of subservience. I didn't want us to be dependent on them even if I had to starve. At the same time, I didn't want to fight. All my life I just wanted to escape controversy.

Mrs. Arsht didn't understand my attitude. She had seen large Jewish families in St. Louis find places in their stores for all of the succeeding generations. That practice was a pattern. She saw nothing wrong with a future for Ray in Foley Bros. even though he had been trained as a lawyer. It was hard to explain my opposition to her. I just said, "No, never."

Shortly before Christmas that first year, Julius Levi, a highly successful insurance agent in Houston and a longtime friend of my family, approached Ray. He said, "I've decided to open my own agency, and I want you to come to work for me. I know you don't know anything about the insurance business, but I'll teach you. You have a wonderful personality, and insurance is a 'people' business." Ray was very happy to get out of the law office and into something new. Not to be ignored was the fact that Julius would pay him two hundred and fifty whole dollars a month with commissions, if there were any.

Ray settled comfortably into the insurance business. Affable and charming, he made friends easily. We plodded along without many commissions but with enough of a stipend not to deplete that first three thousand dollars Ray's parents had given us when we married. I insisted on frugality. Our friends went to the top floor of the Rice Hotel every Sunday night for a buffet dinner and dancing to the music of a full orchestra. The evening cost five dollars a couple, which I considered extravagant, so Ray and I generally stayed home or went to a movie that cost fifty cents apiece.

We appeared to live an uncomplicated life. Every so often we played bridge with some of my newly married Yoakum friends who had moved to Houston. Men against the women. We used matches for money, but no contests were ever more intensely challenged. Every Friday night we went to Aunt Esther's for dinner. Uncle George was very active in Temple Beth Israel, where he served for a number of years on the board of trustees. He insisted on short sermons and timed Rabbi Hyman Schachtel's sermons to the second; they were not to go one second over twenty minutes. Also, he demanded a six o'clock service. Eventually, Hy rebelled, asserting his right to more freedom in addressing the congregation. Hy also persuaded the board of trustees to cancel the early service because most of the members of the congregation no longer supported it. Uncle George was furious, and thereafter the six o'clock service was held in his own home before dinner. He never attended services at Temple Beth Israel again.

Aunt Esther spent most of every Thursday setting the table for Friday night's dinner. It was a major undertaking that took on the characteristics of a ritual, and justifiably so. She had seven brothers living in Houston, along with their wives and assorted children. The main dining table seated eighteen. When there was an overflow, the married nieces and nephews—Pauline and Harold, Gina and Morey, Ray and I—sat with the younger children at a second smaller table. Very often one or more of the brothers went to New York on a buying trip for Foley Bros., so the number present varied from week to week.

Aunt Esther, usually fairly calm, was not at all placid when it came to setting or unsetting that table. Adding a place for a sudden unexpected guest was just as bad as removing one or more settings. Mama knew all about this, of course. Her favorite ploy was to arrive in Houston on Friday, generally without notice. She seemed to delight in my consternation when she walked through our door. I never knew what to do. It was a no-win situation. I could call Aunt Esther to tell her Mama had come in from Yoakum and ask whether she could come to dinner, or I could say that, because she was in Houston, Ray and I would stay home. Either alternative would disrupt Aunt Esther's plans. And either way, it placed Mama back in control.

Ray had never gone to temple very much. Moreover, although he sometimes went to sleep during the service, he didn't complain about our Houston regimen. Ray's parents, of course, were thrilled that he was attending services, never mind where. Nevertheless, they also sounded some discordant notes in our otherwise regulated pattern of living. Every Sunday morning between daybreak and noon, they telephoned. "How is the weather?" they would ask. Our response was routine—hot, cold, rainy—depending on the season. "How is *your* weather?" we asked in return. When they had finished telling us, the next regular question followed. "How do you feel?" Mr. or Mrs. Arsht would ask. "Why, fine," we would respond, "and how do *you* feel?" Their reply to this question took up the rest of the conversation, including a long list of their various current ailments and medicines.

Every Sunday.

I've been told that in most large, demonstrative families full of dominant personalities there is usually one person who functions as the peacekeeper—or tries to. I think that was my role in this period of my life. I had grown up in an atmosphere of constant strife—arguments between my parents and my mother's diatribes against the Meyer family, against her father's family, and against her brother and neighbors. Because of that experience, I forced myself to take every measure to avoid the same thing in my married life. I had vowed that my home would not be a center of discord. I was also determined not to complicate Ray's life by complaining about his parents as my mother had done about the Meyer family, so I kept my troubles to myself. I stuffed them down into a well that I dug deeper and deeper. As a result, I found myself in a continual state of anxiety.

Although I seemed to spend my time and energy trying to avoid trouble for both myself and others—in itself a nerve-wracking endeavor—I somehow always ended up in the middle of it. Mama would find fault with Aunt Esther. To defend or not to defend was the question, especially when the criticism was unwarranted. Similarly, my uncles would come to me to complain about the behavior of one or the other of my parents. Once, Uncle Hyman, who was in charge of the major appliance department at Foley's, wrote a letter to my father responding to an inquiry Daddy had made about stocking some stoves in the lumberyard. My father, instead of writing him back, simply returned his letter with a note on the bottom of it. "These stoves [are] too expensive for Yoakum." Uncle Hyman was furious.

Waving Daddy's letter at me, he said, "Look what your father did! Isn't this insulting? And I thought I was doing him a favor. You tell him I said I thought he had better manners." I should have said, "Uncle Hyman, *you* tell him," but then he would have considered me impudent, a fatal mistake for a niece. So, on our next trip to Yoakum, I dutifully reported the problem. Daddy was justifiably annoyed. "You tell your Uncle Hyman I don't have to make apologies to him for anything I do."

I carried messages back and forth constantly, feeling I had no choice but to obey other people's instructions. Consequently, I always ended up in the bad graces of both sides. Once I considered writing a book and calling it "You Tell Them I Said."

My first daughter, Margot, was born on March 22, 1940. It was a long, hard delivery because my pelvic bones didn't expand as they should have. I didn't learn why until the 1990s, when an orthopedist, examining my back, told me, "The X ray doesn't show anything but that long-ago broken pelvis."

"What broken pelvis?" I asked.

"The broken pelvis that shows on this X ray. It looks like an old break."

I thought back to the only occasion on which it could have happened: the automobile accident with Al H. Sakowitz.

"It certainly is old," I said, "about fifty years old." Apparently, at the time of the accident, the physicians were so concerned with my other injuries that they overlooked that one.

Margot was frail from the outset. I was a nervous wreck from worrying about her. She didn't eat enough, and she didn't cry enough. I called Henry Meyer, our pediatrician, every day and sometimes more than once. Finally, one day she seemed so listless that I took her to his office. After a brief examination, we went directly to the hospital. A few hours later she underwent surgery. Six-week-old Margot was diagnosed as having pyloric stenosis, a constricted passage from the stomach into the intestine. Breaking with my usual habit of not calling long distance because it was too expensive, I telephoned my father in Yoakum. I described both the problem and the operation. I added, "I'm told this is not uncommon."

"What do you mean, it's not uncommon?" my father barked over the telephone. "*My* children never had it!"

Our apartment became more crowded, of course, after Margot was born. The guest bedroom had twin beds, a chest of drawers, a chair, and Margot's crib. My daydreams of a cute, frilly, pink nursery were placed on hold.

As tactfully as I could, I tried to persuade the Arshts not to come visit for a bit, but, two weeks after Margot came home from the hospital, the doorbell rang. Mrs. Arsht was at the door.

"Surprise!" she called out gaily. "I brought a cure-all tonic for Margot, one that I gave Ray when he was sick." She extended an unlabeled bottle filled with a thick, dark-colored liquid. Staring at my mother-in-law standing on the threshold, I took the bottle gingerly. *I wouldn't let this awful stuff in the same room with Margot,* I thought. Still in shock, I looked over Mrs. Arsht's shoulder and saw an unfamiliar dark green car with a man sitting in the front seat. Recovering my equilibrium, I asked, "Whose car is that? How did you get here?"

"Oh," she said, almost coyly, "That's part of the surprise. Dad and I decided your Packard convertible wasn't good for a baby, so we traded it in and bought this solid, sturdy Chevrolet for you. Louis from the store drove me down, and he'll drive your Packard back to the store. I'll return on the train. The car trip was too hard for Dad. I just couldn't wait any longer to see the baby."

I felt faint. I thought, *Don't scream. Don't throw anything. I adore the Packard. I hate dark green* (I was remembering the dark green Brougham). *How could they do this without discussing it with us? What will Ray say? He* loves *the Packard.*

Mrs. Arsht misunderstood my silence. She didn't recognize it as a fight for self-control and went on talking. "I know you're surprised to have a brand new car, but we're pleased to have arranged it. I know I promised you a diamond watch if you had a boy. Well, you didn't. So this is a present anyway."

I sat down abruptly. I truly cannot remember what I said, but I think I murmured, "I like the Packard." I didn't trust myself to call Ray at his office.

When he came in, Mrs. Arsht met him at the door. "Surprise!" she called in a sing-song voice. "First, here *I* am! And something else—we traded in your car for a new one!"

I saw Ray gulp, but as usual, he maintained his calm demeanor. Looking at me, he said, "Well, I guess the Packard has seen better days." With his eyes still fixed on me, he asked, "What kind of car is it? Is it pretty?"

It was my turn to gulp. I couldn't think of anything to say except "It's dark green." Late that night I had a talk with myself. I thought again about how Mama had argued with Daddy over the Brougham. My final thought was, *I will not be like that. I'll make the best of it.*

Stupid and frantic are the correct words to describe my conduct as a new mother. One day I went to our pediatrician's office, sat down, and burst into tears. "What's the matter?" Dr. Henry Meyer asked, thinking some calamity had befallen us. He reached out to comfort me. Unashamedly, I blubbered at the top of my voice, "Margot hasn't eaten anything but one carrot this whole day!"

Henry calmly replied, "So, she just ate a carrot, so what? When she's hungry, she'll let you know."

In the midst of the household confusion brought on by a new, not-at-all healthy baby, Mama wrote me a letter:

July 15, 1940
Dear Marjorie,

I want you to give a party for Elène at the Country Club. She is sixteen and it's time she met some people in Houston.

I think the middle of August would be nice. Just let me know when you have confirmed a date at the Club.

Love, Mama

It never occurred to me to say, "I don't know any teenagers. I don't have time. Maybe next year." Instead, I started calling everyone I knew. "Do you know any teenagers? What are their names?" I developed a list of twenty girls and decided I would ask each of them to give me the names of some boys to invite. The problem with that tactic was that every girl I called wanted the same one or two boys.

Then I started calling a list of boys, thinking I would just tell them which girl to bring. Every single one of them insisted on bringing the same girl: a visitor to Houston. At that point, anyone else but my mother's daughter would have said, "The hell with it," but, of course, I couldn't. Finally, I called one girl who had sounded reasonably accommodating and one boy who had been the least emphatic, brought them to my house, and explained my problem. They actually worked it out, except that the party would be smaller than I'd hoped. Some of the invited teens just wouldn't come. The list shortened—from thirty-six to twenty-eight.

By the time the day of the party finally came, I was exhausted. Mama and Elène arrived the day before so that Elène could rest. They had the opportunity to observe, during that last twenty-four hours, my cajoling responses to those miserable young people who kept calling to ask whether they could change their dates.

After the party I thought everything had gone very well, but Mama said, "You certainly didn't put yourself out. There were too few people." I tried to explain the difficulties, but my words fell on deaf ears. Mama's reaction to a recital of my efforts met with the rejoinder, "You should just have invited more people."

All in all, Margot was a constant worry. The apartment was crowded. The Arshts wanted to be generous, so they repeatedly offered to buy me all kinds of things, but I had only one wish: for them to go to a hotel. However, I couldn't say so, and neither could Raymond. Once in a while I would suggest to him that he do something. He would answer apologetically, "I cannot ask my parents to go to a hotel. I'm sorry." We just had to have a larger house.

Theo Keller, an architect in Houston whom I had dated as a young girl, drew some plans for a new home for us. I showed them to my father. "You have drawn four walls around a bunch of closets," he commented. My enthusiasm for closets has never diminished. "But," he continued, "I approve of your owning a house, and I will provide the oak floors, send Oscar to install them, and give you the roof shingles as a house present."

Mama—and Daddy as well—were extremely sensitive about gifts to me from Ray's parents. After the first time I mentioned the diamond pin I received from them for an engagement present, I saw Daddy grow rigid. Mama drew her brows together and pursed her lips. After that, I never discussed with my family anything I received from the Arshts.

We built a house on Glenhaven, in the Braeswood subdivision, down the street from Gina's house. In June 1941, when Margot was fifteen months old, we moved into the spacious new two-story home with three bedrooms, two and one-half baths—and a maid's room and bath attached. It cost us thirteen thousand dollars.

We didn't begin to have enough furniture to fill the house, but I looked forward to acquiring pieces little by little. Just after we moved in, Mr. Arsht arrived to make an inspection. He came home with Ray one evening and announced he had bought furniture for the porch. I thought, *This has to stop sometime. I'll just lie.* Out loud I said, "How thoughtful of you, but as it happens, I've already purchased some and made a down payment. We'll just have to cancel yours. I'm sure it was lovely." Ray knew I was lying but didn't protest.

Around that time, a new appliance had come on the market: a Bendix washer and dryer combination. Until then I—and everyone I knew—had our washing done by hand on a washboard, and we hung it on an outside line to dry. During a wet winter, with a baby in Bird's-Eye diapers, laundry piled up. Even with a maid, hand-washed laundry was a headache. I just had to have a Bendix. It cost us fifty dollars, and I installed mine in the garage. When Aunt Esther came to visit and saw the machine, she exclaimed, "I cannot believe you bought that thing when you have no *chairs!"*

The morning after Mr. Arsht arrived on one of his early visits to our new home, he announced, "Ray, I want to go to the office with you today." No one suspected he might have an ulterior motive.

Contrary to his usual custom of staying in his robe all day, he seemed energized. "Don't worry about me," he said. "Just go call on your customers. I'll visit with Julius, and then I'll wander around town until time for the office to close." As soon as Ray left his office, Mr. Arsht entered Julius Levi's always open door, made himself comfortable in a chair, and presented his proposal.

"Julius, I'm not a well man. Before I die I want to see Ray permanently established in a solid future. Mrs. Arsht and I want to buy a participation in your company for Ray. It doesn't matter if it's just a small percentage to begin with, of course, as long as he has the option to increase his share as the years go by."

Julius was a jolly man, his cherubic features topped by a mass of silver hair, a broad smile his trademark. His generally good humor contributed to his success as a top-rated insurance specialist. "I'm sorry, Mr. Arsht," Julius replied. "It's out of the question." As respectful as Julius had been gentle, Mr. Arsht asked for a reason for his peremptory refusal. Julius equivocated. Mr. Arsht left, telling Julius to think it over, he would be back the next day. And he did return. Every day for three days. Ray and I simply thought he must be feeling better and didn't want to stay at home. Mr. Arsht's measured, civil persistence finally wore Julius down, and eventually he capitulated. "Okay, Mr. Arsht, I can't sell any part of this business because I don't own it."

"Who *does* own it?"

Julius paused, choosing his words carefully. "Marjorie's uncles didn't want Ray and Marjorie to know. I explained your visits, that the jig was up and I was going to tell you the truth." Julius sat back in his chair and coughed. Mr. Arsht waited. "Leopold Meyer and George Cohen own the company."

Mr. Arsht was dumbfounded but not horrified. When he returned to our home that evening and related the events of the day, I was both. I was also furious. Distraught, I walked the floor. I didn't know what to do. With a new house, a small baby, and very little money, we were hardly in a position to withdraw. Even more than horrified at their perfidy, I was devastated at the prospect of telling my parents that I, too, had been snared by the Meyer trap. I knew my father's views on that subject. While I was at Rice during the Depression years, when the Yoakum lumberyard was at its lowest ebb, Uncle George had offered Daddy a job with a sawmill he considered acquiring. It was a tempting prospect, but in the end I remembered Daddy saying, "I've been my own boss for too long. I'd rather be a big fish in a little pond than have to take orders from my brother-in-law, George Cohen." He turned down the proposition.

Neither of Ray's parents understood my anguish. Actually, Ray didn't either, completely, although Bobby Cohen, Uncle George's nephew and best man at our wedding, warned him before we married that he could expect to take orders the rest of his life by just *marrying* into the Meyer family.

War clouds grew blacker. Hitler had marched into Poland on September 1, 1939, our first anniversary. During the succeeding months, which lengthened into agonizing years, European countries toppled under the Nazi onslaught one by one, while America grew more anxious.

In August 1941, before Pearl Harbor, Mrs. Arsht informed us that the manager of the shoe store in West Frankfort, a bachelor with a low draft number, had been drafted. I saw a way out of my dilemma. "Your father is ill, Ray. We just have to go back to West Frankfort so you can manage the shoe store. We'll sell the house and probably make a profit."

Completely shocked, Ray exclaimed, "Go back to West Frankfort?"

The Arshts were horrified. They had done everything possible to get Ray out of the restricted environment of the little mining town. Not just giving up the opportunities of a metropolis but also foregoing the association with such a prominent family seemed to them unbelievable. I just kept pressing, gently arguing, and persuading.

A family named Chunn from Beaumont paid $15,000 for our house, which we had lived in for only four months. When I proudly told Mama and Daddy about our profit, Mama said, "Well, now you can give your father back the $1,000 he spent on your flooring and the shingles for your roof." His eyes downcast, Daddy looked embarrassed. I was ashamed for Raymond to hear this. To his enormous credit, Ray never discussed Mama's avarice with his parents. When we closed the sale on the house, I sent Daddy a check for $1,000. When he hadn't objected to Mama's demand for a refund, I assumed his silence was justified by a great need for the money.

We packed all of our household belongings into a moving van and sent it on its way to West Frankfort. Stowing our immediate needs for the cross-country trip in the green Chevrolet, we went to Yoakum for a final visit before making our way toward our new life. While we were there, Mama wanted to talk only about the Meyers and Julius—how they had pulled the wool over our eyes and how deceitful they were. It served me right for buttering up the aunts and uncles all the time. Mama's definition of "buttering up" people meant getting along with them. I found myself, despite my own resentment, defending them.

"Where are you going to live in West Frankfort?" Mama asked.

"Oh, the Arshts have room for us temporarily in their new home," I answered. "I told them not to make any permanent decisions about our living arrangements until I got there."

But then came the regular Sunday call from the Arshts, right there in Yoakum. I heard Ray say, "What surprise?" When I took the telephone, I had a premonition. I had learned to be suspicious of surprises. His voice trembling with excitement, Mr. Arsht said, "Marjorie, you just aren't going to believe what we did to the apartment. We put in new floors and new windows. It's just beautiful. I wanted to wait until you got here, but I just couldn't keep it to myself any longer."

"What apartment?" I asked gingerly, thinking, *No, no, no!*

"Why, our old apartment. It's right across the alley from our new house and so convenient."

I thought I was going to have a stroke. They knew how I hated that place. The first holiday visit we'd made to West Frankfort, I had nearly collapsed from the heat that infiltrated the second-floor space from the store below—steam heat that could not be regulated. I had even made it clear to everyone that I didn't want an apartment, *any* apartment, least of all that one. I swallowed hard and struggled for control. I couldn't breathe. I had been so determined to leave the aggravations of my immediate family and the pressures of aunts and uncles behind that I hadn't given much thought to the prospect of changing only the venue of problems. Was that what I was doing? I cried most of the 850 miles to Illinois.

Ray did his best to comfort me. "My parents mean well. They want us nearby so they can see Margot often. I promise you, on my word of honor, we'll find a house."

"And when will that be?" I asked, not at all nicely.

Having grown up in the South surrounded by a multiracial population and with a household always staffed by blacks, I found it astonishing that no black people lived in West Frankfort at that time. Mr. Arsht explained that, years before, a rape at the mines involving a black man had so enraged the community that all the blacks living there felt endangered. They quickly moved out. "But," I said, "I've seen a few during the day, shopping." Without embarrassment, he shrugged, "Oh, that's all right. They just leave before dark." Mr. Arsht didn't even notice my dismay.

White help required adjustments for me, however. A middle-aged white woman from a local mining family, Mrs. Wilson was short, stocky, tight lipped, and serious and always wore a frown, with her mouth resting in an upside down "U." I felt uncomfortable instructing her to mop the floor.

Mrs. Arsht never became accustomed to my having a maid, even less so after I moved to West Frankfort. With a superior air she would remind me, "The young women here have no maids, and yet they spend their days at the country club or shopping. They generally enjoy life." Only people who *worked* had maids. Mrs. Arsht worked, and therefore her maid was justifiable.

But then, at the West Frankfort Country Club, I met some of the young married women to whom she referred, and I found out Mrs. Arsht was absolutely correct. I just didn't understand how they did it.

The club, the center of all social life in West Frankfort, was established by the mine owners for their executives and provided an exceptional facility for such a small town. In addition to comfortable party rooms, it boasted an excellent golf course, where Ray had spent every waking hour when not in school.

There I met Margaret Ellen Johnson, known as Maggie, an athletic, well-put-together blonde; Lucille Simpson, a retiring brunette with a lively sense of humor; and Pat Newsom, buxom, with brown hair and a hearty laugh, always ready with a joke, most often off-color. They became my familiar, frequent companions. With small children not yet school age and no help at home, these women would play golf all day and gin rummy into the night. On rainy days, the rummy games that began in the morning continued after lunch. There was seldom an unoccupied table in the card room. Often, when the club closed at midnight, the rummy game moved to one or the other of their homes. I joined those late-night outings only when Ray traveled out of town. When I expressed astonishment at their management skills, Maggie explained.

"This morning I had just sprinkled a pile of clothes when Pat called for a game. I telephoned my mother, stuck the damp clothes in the refrigerator, put the dirty dishes in the sink, dressed Hal Jr. and Mary for Grandma's house, and shut the door behind me for a day of fun."

"Do you mean to say your husband will walk into the house tonight and find it with unmade beds, unwashed dishes, and damp clothes in the refrigerator? He won't say a word?"

"You bet your boots," she replied without a pause. "When I clean house, I clean house. I wash the walls, the curtains, even the ceilings. I beat the rugs. But when I play, I play. Hal understands." I couldn't wait to tell Mrs. Arsht how my new friends managed their lifestyle, but she wasn't impressed. In her view it was enough that when they cleaned, they did it themselves.

In both Yoakum and Houston, daily housework required dusting. Not in West Frankfort, though. Everyday housecleaning there demanded washing windowsills, furniture, and walls, which most people covered with a washable oilcloth-like fabric. Only a few weeks in West Frankfort helped me understand the need for this strategy: Fine coal dust permeated the air. To dust meant smearing these powdery coal particles. This also explained why Mrs. Arsht had been shocked in Houston when she saw the white leather chairs in our living room and the white rug in our bedroom. After just a few months, I had washable slipcovers made for those white leather chairs, and the white rugs disappeared. I dared not wonder about the color of our lungs.

In that atmosphere, Margot did not flourish. Too many chest colds left her drained and without appetite. I worried about her constantly. One day I noticed a lump on her throat where an Adam's apple would be. Frantically I rushed her to St. Louis to see our pediatrician, Larry Goldman. Larry's diagnosis: a thyroglossal duct cyst that required surgery.

Unlike the pyloric stenosis surgery Margot had at six weeks, we were now dealing with a rare ailment. While an embryo is developing, a sac at the back of the tongue normally disappears before birth, very much like the tail on a fetus does. In rare cases, however, the sac doesn't drop off. Sometimes, after repeated colds, it becomes infected and accumulates fluid. Such sacs have many tentacles, which are identified by injecting a dye before surgery.

In Margot's case, not all of the extremely fine tentacles could be excised. As a result, six weeks after her first surgery, the lump reappeared. The surgeon insisted that we wait until the remaining tentacles inflated enough to ensure that every single one could be identified for removal the next time. For six more months Ray and I watched that lump get larger and larger. The condition wasn't painful, fortunately, and Margot didn't suffer. Moreover, since she was not yet three years old, she didn't care how it looked. But we agonized. Ray and I drove the three hours back and forth to St. Louis off and on for six months, wondering each time whether the lump justified excision. I blamed the damned apartment, its radiators, and the environment's polluted air.

My constant prodding for a house of our own became a front-and-center consideration after Alan's birth on May 2, 1943. I didn't think I could face another winter in that overheated, miserable apartment with a new baby. Houses, however, were nonexistent in West Frankfort during World War II. Young people who married lived with their parents, grandparents, or in-laws until the host families died. If West Frankfort had any real estate agents, they must have starved.

Like a burglar who looks for notices of weddings and funerals to see when a house's occupants might be absent, I scanned the little weekly town bulletin for notices of people who were being transferred to another city. The obituaries offered no help since heirs for those homes already stood by, waiting their turn.

The Arshts argued vehemently against our moving, which would have cancelled out their alley access to our apartment. Any suggestions that we build a house fell on deaf ears, even though they themselves had built one. Their excuse was that they already owned the lot and couldn't sell it. They had one good argument, however. Workmen in West Frankfort were hard to find, unreliable, and unskilled. I had to admit (to myself) that their house validated the observation that labor was unskilled.

I kept hoping for a miracle, an available edifice that might present them with a fait accompli. "If you hear of a house for sale, *please* let me know" became my incessant incantation as I buttoned-holed everyone I knew and strangers as well. My friend Maggie, tall and lanky, her usually matter-of-fact voice raised to an excited pitch, almost sang the words over the telephone one day. "I've found a house for you! It's around the corner from mine."

I didn't ask for details. "I'll pick you up in five minutes!"

The house, its once-white paint peeling, had a dejected air about it, perhaps because it tilted a bit. Scraggly bushes that were scattered around the front porch looked forlorn. The yellowish grass, which needed mowing, made the whole large corner lot with its unkempt house appear abandoned. I'm sure in another life I would have rejected that house on sight, but considering the way I was living, desperation transformed that pitiful sight into a mansion. Without hesitation, I rang the doorbell. With her gray hair in curlers, Mrs. Canfield, a small wiry woman in her sixties, came to the door, straightening her apron.

I didn't wait for an introduction from Maggie. "I'm Marjorie Arsht. I was passing by and just fell in love with your house. Are you by any chance interested in selling it?"

She was obviously surprised. After a moment's hesitation, she said, "As a matter of fact, we've been thinking about just that. Won't you come in?"

An hour later I called Ray. "I've found a house on East Poplar Street. It needs a little work, but it will do just fine."

He asked all the usual questions about how I found it and finally, "How much?"

"Nine thousand dollars. I'm sure they'll take less, but that's your department. By the way, wouldn't it be wise not to tell anyone until you've seen it and perhaps negotiated the price?"

As we pulled up to the curb of 1201 East Poplar Street, I saw Ray catch his breath. Before he could protest, I said, "Look, it has three bedrooms and a bath downstairs and two rooms and a bath upstairs for guests and a maid." Hurriedly I added, "I told you it needed some work. Paint, wallpaper, even mowing the lawn will make an enormous difference." Once inside, he admitted that the rooms were large and airy and the arrangement was gracious. Ray definitely had a talent for dealing with people. Before I knew it, the Canfields were willing to accept seventy-five hundred dollars. As we drove away, anticipating his concern, I said to Ray, "I'll tell your parents this afternoon while you go to the bank to arrange for a loan." I didn't miss his sigh of relief.

Left to right: Alan, Myrtle, Marjorie, Elène, Marcell, and Margot in Yoakum, 1943.

A feverishly busy month that I spent with paperhangers, roofers, furnace repairmen, and gardeners did wonders, although a foundation repair proved hopeless. The front-to-back and sideways tilt provided a kind of quirky charm to the house. I loved it.

The World War II years—1941 to 1945—encompassed enormous changes at home, abroad, and in our personal lives as well. The United States had been unprepared for war. Long steeped in the "no foreign entanglements" tradition, our country had been lulled by the isolationist lectures of one-time hero Charles Lindbergh and the fiery voice of radio broadcaster Father Coughlin, a Catholic priest from Michigan who was a fascist anti-Semite. The American people, though aghast at the happenings in Europe, still wanted no part of the conflict.

Then came Pearl Harbor: December 7, 1941. Ray and I had spent a rare fun weekend in St. Louis and, oddly enough, for once drove back home to West Frankfort on a sunny afternoon without turning on the radio. We didn't know about "the day that will live in infamy" until we reached the Arshts' house late that Sunday evening to pick up Margot. The news of the Japanese attack was so startling and unbelievable that I don't think we fully absorbed the impact of the devastation, the loss of our fleet, and the toll on human life until later.

Suddenly young men from the colleges, factories, and farms stood in line at draft offices to volunteer for their country's service. Their mothers, girlfriends, and wives, often with tears not yet dry, went to work in the stores and factories. From their former occupations—keeping house, teaching school, or nurturing children—those women of the early forties were depicted in cartoons as Tillie the Toiler and Rosie the Riveter. For the first time American women were more than army nurses. Delivering airplanes, tanks, and munitions across the Atlantic to the British, they were an indispensable part of the war effort.

The American family and its landscape changed, and so did the discourse. "Can we get ready in time?" was the question Americans asked of each other, and the unspoken prayer in their hearts was "Please, God, help us do the job."

The volunteers and the draftees, who were trained quickly and frantically, shipped out to places no one knew how to spell or even pronounce. Billboards appeared showing a pretty face with her fingers to her lips, the caption reading, "Loose lips sink ships." German U-boats were devastating the Atlantic, and some were even spotted within view of the Texas Gulf Coast.

Patriotism was in style: soldiers marching, flags waving, and bands playing produced fast heartbeats, hands over the heart in salute, and goose bumps on our arms. *Stories from the Pacific,* written by Ernie Pyle, the acclaimed reporter who would not survive the war, told of the heroism those brave young men and women exhibited. They had probably never realized they possessed such courage.

Ray and I, as well as our friends and neighbors, lived with the radio blaring. Televisions did not exist then, but the newspaper pictures of those far-flung fronts etched themselves forever in our souls. After the first year, our rummy games dwindled. Instead, my ever-faithful friends and I worked countless hours doing what we could to help: Pat, always finding humor somewhere; Maggie, her quiet dignity reassuring us that all would be well; Lucille, bringing serious concentration to any task. Together we wrapped stamps with cellophane, which we then fashioned into corsages to raise money for the Victory Bonds, similar to the Liberty Bonds of World War I. We stood on street corners and offered the war stamps for sale: $5 for a small arrangement, $10 for a medium-sized one, and $25 for a bouquet for centerpieces, which Mrs. Arsht also sold in her store. We knitted sweaters, shawls, and mittens for the Red Cross.

In our new house, with the help of our new maid, Shirley Gillespie, and with Margot now in a nursery school, I thought our lives, in spite of the war, had reached an even keel. Not so.

Ray was a charmer, easygoing, handsome, and good company. He had studied law because his parents wanted their son to be a lawyer, but he didn't complain. He more or less fell into the insurance business, and again he didn't complain. We moved back to West Frankfort so that he could manage the family shoe store. Still, he didn't complain. I never suspected how much he really hated selling shoes.

Because the Arsht stores were Mrs. Arsht's bailiwick, Ray's father didn't spend any time in them. Instead, he dabbled in various business enterprises and invested in the stock market. He had an interest in a movie theater, some outlying real-estate ventures, and, significantly, an oil well just outside the city limits. When a lawsuit developed between the coal companies and the oil companies, Ray, still a lawyer, participated in the defense of his father's interest in that oil well. Because his side won, our lives changed forever. Ray immediately promoted the drilling of an oil well not far from West Frankfort. His father and others in the community provided the funding for that first shallow, not very expensive undertaking. Ray lived and breathed and agonized over that well. As the drillers dug deeper, foot by foot, he brought home samples of rocks that came to the surface.

"Look at this florescence!" he exclaimed, while I, pretending to be impressed, knew full well that neither one of us had any idea what that represented. Nevertheless, a member of the crew had told him it was a significant sign. One evening, when the well was expected to have reached its designated depth, Ray insisted I go with him to the field. I spent most of the night dozing in the car while he paced back and forth around the drilling platform like an expectant father. Finally he shook me awake. "We think we have a well," he said, struggling to appear nonchalant. I had never seen him so excited, so exhilarated. "Move over," he said. "We're going into town to buy beer for the crew."

But then I learned about porosity. When a formation is not porous enough, the fluid cannot be extracted, at least not with the technology that existed in those days. There was no porosity in that West Frankfort well, so it couldn't be produced.

Ray never went to bed. He was gone all the next day, although he didn't go to the shoe store. I worried myself sick. *He'll be crushed,* I thought. I walked the floor. After finally finding what he really loved, he would feel beaten. I was so sorry for him—and worried.

At sundown Ray drove up the driveway and rushed into the house, shouting at the top of his lungs, "Marjorie, I've found a new drill site!"

Even before his second well in Illinois failed, Ray found a third property, this one in Kentucky. Initially a skeptic where the oil business was concerned, I became an outright cynic. Ray's fervor seemed to increase, however, with each setback. I couldn't understand his continued optimism. But for business people in West Frankfort and neighboring communities, Ray's enthusiasm for the oil business was contagious. He never lacked investors who were willing to gamble on this exciting new enterprise that was suddenly emerging in what had been, for so long, strictly coal country.

Meantime, the war raged on and we were losing. In the back of my mind lurked the real possibility of Ray's being drafted. We didn't discuss the prospect, but the threat was out there.

A two-hour drive separated us from the Kentucky field. Ray ran out the door every morning before the sun rose. He seemed to begrudge the hours he spent sleeping. Every day he gave me a running report. "Just another two hundred feet" or "one hundred" or "fifty," he would shout over his shoulder as he left the house, jumping into the old Ford jalopy he acquired when he started traveling to and from the oil properties.

One day he called me at home. "Marjorie, we have a well," his voice crackled over the telephone wire. "And not just any old well—a *good* one!" The words came out so fast they were almost unintelligible.

"Is there oil in the tanks?" I asked, remembering porosity.

"Now, listen. We have to set pipe and arrange for equipment, but this time you're going to see for yourself. You're going to come with me and feel the pipe grow cold as the oil flows into the tank. You'll see, I promise you."

"Congratulations," I managed to say, trying my best to be upbeat for his sake. Still, I wondered whether this might not be a mixed blessing. If there actually was a well, would we be on this roller coaster for the rest of our lives?

I did go with him to Kentucky. And I did hold my hand on the pipe and feel it grow cold. I climbed on a ladder and saw the oil coming into the tank. The McAdams No. 1 was in business.

The next week Ray mentioned offhandedly at the dinner table, as though such a thing were an everyday occurrence, "Venture Energy offered me two hundred thousand dollars for the well." A fortune! I held my breath.

"And . . .?" I waited expectantly.

"Marjorie, I want to develop a *field!*"

At that time neither he nor I knew about Kentucky "hickies," which are little pockets of oil completely surrounded by . . . nothing. Ray drilled well after well in a complete circle like pins in a pincushion. Every single one turned out to be a dry hole. All of the proceeds from the McAdams No.1 funded these experiments. At the end of six months, the property was worthless.

I prayed, *Please, God, help him find something else to do even if it isn't selling shoes.* And then the draft notice came. Ray was called for a physical in Houston, where he had registered before we left in 1941. He decided to return to Texas although he could have transferred the test to St. Louis. "If I have to go, I'd rather be with a Texas outfit," he explained.

Only those who have walked the floor, wrung their hands, and prayed while waiting for a jury verdict could understand my anxiety while I waited by the telephone to hear the results of that physical examination. When the report came, it brought little comfort. The designation: limited service on call. The doctors had discovered a hernia, but that didn't definitely rule Ray out of frontline duty. The rules for drafting fathers changed from week to week depending on the needs of the military. In any event, Ray had to be ready on twenty-four hours' notice to go anywhere in the whole world. The draft designation pervaded our lives. I waited each day for the mail. Would they write or telephone or telegraph? Every time the doorbell rang, I jumped. Ray concentrated on a new venture instead.

"Marjorie, I have the most wonderful news."

Oh, no!

"A man named Snyder called today to offer me a lease on his one-acre drill site in the middle of an enormous producing field."

"Ray, I don't believe in the tooth fairy. There must be something wrong with it. Why would major oil companies let one single acre slip through their title searches?"

"Snyder says they just overlooked it. People do make mistakes, you know. I think it's the opportunity of a lifetime."

"Why doesn't he drill the well himself?"

"He says his health isn't very good."

The problems began again. Ray managed to locate drill pipe, which was expensive and scarce because of the war, but it didn't arrive when promised. The crew, carefully picked by Ray, suddenly had other work to do. He did another search. First one thing and then another delayed the spudding in of that well. Finally, the drill bit hit the earth. Not very many feet down the hole, a tool was lost. There was delay after countless delay, and then the well wouldn't "clean up" because the pipe had been set too high.

I sensed that something was wrong. This time even Ray worried. His carefree air disappeared. When the government called a halt to all drilling because of the war, we went to Washington, D.C., to appeal the fate of our yet uncompleted well and learned the awful truth. A compassionate bureaucrat explained, "We will grant you an extension, but it won't do you any good. You aren't ever going to bring in that well." He continued, "I know all about that property. Mr. Snyder tried to hold up the major oil companies for an exorbitant amount of money. He thought they couldn't refuse him since his one acre sat squarely in the center of their lease. Not only did they balk, but they promised him that no matter what it took, he would never produce that one acre."

"But sabotaging our well is illegal!" I screamed. In that quiet office my words sounded like machine-gun fire.

"Of course it is, but even if you get proof of their complicity, and you sue them, do you know how long the major oil companies will keep you in court? Is it worth it?"

We had to walk away. Was Ray discouraged? Not at all.

It was 1944. Ray phoned me from the shoe store and said, "Marjorie, I'll be home in a few minutes to pack a bag. I'm going to Texas."

I held my breath. "You heard from the draft board?"

"Oh no. I'll tell you all about it when I get home," he said and hung up. *It's another oil deal,* I thought. *I can't stand this!*

As he packed his bag, he gave me a running explanation. "A man named Edelman called me about a producing oil property that's for sale in East Texas. Dad knows the man and says he's a reputable broker."

"How much are they asking for the property?"

"Edelman thinks it can be bought for about $250,000," Ray answered as he methodically placed his folded shirts into the suitcase.

"And just where do you think you're going to get $250,000?"

"I don't know, but when I see the property and, if it checks out, I'm going to see Uncle George."

"Ray, you just can't."

"Oh yes, I can. Now don't worry. If this is as big as I think it is, there's room for more than one investor. I'll keep the lion's share and be in control."

"That's what *you* think!"

Ray called me next from Livingston, Texas. "Marjorie, this is a fabulous property. Three producing wells in East Texas, together with gas property to be developed in Starr County, down in the Valley."

"Why does the owner want to part with it if it's so good?"

"He's deeply in debt. He needs cash, and he's in the midst of a messy divorce."

"Ray, you really don't know anything about operating wells."

"I'll hire people for that." And so he went on to Houston, first to my Uncle Morris Meyer, the lawyer. *Perhaps Uncle Morris will stop this foolishness,* I thought, but he didn't. Instead, at Ray's request, he drew up papers of organization and debt service and all the other documentation for the transfer of property into a newly created entity, the Starr Oil and Gas Company. Then Ray went to Uncle George, who gave him every indication that he was truly interested. He said he would have his lawyers and accountants examine the details. Ray was ecstatic.

Back in West Frankfort, with Margot's overactive behavior and frail health, Alan just a baby, and the prospect of once again being joined at the hip to my family, I was gloomy. I had little household help. Even when I had some, it wasn't good. I didn't trust anyone with the children. And we were experiencing a bitter cold winter.

In the middle of it I had my thirtieth birthday, the only one that has made me feel really old. No one even remembered it until evening, when Ray called from Houston and a letter came from my father with a check for thirty dollars, his annual gift, each year augmented by one dollar. Mrs. Arsht suddenly remembered and called me hurriedly to pick out a coat at her store. Nothing helped. I had one hope, however: the deadline for closing the deal. Uncle George was not known for impetuosity. I was thinking, *Please, God, let it fall through.*

While waiting for an answer, Ray returned to West Frankfort. A day or two later, he walked in with a sad face and a telegram in his hand. My first question was, "The draft board?"

"No, it's from Uncle George. I just can't believe he turned me down."

Thank you, God, I thought. Of course, I didn't tell Ray I was experiencing one of the happiest moments of my life. Instead I said, "Oh well, that was kind of an impossible dream, don't you think?"

"Not at all. I'm going back to Texas to see if I can't get some other investors."

My Raymond. Never say "die."

By the time he had succeeded in securing the wells, almost enough funds had accumulated from accrued production to pay for the project. Ray retained the lion's share of the stock, and thus his business was launched.

The successful completion of the transfer of the East Texas property meant moving back to Texas. Everyone assumed I provided the pressuring influence to get us back to my home, but that was never the case. I dreaded moving back to . . . family.

In any event, another complication entered my life just then. One morning I picked up a cigarette and then threw it away. It tasted funny. Thinking the package was stale, I opened a second package. A sharp pang of terror flashed through my brain. Oh, no! I realized these cigarettes tasted just like they had two other times in my life. I just couldn't have a baby right now. In the middle of my bedroom floor, I stood stock still. I felt like the eye of a hurricane with gales of problems swirling all around me.

My other two children had been planned. Alan was eighteen months old, and Margot, with all of her problems, just four. I had no domestic help. Ray was in Texas more often than in Illinois, settling into a new office and gathering a staff. He also remained on call for the war. I called Warren Kaplan, our West Frankfort friend and doctor, and told him I was contemplating suicide. He examined me and performed a rabbit test, the prevailing technique in those days. When he called me, I could see the smile on his face beyond the telephone. "Hey, girl, quit worrying. The rabbit says no. Change your brand of cigarettes."

An addicted smoker, I had never been able to stand or smell a cigarette during a pregnancy. Each time my father had said, "Maybe this time, you'll quit for good," but each time on the way to the delivery room I wanted a cigarette. My taste buds, however, were accurate. It was just too early for the rabbit.

I sat down to write my parents because I had to talk to somebody. As horrible as the thought was, I simply had to have an abortion. I didn't want to worry Ray in the middle of his big moment, starting his new business despite his precarious draft status. So I stewed. When Ray came home, he, too, was distraught. The thought of an abortion was too painful to comprehend, and yet he knew how hard it would be to leave me with so much responsibility if he were called into the service.

In the middle of our painful discussion, the telephone rang. My father, who still made a long-distance call only for catastrophic occasions, spoke gruffly without any preliminaries. "Marjorie, I forbid you to consider doing anything about your pregnancy!"

"But Daddy," I wailed. "I don't have any help, and Ray may have to go to the war, and . . ."

He interrupted. "Listen, I don't care what the circumstances are. You'll find a way to manage. And that's final. This child will bring you nothing but joy." It never occurred to Ray or me that there was anything unusual about a father telling his thirty-year-old daughter and the mother of two children, "I forbid you." In retrospect, however, we were relieved to have the decision made for us, even though we didn't admit it at the time.

As the months passed, Ray spent more time in Texas than with his family in West Frankfort. He lived at the Rice hotel, and my aunts, uncles, and cousins entertained him royally. He put his laundry in a bag for the maid and his shoes outside the door to be polished. He forgot about being tied down with children. He forgot about being housebound. On one trip back home, he suggested at dinner that we go to the club. When I remarked that we had no help and no baby-sitter, Ray casually remarked, "I think I'll go on alone." I won't repeat here my response, but Ray didn't go to the club that evening and never again suggested going on anywhere alone.

In the early months I was ill, and then later, with my responsibility for the other two children, it became increasingly obvious that I couldn't move to Texas until after the new baby was born. In addition, I would have to find a new doctor because my wonderful Dr. Sam Soule, who had delivered Alan in St. Louis, was far away in India with the war. In that condition, I couldn't go to Houston and find a house. Ray found one he wanted to buy, but I couldn't see him making such a decision without me.

"Just rent something," I insisted.

We also had another requirement. My father wrote to inform us that we would need to make sure our new house had a bedroom in it for Elène. Because of her attachment to "an unsuitable young man," he felt it urgent that she leave Yoakum. We never questioned his ultimatum. I was six months pregnant and thought I didn't need to worry about any of that until later. But it was later than I thought.

Margot got sick. She had trouble breathing. Larry in St. Louis said, "She needs her adenoids out. Nothing wrong with her tonsils, and there's a theory now that those tonsils somehow filter out viruses. So just the adenoids." He wrote the orders to a surgeon I didn't know and never met in advance.

Raymond was driving in from Texas and detouring through Yoakum because, he said, my father seemed inordinately concerned about Elène. He was sure he'd be there in time for the surgery.

At the hospital, I explained Larry's directives to the admitting office. Just adenoids, no tonsils. I wrote those instructions in large print on every form I filled out. Raymond hadn't arrived, but we had to proceed anyway. The hospital was on wartime footing, and when they called you, you went. On the way to surgery, I said to the nurse, "Remember, no tonsils." She nodded. Thirty minutes later Margot emerged, crying that her throat hurt.

"Why is her throat hurting?" I asked the surgeon who accompanied her.

"What would you expect when tonsils come out? Give her some ice cream."

My screams of fury were probably heard throughout the hospital. The surgeon apologized. He simply hadn't looked at the chart. He was rushed, and it was unusual to take out only adenoids.

With any child but Margot, the procedure would have gone as expected. Everything happened to her. I was convinced she would now suffer dire consequences. Furthermore, where was Raymond? I looked at my watch. I had been so upset I hadn't realized how late he was.

Five hours past time for him to arrive, Ray called, "Marjorie, I'm sorry. We had an accident. No one's hurt. Elène is with me. We'll be at the hospital in thirty minutes."

"Elène is with you?"

"There were problems in Yoakum. I made Elène say 'Good-bye' to your father. They weren't speaking. She'll help you with the babies and the move."

Two weeks later, Elène insisted I drive her to St. Louis to see a plastic surgeon for removal of a small mark on her back received when she fell off a horse. She had been bored with nothing to do in West Frankfort, so she found a place to go horseback riding—and fell off. En route to St. Louis, my water broke. Leslye was born on June 28, 1945, two and one-half months early.

"Can you at least get me a private room so I don't have to see all these mothers cuddling their newborns?" Tears were running down my face. "Larry, God is punishing me. I didn't want to have this baby."

My unexpected delivery, ten weeks before the baby was due, had landed me in a noisy, overcrowded ward of the St. Louis Children's Hospital. Larry Goldman, a renowned doctor, was my pediatrician. He brought me the bad news. "I'm sorry, Marjorie, but you just can't count on this baby. Her lungs are underdeveloped. We'll do what we can, but I want you to be prepared."

During the next twenty-four hours I squeezed my eyes shut, held my breath, and clenched my hands every time I heard footsteps walking down the hall toward my room. I was so afraid of losing that baby. I wanted to name her Allison, but Ray's mother insisted that her name begin with an "L" for good luck since some long-ago relative of hers named Leah had lived to be very old. So we chose Leslye, using a "Y" since so many boys were named Leslie. When Larry returned at the end of the first day, I started crying.

"Hey, I know I'm not much to look at, but I'm surely not *that* bad."

"I thought you were coming to tell me . . ."

"Stop anticipating the worst, although I still don't want to get your hopes up. We have some hurdles to cross, but there is one curious thing about your baby. Normally, babies who weigh less than a pound and a half are lethargic and sleepy. But this baby is crying and hungry."

"Then I guess she belongs to me."

"Actually, we're afraid to feed her very much besides vitamins through an IV tube because we don't know how developed her digestive tract is."

"Can we get special nurses for her?"

"This is the best experimental nursery for 'preemies' in the world. There are no better nurses anywhere."

"I want to see her."

A nurse wheeled me to the glass window behind which the newborns were kept. A couple standing behind me said, "Look at that little bitty baby. Isn't she cute?" I looked at Leslye, with arms and legs like matchsticks, long black hair, and veins pulsing and showing through transparent skin. *Thank God my father isn't here,* I thought. She was the most ghastly looking infant I had ever seen in my life! I cried all the way back to the room.

The next evening Larry came in. He knew I was holding my breath. I waited. "Marjorie, the baby continues to cry and suck, which is truly unusual. But she isn't jaundicing as normal preemies do. Instead of having a yellowish tinge, her skin is bright orange."

"She looked bad enough yesterday," I told him.

"We don't know if her kidneys can handle this much jaundice, but we're giving her fluid through her ankles to help her flush the dead cells."

Those miniature ankles? "When will we know if she's going to make it?"

"We're traveling in uncharted territory."

Because premature babies had to have breast milk, nursing mothers who couldn't get near their tiny babies replenished the supplies of the hospital's mother's milk bank. Taking a breast pump with me, I moved from the hospital down the street to the Chase Hotel. Elène and Ray were managing in West Frankfort without me. A telegram came from Mama.

"Isn't this birth early?"

After four weeks, walking to the hospital twice a day to deliver my milk, watching Leslye through the nursery window gain weight ounce by ounce, I began to feel we were out of danger. I didn't let myself think about what was happening with the other children in West Frankfort. And then Larry called me at the hotel.

"Marjorie, I really hate to tell you this. I'm truly sorry, kid, but we may be dealing with hydrocephalus. The baby's fontanel is protruding."

I couldn't bring myself to accept another disaster. "Couldn't that be from all the fluid you've given her since the jaundice?"

"Excess fluid shows up in the ankles, not in the cranial cavity. I also have to tell you that I'm leaving town for a month, but I've arranged for a substitute who will take care of everything."

After dealing with all of Margot's idiosyncrasies and Alan's birth, Larry Goldman had become friend and counselor as well as our pediatrician. I went into the hotel room's bathroom, closed the door, and wailed.

At the end of five weeks Leslye weighed five pounds. Her fontanel remained unchanged, but it was time to leave the hospital and discard the breast pump. It was also time to move to Texas.

While I was in St. Louis, Ray found us a house to rent on Roseneath Street in Houston. He reported that it had a downstairs bedroom and bath for Elène, so as soon as the baby could travel . . .

Having to pack didn't stop me from measuring Leslye's head every single day and sometimes twice a day. Slowly, horribly, almost imperceptibly, it enlarged. At night I prayed, *Please, God!* Every morning I awoke thinking, *Oh God, help me through another day, another measurement!*

In the St. Louis nursery, the lights had been on twenty-four hours a day. As a result, Leslye had day and night mixed up. She slept all day and cooed or cried all night, wide awake. I had to employ a woman to rock her from dusk to dawn so I could get enough sleep to prepare for the move.

Eventually, all six of us arrived on Roseneath Drive, our Houston residence. We entered the front door. Most people in shock turn pale. Ray's dark complexion, in startling circumstances, took on a peculiar shade of green. We stood and stared, speechless. Ray had thought the furnishings in the house were quite nice. A slight error. What he had seen were the previous tenants' possessions. The furniture we found in the house had been stored for years in the garage, uncovered, unprotected, and obviously collected from a discard sale. The sofa was covered in a faded fabric, showing some signs of once having been imprinted with roses and vines. The upholstery material, now in shreds, allowed the cotton padding underneath to protrude wherever there was a corner or a curve. The carpet was so stained and dirty that it took a stretch of imagination to suppose it might once have been beige. The coffee table must have been beaten with a hammer or some other sharp instrument because more of the construction showed than the veneer. The dining room, opening onto the living room, had a decent-sized table, but only three of the six chairs had enough legs to stand upright.

Without saying a word I inspected the rest of the house. Every bedroom had beds. A four-poster in our room, twin beds in the other two bedrooms, all scarred and ugly, but beds, nevertheless. The mattresses, however, were quite another story. They must have been placed under the furniture on the floor of the garage. They couldn't have gotten that filthy propped against a wall or rolled up. Poor Ray! He was first distraught, then furious. Margot, five years old, her curls bouncing, arms akimbo, broke the silence. "Is *this* where we're going to live?" There was nothing to do but laugh!

"If you don't throw away that tape and stop measuring Leslye's head, you're going to have to get yourself another doctor."

"But Henry . . ."

"Marjorie, I've told you before, and I'm telling you again, I believe this baby was so premature that her head is still growing faster than her body, which is what happens to a developing embryo inside the womb." A friend before either of us had married, Dr. Henry Meyer was a tall, dark-haired man with a learned look about him, which was enhanced by rimless glasses. He had been Margot's pediatrician and cared for her during her early trials in Houston before we left for West

Frankfort. Now he was in charge of my three children: Margot, five; Alan, two; and Leslye, three months old. Henry was an old-fashioned, conservative doctor, so it was not out of character for him to view my chronic hysteria with equanimity. Facing every new development with "Let's not rock the boat" or "Let's wait and see," he completely baffled Ray's mother, who was a believer in "taking something" for every ache or pain. Henry's favorite prescription was baby aspirin.

I hired two helpers, Iola Caldwell, a good cook from Yoakum, and Elaine Jackson, the nurse, whom we immediately renamed Ellen since we already had one Elène in the house. We moved the tattered living room furniture back to the garage even though I would have liked to put it on the curb for the garbage pickup. Fortunately, I had kept my own sofa and enough of my chairs and tables to furnish the living room, however sparsely. I had the dining room chairs fixed and bought new mattresses. The house could hardly have been featured in *Good Housekeeping,* but it was finally clean.

The year we spent on Roseneath Drive, 1945 to 1946, was filled with difficult adjustments, beginning with the move back to Houston, Ray's new business, Margot's hyperactivity and inability to adjust even to kindergarten, Leslye's potential hydrocephalus—complicated, as usual, by responsibilities to Mama and Elène.

Ray, however, had never recovered from his dismay at the appearance and condition of the Roseneath house, so different from his first view of it. He couldn't wait to move. He didn't like the neighbors, either, a couple our age from New York who looked with disdain on our shabby house. Besides, they criticized Alan, the apple of Ray's eye, because the two-year-old occasionally relieved himself in our backyard.

I kept thinking we could buy the house we were in and remodel it, but Ray wasn't interested. He wanted something else, but in the immediate post–World War II years, little new construction had taken place, and demand outpaced supply. Prices were high, especially when rent control, imposed during the war, was removed. Then suddenly Uncle Leon Meyer died. He was the second oldest brother after my father, who was the eldest of that large Meyer family of eight boys and one girl. Uncle Morris, fifth in line, was the lawyer for his estate. He said to us, "This is a wonderful opportunity for you to buy a house."

I hated the house Uncle Leon and Aunt Sylvia owned on Southmore Street. It was dark, dismal, and out of date, but Ray's father loved it. Unlike our other residences, which he dubbed "cracker boxes," this house had two-inch-thick interior stucco walls with dark brick outside. A sturdy structure, indeed, if you ignored the antebellum kitchen and the mosquelike arches dividing the downstairs rooms. Nonetheless, it had four bedrooms and a sleeping porch—room for everyone, including Elène and Ray's parents on their frequent visits. Uncle Morris urged us to buy it for thirty thousand dollars. "A good buy," he said. What did we know?

Ray's father happened to be in Houston when this great opportunity presented itself. He was ecstatic. "I'll pay for it myself," he said. "Finally you will have a solid brick house with a good foundation."

So move we did. Our sixth move in the eight years of our marriage. And it wasn't our last. Seven years later, after inflation and Houston's growth, we sold that Southmore house for eighteen thousand dollars. I didn't care that it sold at a loss.

In 1948, the threat of polio dominated our lives. Ray was so fearful of that scourge that the children were virtual prisoners. No movies, no swimming pool, no parks. Margot, still delicate, withered in the heat of Houston's long summer. I had to find an alternative, and I did—three camps in Maine: Forest Acres for girls, Indian Acres for boys, and even one for toddlers. We fled to Maine as soon as the facilities opened.

In July, Ray telephoned me there with the news that Daddy was gravely ill and that I should fly home immediately. I hadn't been in an airplane since I had flown across the English Channel years before. My father had earlier admonished me, "You have children now, so if Ray has to travel by plane on business, that's one thing. You have my permission to fly only if you have to fly home to my bedside when I'm dying." His facetious, offhand remark had been prescient.

The owners of Rod and Reel, the camp where I was staying, also owned the children's camps. They insisted on caring for Leslye, then just three years old, at Alan's nursery camp while I went to my ailing father's bedside.

The plane made thirteen stops before landing in Houston, where Uncle Morris and Maxine met me for the drive to Yoakum. When

Daddy, his face pale and drawn, saw me, he said, "What are you doing home? I must really be very ill."

I leaned over his bed to give him a kiss. "Summer's over, and I came for a visit."

"It didn't seem to me that summer was over."

Elène and I sat on either side of Daddy's bed in Yoakum as he took his last breaths. Mama couldn't face those painful moments. She lay on the bed in the front room and stared at the ceiling. She was pitiful, facing a future without my father, the strong shoulder and the center of her life for so many years. Forgotten were all the quarrels, all the screaming tirades. My beloved father died that night after a long battle with heart trouble. Mama's state of helplessness and grief did not last long.

Preparations had to be made for my father's service and his interment in Beth Israel's original cemetery on Dallas Street in Houston. There he would be buried in the large plot established by Aunt Esther and Uncle George in memory of her mother and for the benefit of all of the Meyer sons and their families.

Muted voices and the coming together of families and friends seeking solace for grief generally characterize the preparations for the funeral of a loved one. Not my father's, however. The first explosion came over the selection of a rabbi. Dr. Henry Cohen in Galveston, whom everyone loved dearly, was old and feeble. He had presided over the religious education of all of the Meyer brothers and was made famous by a book written about him, *The Man Who Stayed in Texas*. He was nothing short of a legend.

My favorite story of Rabbi Cohen described his trip to Washington, D.C., by bicycle to see President Taft. Insisting on speaking with the president personally, he sat outside the Taft office for several days. Finally, President Taft agreed to meet him. "Well, Rabbi," he said, "what is so important that you would ride a bicycle all the way from Texas to see me?"

Rabbi Cohen replied, "There is a young man in a Galveston prison who doesn't belong there. He's a stowaway who, if deported, will face death. Only your pardon can bring about justice."

The president chuckled, "I have to say you Jews do take care of each other."

Rabbi Cohen held up his hand. "Oh, Mr. President, I didn't make myself clear. This young man isn't a Jew. He's a Greek Catholic."

Of course, everyone in the family wanted Rabbi Cohen, but his delicate health made his presence too unpredictable to rely on him alone. Mama insisted on Rabbi Bob Kahn, whom she personally knew from the times Bob had visited Yoakum with me when he was the junior rabbi at Beth Israel, the Meyer family's temple. Mama's preference, however, did not meet with the approval of the other family members. Complicating the situation was the split that had occurred in Beth Israel's congregation during the early 1940s, the years when Ray and I lived in West Frankfort. The schism reflected the national division in Jewish attitudes toward the prospective establishment of the state of Israel. At that time, many of Beth Israel's congregants left their temple and chose Bob to be their senior rabbi in a new temple they called Emanu El.

The Meyers felt Bob's departure showed betrayal and disloyalty, the two characteristics the Meyers most abhorred. He became persona non grata. Instead, the Meyer brothers wanted Rabbi Hyman Schachtel to conduct Daddy's service. He was the current senior rabbi at Beth Israel, newly employed specifically because he opposed a Jewish political entity in the Middle East. Some years later Hy changed his point of view when he could no longer tolerate the ostracism by his professional colleagues, every single one of whom supported the founding of a political state for Jews.

Mama insisted, "I don't know Hy Schachtel, and he didn't know Marcell. I want Bob Kahn, who was a guest in this house. He knew the person he'll be eulogizing."

The Meyers wanted no part of Bob, however. "Myrtle," Uncle Lep persisted, "you and Marcell don't belong to a temple. Hy Schachtel is our rabbi. It seems to us that our rabbi should conduct the service for *our* brother. Hy did know Marcell. He met him at Lasker's funeral. And he knows all our family, including Marjorie and Ray."

A brouhaha ensued, resulting in Mama ordering all of Daddy's brothers and their families out of her house in Yoakum. They sat outside on lawn chairs in the July heat. I marched back and forth with pitchers of lemonade and suggestions for compromise. Finally, I put my foot down and issued an ultimatum to the fractious contenders.

"We'll just invite all three. I'll call Bob in Houston and Rabbi Cohen in Galveston. Uncle Lep, you invite Hy. He's in Maine on vacation. Who knows if he'll even come?"

Then arose the matter of where to have the service. The Meyer brothers wanted to hold it at the George Lewis Funeral Home, a firm that had taken care of Uncle Marcus and Uncle Lasker, the two brothers who preceded Daddy in death. Mama was adamant. "After Lasker's funeral, Marcell said he didn't want to be buried from a funeral parlor, and he won't be. That's all there is to it."

I had to persuade my uncles that the service could be held at my house on Southmore. As much as I hated that house before, I hated it even more now. Although the floor plan was traditional—a living room that opened into a dining room with a small sunporch on the side—there was simply no room for a crowd. By the time the service was to take place, I was frantic. Ray finally arranged for a loudspeaker so people could stand outside in the early August heat and hear the rabbis' words. All three rabbis turned up. In those cramped, hot rooms, each one offered his own eulogy to my beloved father. I insisted on only one psalm, the twenty-third, whichever one chose to read it. When it was all over, Mama and Elène were too exhausted to take care of any of the inevitable chores that follow a death, so I saw to the thank-you letters and the unpaid bills.

After three strenuous weeks in Houston, I fled to rejoin my children in Maine. I felt as if the Hound of the Baskervilles was chasing me. Everything had been so contentious that I hadn't had time for my own grief. On the trip back to Maine, the floodgates opened. I couldn't contain my sobs even though I knew I was making a scene on the plane. It was devastating to realize I had lost my only friend in my own family.

As I walked toward Leslye's cabin, she appeared in the doorway. When she saw me, she started running toward me, crying at the top of her voice, "Mommee, I at camp!" Only three weeks earlier she had had a language of her own. When she wanted water, she said, "bomba." We understood her then, but the counselors must not have, and so she had to speak English. Her baby talk was gone. A poignant moment. Another door from babyhood to childhood had been closed. In a flash I knew my little children would not remember the extraordinary man who had been their grandfather, so it would be up to Raymond and me to re-create him for them. Judaic tenet describes immortality as a state of being remembered in the hearts of loved ones. I would have to see to it that, in my lifetime at least, my father would be immortal.

It was 1950, almost two years since Daddy died. During all those months, Ray had been almost completely at Mama's disposal, involving himself in all the minutiae of shutting down the Yoakum interests—selling the lumberyard, the house, and the apartment properties. Mama really liked Ray and generally behaved well around him. Still, not until years later did I realize she had never even once said "thank you" for anything he did. We all just took for granted that, when she wasn't furious, she was pleased.

Mama didn't have a lot of money. There was almost no cash and little, if any, insurance. Nevertheless, the sale of the house on Grand Avenue and the down payment for the sale of the lumberyard provided enough money to initiate a mortgage for the purchase of a duplex in Houston. Ray contacted an agent he knew, and soon we located a wonderful apartment for her on Binz Street. It was a gracious, white, two-story duplex situated near Almeda Road, only a few blocks from our house on Southmore. One of the two apartments in the duplex was upstairs, and the other, downstairs. Mama could rent the lower apartment and have enough income to cover the mortgage on the whole building.

Elène took most of the responsibility for helping Mama move and used some of her own money left from a matured educational insurance policy to make alterations in the apartment. The day finally came when Mama was settled on Binz Street, and it was time for Elène to join her there. In her room in our house, Elène sat in a rocking chair, gripping its arms. "How in the world am I going to live in the same house with Mama? I don't think I'll be able to stand it." She seemed on the verge of tears. Elène had lived with us off and on from the time she was out of college.

"You don't have to move, Elène," Ray said. "You've made your home with us for so much of your adult life. There's no reason at all for you to leave if you don't want to go."

I was silent, at the same time feeling terrible that I couldn't wholeheartedly join in Ray's supportive plea. My stomach was churning, and my hands trembled. Although there was a certain sense of loss on my part, too, since Elène had been an integral part of our family for so long—at ten years my junior, almost like another child—I knew that she most certainly *did* have to go. Nothing else would do. If she didn't live with her widowed mother, people would talk, the worst possible circumstance in those days. Mama would be incensed. And, equally important, I knew Mama would blame me.

"I'm sorry, Elène," I finally murmured. "You know as well as I do why you have to move to Binz Street."

By 1950, Ray was settling into a prosperous time. Oil was $2.51 a barrel and gas, six and one-half cents per thousand cubic feet, although a lot of gas in those days was just flared—burned in the open air. The prices of both products continued on a steady, upward path. The future looked bright.

I began to look in earnest for another house in place of the hated one on Southmore. Since nothing ready built seemed to fit our requirements, Ray and I settled on a lot in Broadacres, two very exclusive blocks near Rice University. When completed, the house at 1404 North Boulevard was a dream house for me, and I indulged myself in giving the parties long since denied by the inadequate facilities of Aunt Sylvia's house. By October 1951, the house and I were ready for parties.

The accepted format for dinner parties in those days was a seated dinner and, afterward, some kind of card game. The men played gin rummy or poker, and the women played mah-jongg or bridge. Assigned places for the games was a rule of paramount importance. It seemed ludicrous to me that the women, especially, wanted to play with the same people they played with all the time, but assigning someone to a table of strangers was the height of faux pas.

Another requirement of those days was a kind of social bookkeeping. People kept track of who had invited whom to a party and when and selected their invitees from that list. It was always payback time. Forget the possibility of having people you just liked or enjoyed or those who hadn't had a party in the required period demanded by the social calendar. In some quarters that ridiculous practice still exists. I made a list and showed it to my cousin Gina.

"Why are you having that couple?" she asked.

"She's in my carpool and I like her."

"That's ridiculous," Gina said. "No one will know them, and what game will you put them in?"

"I'm not going to have any games."

"What did you say?" she exclaimed. "Well, Jerry Chapman, for one, simply will not come. And what are people going to *do?"*

"They might just have to talk to each other."

And then there was the food. Custom dictated that only approved foods be served: ham, turkey, or whole tenderloins. Sometimes theme affairs would determine the menu: Mexican suppers or Italian spaghetti with meatballs. The only acceptable divergence from requirements were desserts, provided the hostess made them herself. Since no one had food catered for an at-home gathering in those days, many people entertained at the country club or a fine restaurant like Maxim's. I was determined to depart from the norm: I would serve oyster patties. These consisted of plump oysters, lightly cooked in a brown roux and served in a miniature pastry cup. When I discussed my proposed menu with Gina, she threw up her hands.

"Oyster patties? You've simply lost your mind. I don't even like to be in the same room with oysters. People just don't *do* things like that!"

"Tough. What's the worst thing they can do to me? Not invite me back?"

When I drew up my unorthodox list, there were too many people even for my large new house, so I decided to divide the guests into four groups—one for each of four succeeding Sunday evenings featuring the same menu. I surmised that, by the fourth party, I would have tested everything we served. Each party would be progressively easier.

Gina's group came first, the forty people most socially correct, although she and her husband, Morey, came to all four parties. At the last minute I lost my nerve about having only the miniature oyster patties for hors d'oeuvres. I added time-tested and approved mushrooms stuffed with crabmeat. The main course was our Yoakum spaghetti, with tomato sauce and curry. I had to have a menu of foods that could be eaten with a fork because I was breaking another unbreakable rule by not having a seated dinner. I was having a buffet supper instead.

I confess my heart skipped a few beats when I opened the door to the first arriving guests. They were lovely Nina and her cynical husband, Jerry Chapman. Ray and I escorted them to the bar, and, while making small talk, I waited for Jerry to mention that he saw no tables set up for formal dining or card games. Not a word. As the room began to fill, people gathered around the bar. They sat around with drinks in their hands, obviously having a good time. Many were occupied with seeing our new home for the first time. Still no mention of games. The maid started passing the hors d'oeuvres on a tray carrying half oyster patties and the other half, the stuffed mushrooms. The oyster patties disappeared. Suddenly there were raves. "These are simply delicious!"

I began to wonder whether I had enough. I thought, *Next time I'm going to have twice as many patties as mushrooms.* I kept watching Jerry. He was having a marvelous time and drinking away. In fact, he had such a good time that he drank too much and overturned the small table on which a large urn of coffee had been set with cups and saucers. Fortunately, by then, most people had been served, so there was little breakage.

I had never had such a successful party. No one even mentioned playing cards. Instead, many remarked, "This is fun for a change." Each succeeding Sunday I had more guests, ending up with nearly one hundred for the last one. By the time of the largest, last party, oyster patties outnumbered the mushrooms, four to one. Gina accepted defeat—reluctantly. "They were all just interested in your beautiful new house. I don't think it will succeed anywhere else." Nevertheless I was credited with the origin of the cocktail supper, which became an accustomed and familiar format. But there was a downside. My friend, Bugga Cohen, who was one of the social arbiters, complained that people now repaid her seated dinner hospitality with a shrimp.

July of 1952 was a busy time as I prepared for August, when Ray, the children, and I would share a house in Colorado with my cousins, the Sterns, for the whole month. We planned to take the long way up by Carlsbad Caverns and return home the short way through the Texas Panhandle. In order to take possession of our rented house in Evergreen on August 1, we planned to leave on July 27.

I knew Elène had been seeing a young man from Tulsa named Leon Davis, whom she had met when she lived for a year in New York, briefly escaping Mama and the apartment on Binz. I hadn't really heard much about him, except once in a while when Mama would make some remark. I asked no questions, however. I had become accustomed to the fact that Elène did not introduce us to anyone she dated.

On July 25, two days before we were to leave, Elène called and said she would like to bring Leon for drinks. I said, "Of course," thinking, *Well, this must be serious.*

Ray had just come from his office when they walked in. I was impressed with Leon. I guessed he was about thirty years old, a nice-looking, sturdy young man with a ready smile. His hair was dark and curly, crowning a full face that showed promise of a jowl but which now merely seemed to display a prominent chin. After the introductions were made, the orders for drinks were filled, and we had chatted a bit, Leon turned to Elène and said, "Why haven't I met your sister and brother-in-law before now?" There was an embarrassed pause, after which Elène mumbled something, and I said inanely, "Better late than never!"

Almost immediately, without changing her tone of voice and without a smile, Elène tossed her head back and said, "Leon and I want to get married right away. We went for the license today. There's a three-day waiting period. There won't be anyone but family. We'll be married here, of course."

"Here" meant my house. My new house on North Boulevard. I looked at Ray and had trouble finding my voice. "Elène, the boxes and suitcases are packed. You have known for months that we're leaving the day after tomorrow for Colorado. Can't you wait a month?"

"What's more important, my happiness or your silly trip?"

My first instinct was to protest vehemently. But where Elène was concerned, I always just stuffed resentment down my throat. I had established a pattern of going along with her and Mama to keep the peace. And I didn't want to make a scene in front of the young man. So, although inwardly fuming, I asked mildly, "How many people will there be?"

The next day I called my cousin Gina. "Sorry, friend, but we aren't leaving tomorrow. I have to put on a wedding, and you aren't invited. No one but immediate family. We'll have to take the short way up and come back through Carlsbad Caverns. We may be only a day late getting to Colorado."

For years Raymond had wanted to rent a vacation house some-

Marjorie and Raymond Arsht at Houston's famed nightspot, the Cork Club, in the Shamrock Hotel, 1950s.

where. I had managed each year to deflect what I thought a terrible prospect—until one night in February of 1952. On a visit to Houston, our Denver friends, Sarah and Sidney Reckler, suggested that we spend a month in Colorado. "We" meant Ray and me, my cousins Gina and Morey Stern, their son, Marc, age eleven, and our three children, Margot, Alan, and Leslye, twelve, nine, and seven, respectively.

Sarah, beautiful and enthusiastic, painted a picture of a blissful and serene vacation irresistible to Ray and Morey. To my dismay, she quickly located a house on the grounds of the Evergreen, Colorado, hotel resort. She said it would be perfect.

The trip did not begin well. Bleary-eyed from Elène's wedding—too much alcohol and too little sleep—we were tired before we even started driving across the country. Raymond's sunny disposition underwent a metamorphosis the moment he walked out of our house and saw his beautiful new Chrysler Town and Country station wagon, its luggage rack piled high with boxes of pots and pans and suitcases of linens and clothes tied down with rope. But he couldn't blame a soul. This trip was his idea.

Gina's husband, Morey—a look-alike for the long-ago movie star Ronald Coleman—had, with great foresight, developed urgent business in Chicago, causing him to miss the car trip. We left Houston in our two cars, Ray driving the Cadillac convertible, and I, the station wagon. Gina and I divided the maids, Iola and Ellen, and the children between the automobiles.

Lovely Gina—once selected as a Rice beauty because of her gorgeous auburn hair and blue eyes—was also meticulous Gina. Every Monday morning of the year, she planned daily menus for each day of the week to come. I had grave misgivings about how she would fare on this adventure. Actually, she was fairly amenable, except on our first night out, when she offered to sleep in the car rather than enter the motel we pulled up to. And so, we drove for hours until we found a place she considered satisfactory. The second night she pulled her bed into the center of the floor because she saw a bug on the wall. Ellen, the children's equally fastidious nurse, joined her.

During the drive, Leslye cried often, usually because Alan, a natural-born troublemaker, would poke or pinch her or stick out his tongue when no one was looking. Gina counted every time. We changed seating in the cars frequently, but Gina gave up counting when she got to ninety-nine of Leslye's crying spells before we ever reached the Colorado border.

The new station wagon came to be known as Car, with a personality all its own, resembling Stove in that wonderful old movie *The Egg and I.* Car had been delivered to us with a leaking gasoline tank and a faulty fuel gauge. It got less than eight miles to the gallon and had only a twelve-gallon capacity, a deficiency no repair could improve. Knowing Ray never liked to stop on any car trip, I decided I would wait as long as possible to get gas. With my small tank and a car that guzzled fuel, it wasn't very long before I pulled into a station. Ray, who was following, pulled alongside. His bad humor had not dissipated. "Why are you stopping?" he asked.

"I need gasoline," I answered pleasantly, attending to changing children between cars.

"You can't possibly need gasoline this soon. Next time I'll tell you when to stop." Not wanting to argue, I said, "Okay." We drove another hundred miles, and I held my hand out the window, making a circle with my fingers, indicating zero. Ray shook his head and waved me on. So I drove on. When we were well out of the little town we had passed, Car started stuttering and sputtering and gradually slowed to a dead stop.

"What in the world is the matter now?" Ray almost barked.

"We're out of gas," I said meekly.

"You can't be."

"All right. See if you can move this monster without any fuel in the tank."

He didn't answer. He just turned around to go back to the town we had passed, while we sat sweltering in the midsummer heat of the West Texas prairie. For forty-five minutes we stared at the landscape of pastureland disappearing into a bank of heat-induced haze. Even the cows we saw seemed motionless, too hot even to flick their tails. After Ray returned with gasoline, he never questioned my stopping again. We staggered, a little over a hundred miles at a time, until we reached Evergreen.

"Where in the hell *is* this place?" asked my formerly affable, easy-going husband. There were no paved streets on the grounds of the resort, just two-track dirt roads winding through the forest. And no house numbers. It was picturesque—if you knew where you were going.

All of the cottages bore the names of their owners. I had been told to ask for the Ferguson house, but the concierge at the hotel was new, so we wandered around until we found a bicycle rider who steered us to our destination. It was a nice-enough-looking little house when we finally found it. Painted green, it nestled comfortably into its environment of trees and shrubs in varying shades of the same color. When the cars stopped, the children exploded in all directions as though they had been wired to an electrical current. At the time I didn't even care if they got lost in the woods.

Walking in the door, I thought, *What a darling little house—for a couple with one child. One very small child.* There was no foyer, just an entry into one single room. One sofa, facing the door, divided the living area from the dining room. Several comfortable chairs as well as the sofa were covered in dingy, flowered chintz, what my decorator, Alliene Vale, would have called "early awful." Sitting on the sofa, one could look to the right and see the lone bathroom at the end of a hallway. Three small bedrooms, one, as requested, furnished with bunk beds for the children, opened off the hall. Another door led to a break-your-neck circular stairway, descending to a lower floor, where there was a small bedroom and bath for Iola and Ellen. Located downstairs, too, were the washer and dryer, which after a week of our laundry, gave up and died.

After we unpacked and stowed our household belongings and clothes as best we could, Raymond met Morey at the Denver airport. Morey was fresh and ready to play. Three days later, Raymond went back to meet his mother, Ida, who was joining us for a week's stay. She slept at the Evergreen Hotel but walked over in the morning.

"I don't eat breakfast," Ida said offhandedly, "but I'll just have a bite and a cup of coffee." Every morning. The end of the week came and went. No one mentioned departure.

Right after Mrs. Arsht's arrival, the phone rang. "Surprise! Guess who this is!" I didn't have to guess. I recognized Elène's voice. "Leon has just always loved Evergreen, so we thought it would be such fun to spend the rest of our honeymoon here. We're at the hotel. How do we get to your house?"

I caught my breath. *Where am I going to put them?* I stared at the small dining room table, around which clustered the eight chairs I had requested. We were now going to be eleven—for almost every meal, every day. We scavenged chairs from the three bedrooms. The kitchen, with its normal-sized refrigerator and pantry, would have been adequate for an average-sized family. So Gina and I drove into the village every day, not just to go to the Laundromat but also to replenish the larder. The beautiful scenery of Colorado went unnoticed on those drives because we were concentrating on what to serve for the next meal.

Meantime, the children were running wild. Margot, a submissive, pretty child, followed everything that mischievous Alan and ingenious Marc devised as an activity. Leslye, sweet and innocent, trailed along after the others. She still cried often.

Margot adored horses. Although the cottages on the grounds were isolated, she discovered that, about a mile down the road, a neighbor kept several horses in the barn behind his fence. Trying to get the horses to come out into the pasture, Margot, Alan, and Marc threw rocks at the barn. Of course, Leslye, good little girl that she was, didn't throw any rocks, but when the owner heard the noisy barrage and came outdoors to investigate, Leslye was the only one left standing by the fence. Our irate neighbor brought Leslye by the hand to our door, tears streaming down her face. She didn't want to tattle, so she just wailed. Finally, Marc, the hero, confessed. Who would think to tell children, "Don't throw rocks at a horse barn"?

A rocky creek ran near our house. Typical of Colorado creeks, it was charming but also dangerous. We cautioned the children, "Don't try to cross that creek!" Big mistake. One day the children wandered in for lunch, and Gina looked at Marc. "Where's your shoe?" she asked. He stammered and spun a long story about a cliff (there were no cliffs near us), when Leslye started bawling. "It's my fault," she blubbered. "Everyone c-c-crossed the creek, and I got halfway. I was too s-s-scared to move, so I just cried, and so Marc came to get me, slipped on a rock, and lost his sh-o-o-o-e!" This last came out like a shrill screech, followed by more uncontrolled sobbing. We went into the village to get Marc another pair of shoes.

The children often used the bathroom downstairs, but the adults, eyes peeled down the hall, watched the upstairs bathroom door from their perches either on the couch or, if there wasn't room, on the arms of the couch. Every time the door opened someone made a mad dash for the facilities. I thought longingly of my four bathrooms at home and wondered why sane people would deliberately punish themselves in the name of "vacation."

One day Morey decided we should take a trip through the mountains. Of course, to hold everyone, we had to use the station wagon. For this particular drive, I was careful to fill Car's tank before we started down the mountain. Halfway down, the gauge moved toward "E." The gas tank was leaking again, so we had to coast, driving on the narrow outside lane, afraid that if we ran out of gas, the engine would stop and we would lose the power steering, not to mention the windshield wipers. It had started raining, and I was driving. No doubt about it: Car hated me, and the feeling was mutual. The only good thing about our mountain adventure was that we survived it.

We had one good weekend out of the month. In the summer of 1952, candidates Dwight Eisenhower and Richard Nixon announced that they would be at the Brown Palace Hotel in Denver. Ray and Morey decided we should go in to see them. We were all Republicans and devoted Eisenhower fans. Morey's Aunt Amy lived in Denver. Regal and statuesque, she was probably 80. When we remarked that she looked very well, she said her mother had lived to be 104. "However," she added, "actually, she began to fail at 100." I thought, *But I bet she never rented a house on the grounds of the Evergreen Resort.*

As we were passing down the receiving line, waiting to shake hands with the soon-to-be-elected president and vice president and wearing our "I Like Ike" buttons, the television cameras zeroed in on Ray. Pathé News, shown in movie theaters all over the country, captured Raymond Arsht shaking hands with Dwight Eisenhower. His fifteen seconds of glory.

Strangely enough, Leslye remembers that month in Colorado as the most enjoyable time of her whole childhood. She has reminded me that in Denver she ate her first chocolate éclair. Moreover, when Alan's daughter Jocelyn was very young, she would say, "Aunt Lelly, tell me again about Colorado." For both Leslye and Jocelyn, it was their favorite "story." Funny what children recall.

I remember the events of August 1952 very differently. I recall Leslye crying the entire month and that every time my feet got level with my head, I fell asleep. I remember that my smiling Raymond did not smile for thirty days. I remember wanting to kiss the ground when I got home—because our vacation was over and our marriage was still intact. And I thanked God that Ray would never again want to rent a house—anywhere.

We had come home from Colorado, and before I could unpack, Mrs. Arsht was back, dogging my every step. I couldn't shake the fatigue I felt. I had trouble getting out of bed in the morning. The days dragged. Sometimes I was overcome with nausea. Ray thought I had a virus, and Mrs. Arsht suggested I take a tonic. Every single day I had a letter from my newlywed sister, Elène. "Marjorie, Mama says some presents have come. Just pack them up and send them on." Or "Marjorie, how do you cook eggplant?" Or rice dressing. Or okra and tomatoes. Every day. It got to be funny, and I made jokes about it. Also, Mama called me at least three times daily. "How do you think Elène and Leon are doing?" "Does she seem happy to you?" "Elène needs some of these dishes exchanged. I have them boxed for you to take to the post office tomorrow." Endless chores.

Once a month I felt such pain I thought I was having a baby. Some postpartum repair had left scar tissue. Dr. Julian Frachtman gave me a strong pain capsule, which put me into a heavy sleep for relief. One morning when Mama called, before she could say anything, I said, "Mama, I didn't sleep all night. I'm really suffering. I'm getting ready to take one of those knockout pills, and I don't want to be disturbed. Tell me everything you want, and I'll take care of whatever it is tomorrow. Today I have to sleep."

She said, "I didn't want anything in particular," and hung up. Just as I was dozing off, the telephone rang again. "I know you're trying to sleep, but I started a letter to Elène, and I've forgotten how to spell 'dissociate.'" I spelled the word, hung up the telephone, and started crying.

School started after Labor Day. Leslye was having trouble in the second grade. Her first-grade teacher had assured me she would outgrow the difficulties of the first grade—not being able to color within the lines or form her letters. Well, she hadn't. Leslye's tests showed a special kind of intelligence. In certain areas she scored far above average, but in others she was lacking. She didn't have behavioral problems, Margot's kind of trouble. Everyone loved Leslye, but she had difficulty reading and writing. And, unlike Margot, who had trouble focusing, she tried very hard.

At the same time, it became obvious that Margot simply wasn't ready for the fifth grade, even though she had been held back a year. I didn't know what to do about it. We consulted tutors, psychologists, and counselors. Margot tested slightly below normal, but not enough for special education. Her attention span was brief.

Considering the kind of student I had been, the reality of my daughters' scholastic problems was incomprehensible and heartbreaking. I kept trying, fruitlessly, to fix whatever was wrong. Fortunately, Alan was fine academically, but he wasn't being challenged. As a result, he misbehaved. He had thick notebooks filled with repetitive sentences: "I will not throw spitballs again," "I will not giggle in class," or "I will not tease Mary Alice any more," written hundreds of times. I reluctantly withdrew him from public school and enrolled him in the fifth grade at St. John's, where they really put his feet to the fire.

By Thanksgiving Day, however, my nerve endings were raw. The problems with Mrs. Arsht escalated. Each time she arrived, she would say, "Next trip I'm going to look for a place to live." Perhaps she expected some protest, although none was ever made. Before each visit, she sent a box of clothes ahead so she didn't have to be bothered with luggage. Even though she had sold the Fashion Shop, her former store, she still utilized their shipping services.

In those days, when in-laws or parents visited, they were always included in parties or other events. Still, guest status was difficult to maintain when the visitors were in residence eight months out of the year. For Thanksgiving Day, Alliene and Wylie Vale had invited us to their house to spend the day and watch the football games. Alliene said, "I'll just fix a big ham and potato salad. We'll eat when we feel like it." They had a son about Alan's age, and we were taking our children. Alliene added, "What's the difference? Bring Mrs. Arsht along." I told Mrs. Arsht she was invited.

"I don't like football, and I don't eat ham, so I'll just spend Thanksgiving Day all by myself," she said petulantly. I've often wondered whether she expected us to stay home. As it turned out, I wish we had.

We came home late in the evening. The children and I called in a "Good night" to Mrs. Arsht and went upstairs to prepare for bed. Ray stayed downstairs to visit with his mother. I was reading when Ray walked into our bedroom. His dark skin had turned a sickly green as it usually did when he was under stress.

"What in the world is the matter?"

"While we were gone, your mother called." He looked like he was in pain.

"So?" I prodded.

Ray sat down at the foot of the chaise and put his head in his hands. "It's a long story. You know how often we've heard your mother say, 'I'm using Morris Meyer as a lawyer, not as my brother-in-law, and I expect him to send me a bill. Every time I go to his office, I tell him so.'"

Uncle Morris had offered my father's will for probate and helped Mama with all kinds of problems, managing to reduce appreciably any taxes she owed. The association had not been without incident, however, centering around the fact that Daddy left everything to Mama unless she remarried. I imagine it was one of those cookie-cutter form wills. There wasn't very much of an estate, but Mama was furious, and Elène made a scene. She stormed into Uncle Morris's office, blaming him for having written such an insulting will. Despite this episode, Uncle Morris had continued to help Mama with her affairs.

Ray sounded like he was in a deep well. "I was in Uncle Morris's office recently on my own business, and he said to me, 'Ray, your mother-in-law keeps telling me she wants me to send her a bill. What do you think I should charge her?'

"I threw up my hands and said, 'For God's sake, keep me out of this. I don't want to have anything to do with what you charge her.' I guess Uncle Morris was uncomfortable about asking her for anything. According to my mother, as he presented your mother with a bill, he said to her, 'I discussed this with Ray.'" Ray sounded like he was choking. "The fat is in the fire. She's livid. She thinks I told him what to charge her, and so she unloaded on my mother, called me all kinds of names, and accused me of meddling in her affairs. She said she was going to start interfering in my office. I think she's just angry he sent her any kind of a bill."

It was not yet ten o'clock in the evening. I reached beside my bed for the telephone and called Uncle Morris.

"Did you tell Mama you had discussed your bill with Ray?"

He was silent for a moment. "Well, I did discuss it with him."

"And what exactly did Ray tell you?"

He cleared his throat.

"Do you know what you've done?" I was shrieking. "You know as well as I do, Mama never expected you to send her a bill. You know Mama. She just wanted to feel like she didn't owe you anything. And you used Ray for a crutch because you felt she did, in fact, owe you. Maybe she did. Maybe you were entitled, but you had no right to hide behind Ray. Now Mama is simply furious. How could you *do* such a thing?"

"I'm sorry, Marjorie, I never meant any harm."

And I'm sure he didn't.

Perhaps at another time of my life, when I hadn't been so burdened or so fatigued, I would have shoved it all under the rug, pushed it down into that well I used for storage and escape, but this time there wasn't any space left. At first I felt a kind of terrible pressure on my chest. I couldn't breathe. My mind raced. *Mama insists on help from us for everything . . . Ray has been tireless in assisting her after Daddy's death . . . She demands we be at her beck and call even if she takes everything we do for granted . . . All these years I've consciously shielded Ray from any unpleasantness with my family . . . I've never allowed him to be on the firing line . . . I've taken care of what has had to be done with his mother, too . . .*

I heard the sound of dry sobs and wondered whether they came from me. It all seemed so hopeless. How could I survive? After the dry sobs came a flood of tears as though a dam had been unleashed. I couldn't stop. Ray tried to console me and after an hour called Alliene. She recommended ice, her prescription for everything.

Early the next morning, Alliene came. Ray, poor thing, had not slept a wink because I had walked the floor like a zombie and cried all night. Alliene called an ambulance, which took me to St. Luke's Hospital. Our doctor, Julian Frachtman, was almost family. He called me "Cuz" because he had married my second cousin, Mary Jane Lowenstein. A tall, strapping, good-natured kind of guy, Julian and I had been classmates at Rice. He knew Mama well. He told Ray I needed sedation and rest.

The word got around, and Mama came to the hospital when Julian happened to be there. He asked me whether I wanted to see her. I became hysterical, so he told Mama he thought I'd be better off without visitors.

Ray called Elène. We were scheduled to go to Tulsa the following week for a meeting of the Independent Petroleum Association of America (IPAA), of which Ray was a director. "Elène, we won't be coming to Tulsa next week," he said. "I think you had better come here as soon as possible. Your sister needs you. There has been trouble with your mother, and Marjorie is in the hospital." She didn't come.

I came home from the hospital after a five-day stay. Ray told the servants to answer the phone and take messages. There was no doubt I was still fragile. Noise and sunlight bothered me. I didn't even notice that the children were whispering and the curtains stayed drawn or that Ray came home several times a day. Ellen or Iola brought my meals on a tray.

When I was first taken to the hospital, Mrs. Arsht, around whom the current dispute swirled, asked Ray whether she should go home. He said, "I think you should." When the servants told me that he had actually encouraged his mother to leave, I knew he was taking my breakdown seriously. After I had been in bed at home for ten days, Ray said to me, "Marjorie, you need to go to the beauty parlor. I'll make an appointment." I started crying. "Well, you don't have to go, but I think you'll feel better. I'll go with you." For the first and only time in his life, he sat in a beauty parlor and looked at magazines while an operator cut and set my hair.

One day I remembered we had planned to go to Tulsa for Ray's IPAA meeting. I had written Elène such an enthusiastic letter. "Oh, I just can't wait to come to visit you, a married woman in your own home. There will be so much to talk about." How long ago was that? Had the meeting taken place? And it was then I realized that I hadn't heard from Elène. Not a word, whereas, before the episode with Mama, I had had a letter or a call every single day. I summoned Ellen. "What's happened to my mail? Aren't there any letters from Elène?"

"No, ma'am."

"How many days since I came home from the hospital?"

"Three weeks."

"And not a single letter?"

"No, ma'am."

"Ellen, have you heard from my mother?"

"No, ma'am."

After that I waited anxiously for the mailman every day. And every day Ellen brought me the same answer. Nothing. Finally, truly distraught, I called Ray at the office. "Have you heard from Mama?" There was a pause. "Tell me!" I shouted into the telephone.

"Marjorie, don't upset yourself. You know your mother. I suppose she was humiliated when she went to the hospital and Julian told her you shouldn't have any visitors, so, typically, she decided she would go to Elène's. Then I think they went to New York to buy Elène's trousseau since she never had one."

"What about Elène? No word from her, either? I seem to remember you called her."

Another pause. "Well, you know she was so anxious to have children. I think she wanted to stay close to home trying to get pregnant."

"But she could go to New York?"

Ray was still quietly and calmly protesting when I hung up. It seemed to me that I had no sooner stopped talking to him at his office than he appeared in our bedroom. I was staring at the ceiling, my hands balled into fists. "Why?" I asked him. "Why? Why am I rejected by my own mother and sister?" Multiple incidents of imposition, rejection, and hurt feelings over the years circulated in my brain. I was inconsolable.

A few days later, a letter came from New York from Mama. It was all about what they were doing and what they had bought. Not a word about Uncle Morris's bill or the hospital. Usually, when Mama's tantrums were over, she acted as though nothing at all had happened. Like a purged computer memory. A complete blank. She even seemed serene. On other days I had always been relieved when she was calmed. *Whew!* I would think. But not this time. My depressed soul went through a metamorphosis. All that anguish began turning into anger, a kind of fury that bubbled up like lava in an erupting volcano.

I suddenly remembered Elène's birthday gift to me in November, before that momentous Thanksgiving. Two pairs of stockings. The card had read, "Happy birthday, from Elaine," misspelled. The stockings had been ordered over the telephone. At the time I dismissed the indifference as trivial, but now I remembered how I had shopped for hours, trying to find just the perfect bracelet for her on her birthday a few weeks earlier.

I walked the floor of my bedroom until once again I succumbed to self-pity. Was there something wrong with me? Why did other people have loving mothers and sisters? I had friends who depended on *their* sisters for support and comfort. Once again I took to the bed. In the days that followed I vaguely realized that my aunts and Pauline and Gina and Alliene came from time to time or phoned, but I didn't want to see anyone.

One afternoon, Alan walked into my room, all excited. "Mother, guess what!" Then he stopped abruptly and turned away. "Oh, I forgot you were sick." A flashbulb went off in my head. This had to stop. I was neglecting my children and my husband. I got up, found Alan, and listened to him tell me about a touchdown he had made that afternoon.

I finally received a letter from Elène:

Dear Marjorie:

I could tell from Ray's manner that you are both very mad at me. Actually, you have grounds to be peeved. I haven't written. There has been no malice aforethought, though I am sure I could not convince you that is not the case.

It may seem strange that I should be busy in (a) one room (apartment), but there is always a tea or a luncheon which incidentally I loathe—it ruins a whole day. I have taken on the chairmanship of the Council of Jewish Women, a project for the year which has taken all my time for the last weeks and will—for the next three months.

I cook 3–4 nights and with the usual errands, I'm tired in the evening. We go at night because people ask us, but our delight is to be able to stay home.

Needless to say I was most upset over your quarrel with Mother. As a matter of fact it put me to bed for two days—the long distance calls and your being in the hospital.

Mother came up here with her story. What is truth and what is romance is always questionable. Mother can make me madder than anyone in the world. It was unfortunate that you were victimized—but knowing myself, I can say that your nerves were ready to snap and that brought it to a head. Mother is tactless and aggravated a condition, which she has never learned not to do—and more than likely never will. What grieves me is that I am sure there are many strangers who know all the details. Mother, or really none of us, know how to swallow things to get along. I am learning because I must. And it requires working at all the time.

I certainly hope that when Mother comes back you will be on decent terms.

We are both sorry you won't be in soon.

Sunday we looked at houses. There are some awfully nice ones in a new addition, ranch style. One we saw was laid out beautifully. Needed several hundred more square feet to allow for deep enough cabinets, etc. Would much rather buy than build. If we can find one going up we like, I can pick the décor. Can't take two tone bathrooms and kitchens.

But that remains to be seen. There is no rush, but we are beginning to get enough of our apartment. I am sure that in the future I will look back and wonder why I didn't want to stay.

Alan's letter was so cute.

Our love to the children,

Elène

I had trouble digesting what she had said. Its tone was so trivial, like nothing important had happened. I read it again. Teas? Luncheons? *She* was in bed for two days? Yet never once did she pick up the phone to check on me? Did she even know what was wrong with me? Or didn't she care? I was deeply hurt. Before long, however, my distress turned to fury.

The next morning, after a sleepless night, I sat down at my typewriter and wrote a letter to my sister. I didn't keep a copy of it, but I remember its contents. All of the stored-up resentment spewed out onto the paper like bile from a sick stomach. The time had come to draw the line and put a stop to their lack of respect, not to mention their ingratitude. Forget love. We had never been a demonstrative family. Instead, our relationship revolved around the ideas of duty and obligation. But was this a one-way street? Was I the only one who felt the imperative of responsibility? Suddenly I realized that neither my mother nor my sister had ever shown any real affection for me. All of the effort and energy had been flowing from me to them.

I made a number of drafts, each one more virulent, each time remembering another slight, another knife wound, some just skin deep but others visceral. When Ray came home, I said, "Please read this letter."

Glancing at the salutation, Ray held it above his head, away from the children's noisy welcome, and said, "I think we should save this until after dinner." After our meal and with the children dispatched to homework and the house quiet, Ray put his feet up on the large, heavy coffee table on the lanai and began to read. I watched his face closely and held my breath as I saw him reach the bottom of the last page. But he didn't look up. He just put the pages in order and started reading from the beginning again. When he finished, he looked up at me, puffing his cheeks out as if he were going to blow up a balloon, and seemed to hold his breath. I waited. With a kind of sad sigh, he said, "Do you think you're going to feel better about yourself if you mail this letter?"

I thought about that for a few seconds and then said, "It isn't a question of how I would feel if I mailed it, but how I will feel if I don't."

"I guess, then," he added, "the matter is settled."

I wondered how Elène would react to my diatribe. Would she fire back? Make excuses? Be remorseful? Would she answer at all? I couldn't quite analyze my own feelings. I certainly wasn't sorry I had vented my anger. I wasn't sad or mad or glad. Now I just felt drained.

I had a few anxiety attacks like the ones I had when Margot was an infant. At least this time I recognized the sinking feeling, the beads of perspiration on my forehead, and the shortness of breath. I went to Julian Frachtman for vitamin B-12 shots.

Finally, after ten days, I held a letter from Elène in my hand. My heart started pounding, and I wondered whether I was going to have another attack before I even opened it. Somehow that struck me as funny, and I laughed. My maid, Ellen, had brought the mail, and she stood there waiting. When she saw me chuckling, she said, "Miz Arsht, aren't you going to open that letter from Miss Elène?" Jarred out of my reverie, I opened the envelope.

Dearest Marjorie:

I received your letter today, and must say I didn't expect one of that variety.

However, I want you to know that in the three weeks that you didn't hear from me, we had a crisis of our own. A great deal of the time Leon spent in doctor's offices and what time was not spent there was spent in worrying. It was of a serious nature and we felt so low, we hardly had the spirit to go about our daily business. But everything turned out O.K. so we don't even talk about those three nightmarish weeks. It wasn't actually the cooking of the "grub" or the "project" which prevented my writing. I just sat at home and did nothing.

But none of that is really important now. I know that all the rancor and bitterness you have was there before and my failure to write seemed to be the incident [that brought it out]. I'm sorry you feel the way you do about me. I'm sure there is nothing I could do to change that.

Leon and I hope you are feeling better. We both wish you well.

Our love to you all,

Elène

Ellen was still waiting. She must have seen a strange expression on my face. "Well, ma'am, what did she say?"

"Nothing."

Ray looked at the letter when he came home and, shaking his head, said, "This truly takes the cake. What happened to the teas and lunches and house hunting?"

"Well, it's just really over," I declared. "She thinks it will be business as usual, the way Mama always does, but I have news for them both. Not this time."

Mama called sporadically. Sometimes I told her I was busy and would call her back—and didn't. Usually I tried to be as matter-of-fact as I could. Each time she tried to talk about Elène, I changed the subject. Once in a while I invited her to dinner but made it a point to have someone else there as well so there was no opportunity for personal conversation. For nearly thirty years thereafter I had no meaningful contact with my sister.

During the fifties, I moved into what I called my period of "underwater basket weaving," doing the kind of busy work given to hospitalized mental patients in the 1950s. I found I relaxed when I worked with my hands. My underwater basket-weaving therapy lasted almost a year. I had started making fringed, felt "theme" Christmas tree skirts, personalized to the interests of the recipient. I used glitter, beads, and gold and silver cording, with figures cut out of contrasting colored felt, and lots of fancy embroidery.

When the Christmas season ended, I moved on to fashioning men's ties out of unusual fabrics. Ray received so many compliments on the first one I made for him that he commissioned more. Soon all of our friends had new ties.

When that effort eventually palled, I took up ceramics. The children's upstairs playroom became my studio. There I made personalized monogrammed ashtrays. I gave one to my doctor with his initials drawn around a caduceus. Next I tried my hand at mosaics. I even completed two mosaic end tables to place between the sections of the circular sofa on our lanai. Throughout this period I refused to think about my sister.

Time passed. More than a year. One day I told Mama, "The IPAA meeting is being held this year in Tulsa, Oklahoma. You can tell Elène I'm going. If you remember, I had to cancel the last one. Even Ray didn't go, and he's an officer."

Mama's black eyes flashed. She blinked them rapidly as she always did when she was angry. Her lips formed a thin white line under a twitching muscle in her cheek. She was gritting her teeth. "I forbid you to go," she said in a controlled monotone.

Anger welled up in my throat. I swallowed the sour fluid that collected in my mouth and forced myself not to yell. "Why on earth shouldn't I go?" I sputtered.

"Because I forbid you, that's all."

"Would you please tell me why I shouldn't go with my husband to Tulsa just because my sister lives there? I'm not expecting any hospitality from her, even though she lived with us most of her life."

"What you did for Elène was your duty!"

"Okay. Granted. What, please tell me, is Elène's duty to me?"

No answer. Mama started walking toward the door. She paused and then, over her shoulder, called back to me. "If you insist on going, it will cost you." Contrary to custom, I didn't call Mama before we left Houston.

As Ray and I approached the check-in desk of the grand old Mayo Hotel in Tulsa, where the IPAA was holding its convention, I found myself wondering whether there might be a message from Elène. Would she really ignore our presence in Tulsa?

No message.

We made our way to the opening reception. Because Ray knew so many people, we were immediately surrounded. I spotted Elène's brother-in-law, Eliot Davis, and his wife, Hannah, across the room. My initial thought was a good one: Avoid them at all costs. We had met only one time at our house on the occasion of Elène and Leon's wedding. Perhaps they wouldn't recognize us. Ray was so engrossed I couldn't get his attention. Before I could point them out to him, the Davises had disappeared.

Back in our room before nine o'clock, I finally had a chance to tell Ray I had seen Eliot and Hannah. "Why didn't you go speak to them?" he asked.

"I really don't know. Actually, I'd like to call them."

"Go ahead, if you want to," he said offhandedly. It was obvious that his mind was on the business of the convention.

I can't remember ever having felt the way I did that evening, either before or since. I wanted to fight. I wanted to hurt someone. I understood manslaughter. Mostly I was furious with Elène since it seemed to me that the least she could do was to acknowledge my visit to her town. I called the hotel operator and asked to be connected to the Elliot Davis household.

"What a wonderful surprise to hear from you!" was Hannah's excited reaction to my greeting. "It's early. I insist that Eliot come get you and bring you to the house. This is the only free evening for this convention, and we would just love to visit. Please say you'll come."

Ray shrugged at the suggestion and said, "Why not?"

The Davis house was comfortable and attractive. It was a proper setting for an up-and-coming young family. A few years older than Leon, Eliot was a trim, well-groomed man. I estimated him to be in his midthirties. Hannah was an attractive brunette with sparkling eyes and a ready smile. They couldn't have been more gracious. Eliot served us Johnny Walker Black Label scotch, and Hannah brought out assorted cheeses and peanuts. We talked about problems in the oil industry and issues that would be covered during the convention. We chatted about children and the weather—until Eliot said, "Leon didn't tell me you were coming." Silence.

I broke it by saying, "I'm not surprised since we weren't invited to be with them."

Hannah and Eliot looked at each other. Eliot said, "You might as well know that, unfortunately, our relationship is very strained. Elène doesn't speak to us. She and Leon come by every morning to drop Leon off so we can go into town together. She doesn't turn her head or respond to my 'Good morning.'"

Hannah added, "You know we're more orthodox than your family. Well, when your mother was here, she and Elène openly made fun of our customs. Elène has treated Miriam shamefully."

I remembered Leon's mother, Miriam, as a lovely, pleasant, blonde woman, but Hannah's revelation did not surprise me. This was just the latest example of Mama's thing about in-laws: a running feud with all of Daddy's family, a frightful relationship with her own father's family, and overt disdain for Ray's mother, Ida.

The liquor flowed and tongues loosened. Nothing they told me contradicted my own experiences. They just poured gasoline on the fire of my resentment. And I said things I should not have said. Some of my revelations may have been liquor-induced, but undoubtedly my anger and frustration were deep-rooted. I told them about Elène's treatment of me. I even revealed that, at my suggestion, she sought counseling before she made up her mind to marry Leon. I should not have disclosed that.

We stayed late, and the next morning I had a hangover. My hangover turned out to be more than a headache. As we were having breakfast, the phone rang in our hotel room. Mama was hysterical. Livid. Wild. Eliot had surely wasted no time getting word to Leon. He must have phoned him at daybreak.

Mama was screaming into the phone, "To think that you would do what you did to your sister last night! I hope you rot in hell and that your children are cursed as long as they live." She hardly paused for breath. "You are going to pay for what you have done. I'm going to disinherit you."

Then I made another mistake. I told her I didn't think the Louisiana courts, which had jurisdiction over the Bendel property, a major part of her estate, would allow that. "You don't know what I can do," she declared in a suddenly normal voice and hung up. I felt like I had been run over by a tank. Mentioning the courts to Mama was like waving a red flag in front of a bull. When I was a small child, she had once sued her father's brothers. Ray was looking at me with a sad expression on his face. I knew he didn't have to ask about the conversation. He had heard it all.

Later that day I talked to Leon. I cannot remember whether I called him or he called me. I do remember he insisted they didn't know I was in town. "I'm sorry you came," he said. "Everyone is terribly upset. Elène is pregnant again and has taken to her bed."

Had Mama never told them that we were coming to Tulsa? It was possible. At the same time, I had been sure she would. Mama wasn't known for tact or keeping secrets. Of course, it was equally possible Elène had known of our visit and not mentioned it to Leon. I have never really known the truth.

I have often wondered why Mama was so adamant about my not going to Tulsa. In retrospect, I can only suspect that she may not have wanted me to discover the rift between Elène and her in-laws.

Somehow I got through the day and evening. I walked around like a ghost. I have no recollection at all of the people we saw, the convention program, or even Ray's part in it. I couldn't wait to leave Tulsa. For the first time I felt scared.

When the Arsht name sounded over the loudspeaker as we waited for our plane in the airport, I was so irrational I wondered whether I was going to be arrested. I clung to Ray's arm. I was having another anxiety attack. The summons was just a message from one of Ray's colleagues.

A few days after I returned home, a letter arrived.

Dear Marjorie:

I feel like I probably committed a very great wrong in telling Leon about your visit. Hannah and I are very sorry for the trouble we have caused.

But Leon is, after all, my brother. And I thought it my duty to tell him about our conversation.

Regards to Ray,
Eliot

Chapter 4

Public Life

The balance of the fifties was a strange period for me. I had no desire for any contact with my sister, and yet, since she had been so much a part of our lives, there was a void. In the absence of continual absorption with family matters, I found myself focusing my attention on public affairs.

Temple Beth Israel is the oldest Reform Jewish congregation in Texas and one of the most respected. It, however, had always been a socially conservative temple, and the majority of its members had been in the United States for generations. They were Southern and very "American." During periods of social upheaval, they avoided controversial issues of any kind, from integration to the special relationship with the state of Israel, at that time a topic at the forefront of everyone's mind.

It is a tenet of political Zionism that Jews everywhere in the world have a personal obligation to the state of Israel. They shouldn't just give money and visit regularly but also defend the state's behavior and, if possible, move there, which they called making *aliyah.* Before the Hitler years, Zionism was just a bad word to most Jews, especially those at Beth Israel. The truth is, no one knew much about it; no one knew the difference between political and religious Zionism or between any form of Zionism and Judaism. More importantly, no one cared.

Then came the Holocaust and with it a schism in the Jewish community—a rupture that in one form or another still exists. When more and more of the atrocities committed by the Germans upon their Jewish citizens became known, the actual creation of a political state for Jews loomed on the horizon, with protagonists and antagonists at each other's throats. The issue divided Beth Israel. Many members of the congregation who favored the creation of a state for Jews resigned to form Temple Emanu El. They asked Bob Kahn, the associate rabbi at Beth Israel and a former beau of mine, to be their rabbi. A majority of those who remained at Beth Israel feared that the existence of a political Jewish state would blur their American citizenship and lead to confused concepts of nationality. Such concerns were shared by the American Council for Judaism, the premier American anti-Zionist organization, of which a considerable number of Beth Israel's congregants were members.

This "war of the temples" took place during the early 1940s, the World War II years, when Raymond and I lived in West Frankfort, Illinois. Every letter from Houston dwelt on the local turmoil, the division of families, and who was or wasn't speaking to whom. It would even take years for Bob Kahn to view me as a long-time good friend rather than an enemy, even though I wasn't in Houston when the breach came. Passions on this subject took precedence over reason.

In 1945, when we returned to Houston, the horrors of the death camps and the revelations of the tortures of innocent families, along with the fate of refugees, dominated the newspapers and exacerbated the divisions in the Jewish community. In 1948, after President Truman recognized the state of Israel, the position of anti-Zionists was politically and socially untenable. They had lost. The American Council for Judaism became anathema, the equivalent in some Jews' minds to the anticommunist Birch Society. Members left in droves. Rational discussion in the face of so many pitiful victims was out of the question.

I had been and continued to be a committed anti-Zionist and a member of the American Council for Judaism, although I am no longer one of its national spokespersons (which entailed lecturing at universities and other public forums). However, I have never forsaken my position that Judaism is a religion, not a nationality, and that when religion and the state are intertwined, religion inevitably suffers. At the time of my active participation in anti-Zionist affairs, my sympathy for the tragedy of people's suffering carried no weight at all. I was respected—but scary. People with strong opinions they defend with valid arguments generally are. When I intensified my involvement in the Beth Israel Sisterhood, this became an issue.

In the 1940s, many families who were formerly traditionally Conservative or Orthodox Jews began sending their children to Beth Israel for social reasons as much as for a change in their form of worship. At that time, the confirmation ceremony for girls and boys at age fifteen had gradually become so elaborate and expensive that it resembled a debut. As the classes grew larger, the expense became a burden for many families. An extravagant gift for Hy Schachtel, the rabbi, was always a part of the obligation. Everyone worried about the cost problem, but no one dared touch it.

The Beth Israel Sisterhood had a hierarchy of its own. Four vice presidents, each in charge of a certain department of the temple's activities, were expected to progress up the ladder and finally become president. The fourth vice president supervised the religious school and was therefore responsible for making the arrangements for confirmation. By 1960, my children had already been confirmed, and, since I had done my share of complaining, I was urged to be the "reformer." I finally agreed to be the fourth vice president—on one condition: I would not have to be president, the thought of which I found appalling. Absolutely, positively, not a chance. Everyone agreed.

And I did reform the confirmation experience. We inaugurated a library fund in Hy's honor and, for the class gift, gave him a plaque. That fund became a wonderful memorial to him and flourishes to this day. However, for that day and time, it was a heretical act. Under our new system, the confirmants drew numbers for gifts; thus they had only one to give. In addition, there was one very large, nice party, so the girls had only one dress to buy. Not that I didn't make some enemies, but as the French say, *on ne fait pas d'omelette sans casser des oeufs* (you can't make an omelet without breaking eggs). Nevertheless, the majority of the mothers were profoundly grateful.

Assuming that my job was done and the agreement for not moving up the Sisterhood ladder was in effect, I was preparing to spend my time on other things when a series of impossible-to-predict events occurred. The temple secretary called me. "You aren't going to believe it, but in forty-eight hours the vice presidents ahead of you have vanished into thin air. One has to have a hysterectomy, another's husband is being transferred, and still another broke her leg this morning. So, my friend, you are *it!*"

Taken aback, I said to her, "I just won't do it. Hortense Sher is a faithful, energetic Sisterhood member. She's due to follow me. *She* can be president."

Following that conversation, I began showing Horty the procedures and sharing my records with her when I suddenly realized that no one at all was pressuring me to stay on. The silence was deafening. I made a few subtle inquiries and found that most people were enormously relieved that I would not be the president and spokesperson for Beth Israel's Sisterhood—because I was too controversial. Not only was I still an outspoken anti-Zionist, I was also an equally vocal Republican. In those early years, there were very few Republicans in the state of Texas, few Jewish Republicans, and even fewer "public" Jewish Republicans (whatever I have ever been has always been public). Accustomed to being courted and cajoled into taking any job, I was rudely awakened by this insight. I felt very silly. All that trouble to have everyone assure me I wouldn't have to be president, and now no one wanted me to hold that office anyway. It was a humbling realization, but it didn't last long. I said to myself, "To hell with them. I'll just be president anyway." And I was. It turned out that Horty didn't mind a bit.

During my presidency, board members kept waiting for the other shoe to drop. Attendance soared because no one dared miss the meetings. Observing their anxiety became my favorite pastime. For the most part, however, I was a paragon of propriety. I had made up my mind that as long as I was president of the Sisterhood, I was going to be a good president. Since everyone knew my personal beliefs, there was a grudging admiration for my impartiality. I did manage a few improvements, however.

Beth Israel had a long list of memorial funds that the members managed in honor or memory of someone. The chairman of a fund received donations and wrote thank-you notes, but no means of auditing anything existed. I reformed the outdated and totally inadequate bookkeeping system for these funds, taking them out of the hands of untrained volunteers and transferring that authority to the temple office. All those who had proudly borne the title of chairman of a fund were incensed.

Longtime members resisted every innovation I proposed. However, my efforts were sustained by my remarkable executive committee, my four vice presidents, younger women whose respect I eventually earned. They gave me unqualified support and in the end proved to be a blessing.

Sisterhood meetings were held once a month and consisted of lunch and a program. Each year one of the programs was reserved for public affairs and usually featured a speaker. I had seldom attended any of them in the years before I became president. But, in 1960, two years before my tenure, I noticed in the temple bulletin that the next program would present a Republican, Bob Overstreet, and a Democrat, Wally Miller, both of whom were candidates for the Texas legislature. At that time, the Republican Party in Texas was so small that a state convention could have been held in almost anyone's living room. I had been a voting Republican for many years, ever since President Roosevelt took the United States off the gold standard when I was in school in France. I had watched then, with horror, as the value of my money declined by more than a third overnight. Before I went to Europe I had been too young to vote, but when I returned, my first presidential vote was cast for Wendell Willkie.

My actual involvement in politics at that time had been restricted to polemics. My father had been a Democrat's Democrat. He fed me the Constitution at breakfast, lunch, and dinner. Arguments and debates were in my blood, along with my father's philosophy that no opinion is worth having if it can't be defended or promulgated. By the time I became president of the Sisterhood, my father's conservative Democrat philosophy had become the Republican Party platform.

At that political Sisterhood meeting, I listened to an educated, articulate, good-looking Republican, Bob Overstreet, debate a stumbling, unpleasant Democrat, Wally Miller. I was committed. I made my first political contribution: I wrote a check to Overstreet for five dollars. That one check put me on what few lists existed at that time. I knew a lot about national and foreign policy, not much about state structure, and nothing at all about precinct-level politics. But I soon learned.

In 1960, Bob Overstreet lost his election, as did every other GOP candidate at the local level. Texans had become accustomed to voting for Republicans nationally, but they remained Democrats at the state level. They contended that a two-party state wasn't needed because Texas actually had two parties, one liberal and one conservative, all within the Democrat Party, of course. No single-member districts existed then, so all of the candidates ran at large. The Democrat races were vigorously contested in the spring primaries. Victory at that time was tantamount to election because seldom, if ever, did a Republican oppose the Democrat nominee in November.

In Houston, most of the conservatives lived west of Main Street, while most of the liberals lived east of Main Street. The conservatives dominated rural Texas and, in those days, composed a larger population than the cities, so they controlled the legislature as well as the governor's office in Austin. However, when it came to national programs and policy, all of the Democrats, however competitive among themselves in the spring, were on one team in the fall, regardless of ideology.

Liberty thrives on competition. Just as people have better table manners when someone is looking, so behavior improved in the Texas legislature after surprising victories in the late fifties' special election of two truly neophyte Republicans, one a stevedore from Galveston and the other a haberdashery clerk from Amarillo. They were not reelected, but their temporary presence stopped many abuses, such as the old practice of voting aloud one way and then having the record reflect another.

After the Sisterhood's political program and my small contribution, I received call after call to help with one project or another. I became a very busy Republican activist at the local level.

In the 1952 national primary between Taft and Eisenhower, a rift developed in the Republican ranks. Both Republican and Democrat conservatives considered Taft the embodiment of their principles. General Eisenhower had spoken out against the red-baiting of Sen. Joseph McCarthy and was generally considered by Taft supporters to be a liberal. After Eisenhower won, their fears were realized when he appointed Earl Warren to the Supreme Court. Reaction to the liberal policies emanating from that court led to the formation, in 1958, of the John Birch Society, a violently anticommunist organization. The fifties were also the heyday of the Minute Women, a national anti-Semitic, anticommunist group with a large following in Houston. I was so concerned about the uproar over the Birch Society that I wrote an article for the then-existing *Houston Press,* a leading afternoon daily. George Carmack, the editor, was so pleased that he gave me most of the editorial page.

My thesis, expanded in print, was as follows: Concern over the Birch Society should force everyone to examine the reasons for its birth. People who support it are reacting to the sharply leftward trend of government policies, which are influenced by the decisions of the Warren court. Extremism breeds extremism. Such a problem existed after the War between the States, when Southerners, having no recourse against the abuses of Reconstruction, formed the Ku Klux Klan. All such organizations eventually fall into disrepute because they are extrajuridical. We should address ourselves to reclaiming balance in our institutions and public policies in order to negate the impetus for creating groups such as the Birch Society.

Bob Overstreet called the day after the article appeared. "John Tower saw the editorial you wrote and has asked me to bring you to Austin next week to meet him." John, then in the midst of his first run for the Senate, began using my point of view in addressing all of the questions posed to him about the Birch Society. That association with John Tower was the beginning of a lifelong friendship, and I became an integral part of every one of the Tower campaigns, holding high-level volunteer positions.

In 1961, Tower, the little professor from Wichita Falls, defeated the very conservative, crusty West Texas rancher William Blakely, with the help of liberal Democrats who wanted to purge their party of conservatives. No one actually celebrated the Tower victory. No one believed it had even occurred until John was sworn in as a U.S. senator.

On election night, everyone on the Tower team panicked because Lyndon Johnson had come back to the ranch. Although every precaution had been taken to impound all of the paper ballot boxes in the Valley, the memory of what Lyndon could do with them was still fresh in our memory (eighty-seven questionable votes had put him in the Senate). But John had won, and his incredible victory brought the Texas Republican Party to life. Because of his election, the state party made exciting progress between 1960 and 1962.

My presidency of the Sisterhood followed closely on the heels of the Tower election. In retrospect, I don't know how I balanced such conflicting and contradictory assignments—the Beth Israel presidency, heading the American Council for Judaism's Houston office, and my Republican activities. Somehow I juggled the three hats I wore without mixing them up—until February of 1962, when push gave way to shove.

Candidate Marjorie and Senator John Tower, 1962.

After the Tower victory, the Harris County Republican Party felt it imperative to field a full slate from governor on down the ballot. I was urged to be a candidate for the Texas legislature for the fall election. My husband was the only one who was thrilled at the prospect. Even though not elated, I did want to do it, but, if I were to be a candidate, I had to file in February before I completed my term as Sisterhood president. First I called a private meeting of my executive committee at the home of one of my vice presidents, Aileen Gordon. I felt obligated to ask their opinion because, if they had thought it out of the question, I would simply have resigned as president or not filed for office. They surprised me. Aileen, especially, thought the whole idea exciting. The others, though less exuberant, were determined I not resign the presidency, so it was decided that no one would say a word until my announcement at the next board meeting.

As president of the Sisterhood, I was duty bound to attend every Friday night service; my family was expected to go, too, often to their annoyance, such as when a high school football game was scheduled. One evening in February of 1962, immediately after that executive committee meeting, Hy gave a memorable sermon. He chose as his text "The duty of every Jew is to participate in his or her community as an obligation of citizenship, religious and political." I couldn't believe my luck. At the reception afterward, with malice aforethought, I led my rabbi into a trap. I said to him, "Hy, your talk this evening was the most meaningful one I've heard you deliver in a long time." He beamed. "You actually helped me solve a problem that has been troubling me deeply." He glowed. And then I said sadly, "I've been asked to run for the state legislature, but I have to file before my term as president is over."

"Why, that is simply marvelous! I'm ecstatic. Absolutely, positively, you must do it." He did everything but jump up and down. I gave a great sigh of relief, thanked him profusely, threw my arms around his neck, and then whispered in his ear, "on the Republican ticket." Someone should have had a camera. His face froze. He turned pale. I had to relieve his speechless misery. "Would you like to think about it?" I asked not unkindly. He nodded slowly, still in the shock of disbelief. However, we never discussed it further. I had both the approval of my executive committee and my rabbi's exhortation to public service, even if he hadn't designated his approved political party.

At the next board meeting I went through my whole agenda. After asking for new business or comments, I said, "I have an announcement to make. I shall be filing for public office as a state legislator on the Republican ticket next week, but since I have no primary opponent, I will do no campaigning until my term is up in May. And I shall not serve the second year as president. The meeting is adjourned." Someone should have had a camera that day, too.

The word of my intentions circulated before I actually filed. Walter Sterling, chairman of the Democrat Party in Texas and son of a former governor, telephoned. "Marjorie," he said, "we didn't know you wanted to be in the legislature. Just say the word and you're in."

"But, Walter, I don't want to be a Democrat!"

In 1961, David Ben Gurion, prime minister of Israel, addressed a Zionist congress in Jerusalem. His remarks were widely reported by the press, including the *Houston Chronicle.* In his comments, Ben Gurion condemned the Diaspora (those Jews living outside the state of Israel). He promoted *aliyah,* the immigration of American and Western European Jews to Israel. Suddenly confronted with an influx of Jews from countries such as Morocco, Egypt, Yemen, and Ethiopia—Jews who, because of the birth of the state of Israel, had to flee their homelands where they had become persona non grata—Ben Gurion made no secret that he was afraid that, without Western immigration, he would be presiding over just another Middle Eastern dark-skinned populace. It was, and still is, widely accepted that Israeli Arabs and dark-skinned Jews from Ethiopia and India are treated as second-class citizens in Israel. The issue even elicited a resolution in the UN, purporting to equate political Zionism with racism. The resolution failed, but the issue remains unsettled.

Newspapers all over the country gave particular attention to Ben Gurion's statement that "All Jews living in the Diaspora are living in exile and are therefore godless." I thought the top of my head would fly off when I read the transcript of his speech. I obtained a certified copy to be sure I wasn't receiving something filtered through someone else's bias. I flew to my typewriter, addressing myself in an open letter to my favorite target, the readers of "Letters to the Editor." I knew my diatribe was too long, but I was in a hurry because Ray and I were leaving for New York. On my way to meet Ray at his office, I stopped by to see Everett Collier, then editor of the *Chronicle.* Everett read the first line and said, "This is terrific." It read, "You have brought to fruition all the fears of those like me who have always opposed the political Zionist movement." Then Everett added, "But it's too long for this paper. You should by all means mail this to Israel."

Half joking, half serious, I accused him of being afraid he would insult his Zionist advertisers and shoved the letter into my purse. When I reached Ray's office, I said to Ray's secretary, "Mrs. Flynn, will you find an address somewhere and mail this to the Israeli prime minister?" I didn't expect an answer, but a few weeks later a manila envelope arrived, postmarked "Israel."

I thought, *They're sending me a solicitation for the bonds for Israel Drive or perhaps brochures describing tourist attractions.* Instead I found a single-spaced, two-page letter from one Mr. Applebaum, who identified himself as an aide to Ben Gurion. He said, "You have written with emotion" and then proceeded to defend Ben Gurion. "You must not have read the entire speech, or you would have understood that Mr. Ben Gurion spoke 'allegorically.'" He tried to explain the historical context in which Ben Gurion had spoken. Of course I had to reply.

When word got around about the exchange, I was invited to speak in Philadelphia at the convention of the American Council for Judaism, a speech that was reprinted in their magazine, *Issues*. I even heard from the editor of the *New York Times,* Arthur Sulzberger, who invited me to visit him in New York. I remember his cavernous office, which seemed to me the size of a basketball court, presided over by the most elegant gentleman I had ever met. His white hair and aquiline features gave him a regal presence. Sulzberger didn't agree with the American Council for Judaism, but he did agree with my objections to Ben Gurion's remarks. Furthermore, he worried about the many anomalies that were developing. For instance, because of Israel's "law of the return," which guaranteed a right of citizenship to every Jew born of a Jewish mother, a Catholic monk from Austria had arrived in Israel, demanding his citizenship rights. His mother was Jewish, and that qualified him.

In addition, every young Jew who came to Israel was eligible for Israel's draft. On such a visit, the son of a rabbi in Chicago got caught and was drafted, much to his distress and that of his American family. For a brief time, the State Department issued a pamphlet warning American Jews traveling abroad that at certain ages they were at risk in this fashion, unless they declared to Israeli immigration, at the outset, their desire to hold *only* American citizenship. Sometime later, that little booklet mysteriously disappeared. Today some Israelis come to the United States and become U.S. citizens without ever giving up their Israeli citizenship. Their children, however, are still at risk of being drafted when traveling in Israel. To my knowledge, no law was ever passed allowing Americans dual citizenship, but, by some kind of gentlemen's agreement, it now exists, so no one ever mentions the issue.

These anomalies derive from the assumption by the state of Israel that Jews everywhere owe Israel their national allegiance. Involuntary imposition of a blurring of citizenship, often confused with nationality, is a gross injustice and deeply resented by people like me. To my surprise, I suddenly found myself in demand everywhere to report on the correspondence and to explain the difference between Zionism and Judaism and between religious and political Zionism.

A word about that is appropriate here. Religious Zionism is what its name connotes, a philosophy founded on the ancient dream of sovereignty for the religious entity of Israel, an event that would prompt the appearance of the Messiah. Early in the nineteenth century, religious Jews from Russia traveled to Palestine seeking to fulfill this dream, but they found Arabs occupying the land, and, because these Jews were pacifists, they went home. Remnants of the credo that prompted their journey remain in the ritual of Passover, when participants recite "Next year in Jerusalem." That aspiration dates from the time when early Jews, driven from Israel, Judea, Samaria, and their capital, Jerusalem, lived in Babylonia for eight hundred years. They believed that their God presided over only the land of Israel and that therefore they were living in exile from Him. Babylonia is now Iraq, and it is interesting to note that several generations ago, one-third of the Iraqi population was Jewish. Today only a few Jews remain.

In Babylonia, synagogues (schools) were established to teach the children the faith of their ancestors. There, too, the Bible was written in the vernacular, Aramaic, not Hebrew. These "exiled" Jews believed their only temple to be in Jerusalem, whereas Reform Jews, like me, consider any house built for the worship of God to be a temple.

The Reform Judaism with which my father and I were imbued is gradually disappearing. The process is called the Judaization of Judaism. It is becoming, as many religions are, more fundamentalist and therefore less and less distinguished from the other branches of Judaism, the conservative and the orthodox. For instance, "synagogue" has replaced "temple" in general usage for all of the different branches.

Political Zionism is a relatively new phenomenon in the history of the Jews. It is a secular movement that seeks to translate that once-religious aspiration into reality. Its aim is to establish a political state for Jews by any means, including war, which is anathema to antiwar religious Zionists. There are orthodox antipolitical Zionist groups left in Lithuania and Germany who consider the "forced" return to Israel to be blasphemous since the return to Israel and the coming of the Messiah should be by the will of God, not human beings. The birth of political Zionism derived its impetus from the pervasive anti-Semitism that characterized the Old World, which included Europe and Asia.

Despite the fact that the French Revolution allowed Jews, for the first time in Europe, to own land, anti-Semitism remained endemic throughout the nineteenth century. A prominent example is the case of Alfred Dreyfus, which involved the false indictment and imprisonment of Dreyfus for treason, even though he was in fact a loyal and devoted member of the French military. (His case was made immortal by the defense described in Emile Zola's *J'accuse.* Many years later, Dreyfus was vindicated.)

The movement found its philosophical roots in 1896, when Theodor Herzl, a Hungarian Jewish writer who was not at all religious, wrote *Der Judenstaat* (The Jewish State). His thesis was that anti-Semitism is an immutable fact and will not be solved by assimilation. The only solution would be a state for Jews that the international political world would recognize. Because of the continued pressure of important British Jews such as Lord Rothschild, England—then the protector of Palestine—issued the Balfour Declaration in November of 1917 and clearly stated these now famous words: "His Majesty's government views with favor the establishment of a national homeland for the Jewish people." It is not widely known that elsewhere in the declaration one finds the following qualification: *"Nothing must be done to prejudice the civil or political rights of existing non-Jewish communities in Palestine or the rights and political status of Jews in any other country"* [emphasis added]. Following this British policy statement, however, the matter remained largely dormant because many Jews, especially in the United States, had nothing but charitable interest in Palestine—until the Holocaust, when world opinion focused on the plight of persecuted Jews, a situation made all the more vivid in the public mind by Leon Uris's novel *Exodus.*

In 1948, Pres. Harry Truman recognized the newly declared, fledgling state of Israel. Subsequently, as we all know, there has never again been peace in that troubled region. In a dilemma that reminds us of Solomon, it seem obvious to me that peace cannot prevail so long as some of the Israeli Jews want all of Palestine and most of the Arabs want it all, too. With the death of Arafat, however, a window of opportunity has opened for forward-looking Arabs to determine that the well-being of Palestinians lies in accepting a two-state solution. Of course, Israel will have to make some accommodations, too.

I loved the opportunity to speak out on Zionism in all its aspects, not just because I am at heart a teacher but also because I felt I was doing a service by clarifying a subject generally considered too sensitive to discuss in mixed company, either between Christians and Jews or among Jews with different built-in attitudes. I particularly liked calling attention to the misuse of words. For example, it is correct to contrast Hebrews with Gentiles (tribes) and Jews with Christians (religions). My involvement with the Ben Gurion correspondence, however, added fuel to the atmosphere of controversy that surrounded me.

Since I was unopposed in the Republican primary of May 1962, no real campaigning was needed before summer. Still, the candidates had regular meetings. None of us really knew anything about the offices we were hoping to fill, much less how to go about getting support and money. I had two large cash contributions: $1,000 from Uncle George and another $1,000 from a loyal friend whom I had taught in religious school. It was understood that their gifts would be anonymous because no one wanted to be on any public Republican list. Only my husband, Raymond, believed there was no way I could lose. Fortunately, his business acumen proved better than his political judgment.

"Coffees" where the "hat" was passed were the chief source of funds. A really successful gathering produced twenty-five dollars. The money wasn't for television, which was unheard of at that time for lowly political candidates, or even major advertising. It was for little things such as bumper stickers and yard signs, the printing of brochures, and little push cards with your "beliefs" on the back.

I concentrated on the newspapers. *The Houston Post,* the most prestigious, made a practice of not endorsing low-level positions, which state legislators were considered to be at that time. Oveta Culp Hobby, owner of the *Post,* had been a high official, head of the Women's Army Corps (WACs), as well as the first Secretary of Health,

Education, and Welfare under President Eisenhower. She thus held no animosity toward Republicans. More important, I knew Oveta personally since the Hobbys had been family friends for many years.

Although I had no trouble getting an appointment, I had never been to her office. When I walked into that enormous, luxuriously furnished room, I could understand how a vassal might have felt when summoned to the palace for an audience with a queen. Friend or not, I considered an endorsement from that forceful and powerful lady highly unlikely. Oveta questioned me at length and—miracles of all miracles—broke precedent and, as the election drew near, gave me an editorial endorsement, a full column long.

The *Houston Press* already knew me well. George Carmack, the editor, did not present a problem. Actually, at the outset I thought he might be the only one in my corner. In endorsing me, he said, "Mrs. Arsht is consistently conservative, but aggressively constructive."

Then there was the *Houston Chronicle,* which everyone assumed was an insurmountable obstacle because it was considered committed to the Democrats. My friend Everett Collier could not help since only the owner and his subordinates made decisions on political endorsements. First, I called on the political editor. Yawning in boredom, he asked me who my opponent was. When I told him it was Wally Miller, he said in an offhand, doing-his-duty manner, "What's his background?" I had my opening. "My goodness, do you mean you don't know who Wally Miller is? He's the incumbent, and you and the *Chronicle* endorsed him last time." That miserable little editor had the grace to be embarrassed.

With that ammunition I asked for an appointment with John T. Jones, owner of the *Chronicle* and heir to the Jesse H. Jones empire. I didn't know him personally, but he knew my Meyer uncles and agreed to see me. When I related my experience with his political editor, Jones chuckled, shaking his head, but he was hardly surprised or shocked.

I thought it time to go in for the kill. I told him that political action in Austin was considered so insignificant that it was printed like a footnote in type so small that a magnifying glass was necessary to find out what really happened. How in the world could the average citizen be an informed voter if a major communicator like the *Chronicle* didn't keep up with its own endorsements? Why would good candidates want to offer their services to a community whose leaders didn't care whether they were qualified? Like a traffic cop, he held up his hand. "Stop!" he said. "You Meyers do have a way with words. You've made your point. Let me think about it." He wasn't frowning, so I knew I'd better leave while I was ahead.

I got the *Chronicle* endorsement. I was just listed along with others the newspaper recommended without editorial comment. And, since it came just the day before the election, it was more a moral victory than a political asset, but it counted.

Next I went to the *Informer,* then Houston's leading black newspaper. Conservative Democrats like Wally Miller were committed segregationists and considered enemies by the black community. I gave them a better choice than usual: I was Jewish. At that time, before the schism between African Americans and Jews, being Jewish was an asset among those voters. In some less sophisticated, less bureaucratic, and less political black circles, it still is. The *Informer* published an editorial, possibly the first endorsement it ever gave a Republican. In part it read: "Mrs. Arsht is a Republican and a conservative, but not a squinty-eyed reactionary. . . . She stands for sound, responsible two-party government in Texas."

I asked our friend and chauffeur, Harold Brown, to put my sign on top of his car, but I assured him he didn't have to do anything that made him uncomfortable. At the time, he seemed reluctant, but a few days later, he came to me, grinning. "May I have one of those car signs? I asked around, and, when my friends heard you were Jewish, they said that made you okay. I'll need some bumper stickers, too."

Then, out of the blue skies came a bolt of lightning. A Jewish reporter, Saul Friedman, wrote a derogatory article about me in a Jewish periodical. It wasn't just my anti-Zionism. By running as a Republican I had broken ranks. Jews were supposed to be Democrats—and liberal at that. I issued a blistering rejoinder that caught the eye of the very conservative Washington periodical *Human Events,* which featured me in their September 1962 issue. Here are some excerpts:

> *Mrs. Arsht Defies Liberal Stereotype*
>
> For the first time since reconstruction, Republicans in the South are making a determined effort to break one-party monopoly, fielding a record number of candidates for state and national office. Symbolic of the resurgent GOP is Mrs. Marjorie Arsht, a Houston housewife . . .

Mrs. Arsht had hoped her campaign would stand or fall on the basis of her discussion of issues. Some opponents had a different idea. Saul Friedman, a former *Houston Chronicle* reporter, now studying at Harvard . . . reported that the Republican Party was "embarrassed" to have a Jewish candidate and attacked Mrs. Arsht as having an "affinity" for the John Birch society. She is not a member.

Mrs. Arsht answered the smear this way: "The so-called liberals have a special pigeonhole for me. They claim to love me because I'm Jewish. They say they're protecting me from Fascists. They're fighting for my faith. They're the champions of my rights. All I have to do to earn my share of this largesse is to stay in the pigeonhole of liberalism. The liberals cannot understand, or refuse to admit, that anyone can be true to his religious or racial or cultural ties and still be a political conservative and, as such, be welcomed into the Republican Party ranks."

There I was—endorsed by the *Houston Post,* the *Houston Chronicle,* the *Houston Press,* the *Informer,* and *Human Events,* with congratulations, if not money, coming from all over the United States. What more could an unknown, lowly legislative candidate hope for? And I had eight thousand dollars in the campaign coffer, which made me a serious candidate.

However, since the contest was countywide, it wasn't all rosy. I should have been able to depend on the west side of Main Street, where those who called themselves Republicans were concentrated, and spend my time with other constituents. But I couldn't. Saul Friedman had been right about one thing: Many Republicans held me suspect. A Jewish Republican who wasn't a communist? Impossible! They were influenced in their concerns, of course, by the Birch Society's paranoiac fear of communism. The Birchers' questions to me revealed their attitudes: Why are most Jews soft on communism, when Russia has had so many pogroms? Why are all the Jews I know Democrats?

One day, I stumbled upon a meeting with a Republican precinct chairman who had a wall map showing little colored flags that marked areas of "concern." The color of the flag in my precinct was red, signifying leftist leanings, prompted undoubtedly because I was Jewish.

The Jewish community, which might have been expected to rally to my candidacy, held back for different reasons. My cousin Gina came to me one day. "Marjorie, I didn't know you were a member of the Birch Society."

"Are you crazy? Of course not. What on earth gave you that idea?"

"Last night at a party, everyone was talking about it."

"Will you find out who started such a tale?"

She later confided that no one seemed to know the source of the information. It was simply accepted as fact. I called the director of the Anti-Defamation League, Ted Freedman, and asked, "Do you have a mechanism to protect Jews from Jews? I'm being maligned, and I don't know what to do about it."

He questioned me at length. "Do you have a clue? Do you have any suspicions, however unfounded?" I had none, except, as I reminded him, "Some Jews assume that being a Republican and a member of the Birch Society are synonymous." Ted did get to the bottom of it, fortunately. Step by step he traced the rumor to a woman who was recognized as a pathological liar. Her friends knew of her condition, accepted it, and ignored it. She is now deceased and, for the sake of her children, shall remain nameless here. Miraculously and instantaneously, the association between the Birch society and me was gone, like a switch extinguishing a light. Ted and I became fast friends.

He was also a very close friend and advisor to David White, editor and publisher of the *Jewish Herald Voice,* a local weekly paper. White, an ardent Zionist, was really a very nice man. When I would visit with him, he was polite but unshaken in his attachment to his belief in the Biblically based, but politically interpreted, right of all Jews to the land of Israel.

Ted and I shared an interesting secret with regard to the *Jewish Herald Voice*. For years until he moved away from Houston, he would call me for my recommendations of "good" Republicans for endorsement by the paper. White, who depended on Ted for political advice, would turn over in his grave if he knew that I was responsible for the Republican endorsements made year after year by the *Jewish Herald Voice,* among them the esteemed Bill Archer, former chairman of the Ways and Means Committee.

Marjorie and Congressman Bill Archer, former chair of the House Ways and Means Committee.

As soon as my Sisterhood presidency concluded, I set about covering the political territory of Harris County. In those days actual rallies were held. People went out in the hot summer nights to open-air meetings to hear political candidates debate. Homes were opened for political gatherings. Because I was such a curiosity, I was invited everywhere. One invitation came from the Texas CIO meeting at a union hall. Many Republican candidates wouldn't go, assuming it was a lost cause, but I went. I went everywhere I was asked. My conservative Democrat opponent didn't show up, so I performed the then novel stunt of debating his empty chair. I even offered a ten-dollar reward if anyone could find him. No one did—until Election Day.

Although the audience in the labor hall was largely Hispanic, I had one thing going for me. I was from Yoakum. In that group, it was an important credential because so many in the audience came from small towns or had relatives in one. Finally, one Anglo stood up and asked, "Mrs. Arsht, are you a Goldwater Republican?" I replied, "I'm a Marjorie Arsht Republican. I agree with myself more than anybody."

The audience laughed. "But," he added, "how can someone of your nationality . . .?" I interrupted him. "Stop right there. My nationality is the same as yours. I am an American." With that, the Hispanics in the room stood up, clapping and cheering and stomping their feet. They, too, have a problem with that kind of ignorance.

When the meeting was over, the head of the CIO, who, having to choose between a Republican and a conservative Democrat, was between a rock and a hard place, came over to me. Shaking his head, he said, "Mrs. Arsht, you surprised me. You got a lot of votes here tonight." The *Houston Chronicle,* leaving out the "nationality" part, reported the meeting this way: "One of the best received was Mrs. Arsht, who quipped, 'Labor can never again be called narrow minded because you have invited me, a conservative, Jewish, Republican female to speak to you.'"

Every place I went, the questions sooner or later would get around to my being Jewish. One evening my husband said to me, "I'd like to go with you tonight, but I don't think I can stand the Jewish question one more time." I told him that, if I had to face it, he had to face it, too, and so most of the time he accompanied me. Routinely, the same questions emerged, in addition to those about alleged liberal or communist sympathies: Why are Jews so conservative in their private lives, working hard and saving their money, but want to give everyone else's away? I had developed a repertory of stock answers: Jews are a minority. When depressions come, people look for a scapegoat, and the Jews are always chosen first. That's where the inside Jewish joke, referring to being "the chosen people," originated: "Please, God, choose someone else!" They have never had the power of numbers, so they join with those who fight their enemies. After all of the pogroms in Russia and the endemic persecution of the Jews under the tsars, if Russia fought Hitler, then the communists couldn't be all bad. The enemy of my enemy is my friend.

Often I told my favorite story. In Yoakum, my father's best friend was the Catholic priest. One day, during Franklin Roosevelt's campaign, he came into my father's lumberyard. "Marcell, everyone in Yoakum is troubled, and I've been asked to be their spokesman. No one can understand how you, a Jew, can walk up one street and down the other ranting against the election of Franklin Roosevelt. He's for good business, good times, good jobs, and everyone knows that the Jews are all rich, they're all smart, and they're all good businessmen."

My father responded: "There are a lot of myths about the Jews, Father. One is that they are all rich, but if they were, they wouldn't have so many fundraisers to take care of their poor. Another myth is that they are all smart, but if they were, Father, they would have made a better deal with Paul. And if they were all good businessmen, they would never have let a paying proposition like the Catholic Church get away from them."

That story usually settled the issue, and we went on to other things. Nevertheless, one evening I was tired of it, so I decided to play a parlor game. I asked, "How many Jews do you think there are in metropolitan Harris County?" I got answers that ranged all over the place: 500,000, even 750,000. I let them wander around. Then I said very quietly, "This year, 1962, there are approximately 25,000 Jewish men, women, and children in greater Houston, which translates into fewer than ten thousand adult votes." Dead silence. Finally, a man in the back of the room held up his hand, "Mrs. Arsht, are you sure?" When I assured him that my figures were accurate, he paused and then said, "Well, if that's true, then they must all live around me." At times, when I ran out of anything else to say to the same old harangue, I told that story, too.

In those days, most of the people who attended the rallies were really political novices. Someone would get together and create a list of questions to which the answers were "yes" or "no." I never once answered a question without some explanation or modifier. Often I would get calls from supporters who had reports of some of those meetings that left us all roaring with laughter. It seems the audience would meet after I had left, with their questionnaires in hand, trying to decide whether my answers to their questions were in the affirmative or negative.

Anyone who makes speeches very quickly senses the audience's response. One evening, at a meeting of a group called Protestants United against Church and State (PUACHS), I opened my usual presentation with what I thought was an amusing story. Grim faces. I tried another gambit. Nothing. Realizing I was going nowhere, I put my paper down and said, "I'd like to know what you are interested in discussing. You ask the questions, and I'll do my best to answer." There was a long pause. Finally someone spoke, "Do you know your opponent, Wally Miller, is a Catholic?" I thought, *Well, that does it.* I answered, "Yes, I do. It's the only thing I don't hold against him." That evening PUACHS held a very short meeting.

Jim McBride, candidate for the state senate, was a character. Tall, bespectacled, thin as a reed, he was brilliant and a member of Mensa. When Jim learned that I had eight thousand dollars at my disposal, he suggested we share an office and employ a staff person. Linda Dyson became our assistant, friend, savior, and critic. We could not have managed without her.

On our slate, we had one candidate, however, who differed markedly from the rest of us. A conservative, fundamentalist Christian, G. Edgar Coleman believed in the old ways—the subservience of women, in particular. It bothered him enormously that I was running for office, which was "a man's job." My religion didn't matter. Fundamentalists revere the "chosen" people, at least in theory, but not necessarily person to person. Another problem for Edgar was that I wasn't an Orthodox Jew. Periodically he would get perturbed, so we would invite him to our house, and Raymond would say forcefully, "You know, Edgar, I had to force Marjorie to run for office." The poor fellow would beam. That would last a while, and then we would have to do it all over again. Behind his back, we called him, " 'G' for 'Godly' Edgar."

Even though the Birch Society slander had been laid to rest, the Jewish community remained silent throughout my campaign. There was not one coffee or gathering among my many Jewish friends. They figuratively walked on the other side of the street. Nonetheless, I understood completely. Whereas political appointments were sources of pride, at that time Jews simply didn't run for public office for several reasons. Candidates, of course, are targets for all kinds of attacks—some true, some false. Also, among Jews there was a fear that if a Jew in elective office did something wrong, all would be held accountable. Even if the charge were false, everyone would still be blamed.

From the time I announced my candidacy until the election, I could sense everyone's bated breath. The newspaper endorsements let them relax somewhat, fortunately. Needless to say, every single one of my friends later assured me I had received their vote. Of course, that is normally the case in elective politics since no opponent can be identified except the one on the ballot.

Election night was exciting. I clearly won the absentee vote, which made me think, *What if Edgar wins, too?* I didn't have to worry long. The returns came in quickly, and the entire Republican slate lost, although I received 48.9 percent of the vote countywide, which was amazing. West of Main Street, I ran ahead of the governor. Part of my platform had been a plea for single-member districts. Had such lines been drawn at that time, my life might well have taken an entirely different course.

The Democrats were watching closely. I had called on all the liberal Democrats at that time: Frankie Randolph, who was the grande dame; Chris Dixie, who was labor's lawyer; and Billie Carr, who remained the backbone of the group until her death. Ed Smith, a diminutive lawyer with a giant brain, became and remained a very good friend. He took me to Austin one time to attend a seminar on the Missouri Plan for the election of judges, long before anyone in Texas had even considered such a process. After more than thirty-five years, Texas and other states as well are still wrestling with judicial election reform.

Barbara Jordan, eventually the distinguished black member of Congress from Houston, had run for the legislature in 1960 and lost, a casualty of the segregationist attitudes of many influential conservative Democrats. I believe she would have made a great addition to our ticket in 1962, but the Democrats heard I was courting her, and that was the end of that. They elected her that year.

During all the years of our friendship, Barbara and I had only one disagreement. In 1964, she urged everyone to "pull the lever." That lever included voting for Wally Miller, who, running for reelection, was one of the most strident segregationists of all of the candidates. She explained to me that there were two candidates named "White" on the ballot. One was Hattie White, destined to become the first African American member of the Houston School Board; the other "White" was running for statewide office. Barbara told me she was afraid "her people" would be confused and that it was more important for Hattie White to be elected than for anyone else to be defeated, no matter how bad a candidate they were. At the time I chided her, "Barbara, I have more respect for your 'people' than you do." Today I am more understanding of her ultimate goal. Sometimes the choice in politics is the lesser of two evils.

The Democrats at that time were smarter politicians than the Republicans because they used the "bell cow system." Farmers often put a bell on the lead cow so that the others will follow. When the Democrats had a popular winner in a particular locale, all of the

Marjorie with former speaker Newt Gingrich at her home, 1984, when he was minority whip.

literature and effort was concentrated on featuring that candidate. In Harris County, Hattie White elected John Connally governor of Texas. He never had to campaign there at all. In contrast, the Republicans went with their "feature," the candidate at the top, like a stampeding herd over a cliff, even if someone else could carry the ticket better.

In 1964, George H. W. Bush was the most popular figure in Harris County. However, instead of featuring him, the politically naïve Republicans, at the insistence of the conservative Democrats, whom they were courting, forced Barry Goldwater's name and face to be widely displayed on every piece of Republican literature. They all went down like stones in a pond.

Raymond and I were personal friends of Barry's. He was a wonderful senator and a great human being, but he had one problem: He was ahead of his time. His solutions to complicated problems appeared too simple, if not simplistic. For instance, in 1964, people thought his idea of a flat tax idiotic. In 1996, though, it became a central, accepted campaign debate topic. In addition, the people around him weren't just naïve, they were also politically illiterate. No one who is interested or active in politics will ever forget his memorable sentence "Extremism in defense of virtue is no vice."

Our whole family was in the Cow Palace in San Francisco when that speech was given. I remember Sidney Buchanan, one of the alternate delegates, coming to where I sat beside his wife, saying "Now, Marjorie, don't be upset. Let me tell you what he meant!"

Marjorie and Senator John Tower, 1985, the year Tower retired from the Senate.

Houston-area Bush stalwarts at a Republican rally, date unknown. Left to right: Nancy Crouch, Rob Mosbacher, Becky Orr, Barbara Patton, Dee Coats, Jack Steel, Marjorie, unknown woman, George W. Bush, unknown man, Liz Ghrist, Hal DeMoss, former Harris County judge Jon Lindsay.

Corinne and I looked at each other with disbelief and, almost in unison, exclaimed, "Don't explain what Goldwater said to *us*—go explain it to those hundreds of millions of people on television!"

In 1963, the conservative Democrats looked at the figures of my election. A very liberal Democrat named Bob Eckhardt from the northeastern part of Harris County was entrenched in the state legislature. The conservative Democrats wanted him defeated before the inevitable creation of single-member districts. Their strategists surmised that, if Eckhardt were not defeated at large in 1964, he would be unbeatable later as a congressman in his liberal northeast area. One of them called to make me an offer. He explained that the Democrats wanted to get rid of Eckhardt, but they couldn't afford to oppose him publicly. They felt that I was the only Republican or Democrat who could beat him and offered me an enormous campaign fund if I would run against him in 1964. They were willing to back a Republican in order to oppose one of their own. It was a compliment, of course, but the thought of running as a Republican with Democrat money turned my stomach. More important, I didn't want political office except on my own terms. By that time, too, I felt that the whole ticket would be defeated because Americans were just not ready for Barry Goldwater as president. The Democrats were right about Eckhardt. He did go on to become a congressman from the Eighth District and stayed there for many years, until Jack Fields eventually brought that district into the Republican column.

People wonder why defeated candidates keep on running for office. The answer is that politics is a disease. Once contracted, it is simply incurable. One Democrat ran so many times for the Senate that voters thought he was an incumbent. Even when a candidate gets elected, somehow there is an itch to move to another office, so when a political party becomes fairly successful, the voters witness a game of musical chairs. Incumbents of one office move "up" to another, creating all kinds of opportunities at the "bottom."

That wasn't the case in 1962, however. A defeat then was a defeat. The Republican Party was looking for new faces and preferably noncontroversial ones. I developed my own definition of "noncontroversial," as someone who has never known anyone or done anything. The energy generated in running for office is part of the addiction, of course. Even losing didn't dampen my enthusiasm. The juices were still flowing.

The very day after I was defeated I set about finding out which precincts had produced what percentage of votes and where they were located. Immediately I eagerly proposed plans to improve the mechanics of the Republican Party and to solve problems I had encountered as a candidate. Anyone with any political experience would have known that getting mixed up in the structure of the party is a sure recipe for trouble if you are interested in a political future as a candidate for office. You make too many enemies. Even if I had known that fact, I don't think I would have cared because I was interested in building the party, not in running again for public office.

Since then, the growth of the Republican Party in Texas has been extraordinary. Along with that expansion, of course, factions have developed, as is common with all political parties. I call this the "us-and-them" syndrome. Sometimes the cause is simply a matter

Marjorie with Sen. Kay Bailey Hutchison and former first lady Barbara Bush. Photo courtesy of David Bray and Associates, Bellaire, Texas.

of the pursuit of raw power. Sometimes the difference is ideological. More often it's both. The larger and more successful the party, the more serious the divisions.

It seems to be human nature to attempt to translate complex issues into simple terms and to apply simple questions to determine what a person thinks about a constellation of issues. The easiest method is to employ a watchword or litmus test to determine whether someone is one of "us" or one of "them." In 1958, and for a surprising period of time thereafter, the defining question among Republicans became "Are you for or against the John Birch Society?" Earlier, McCarthyism used "softness" on communism as the defining issue.

Around the time I became active in "retail" politics—that is, dealing directly with voters—capital punishment became the watchword. I confounded listeners with complex answers. No simple "yes" or "no." Was I for or against capital punishment? I offered the thesis that, until a way existed to exile without parole those offenders who posed a threat to society, capital punishment was a necessary evil.

But there was a problem with the finality of the death sentence. Better a hundred guilty men go free than one innocent person be deprived of life.

Today the words "abortion" and "homosexuality" have replaced the earlier code words of "capital punishment," "communism," and the "Birch Society." Ironically, John Tower could not have won a Republican primary in today's Texas. He was a pro-choice advocate and unabashedly so. However, no one paid much attention to that subject in those days since there were communist fish to fry.

In recent years I have often been asked why so many Republicans do not agree with the Republican platform—particularly its position on abortion and homosexuality. Democrats are often asked the same question about their platform, which tilts as far to the left as the Republican does to the right. The reason is simple. The great majority of voters don't support their respective party platforms because they hold opinions that fail the litmus tests given by single-issue extremists. The people who devote almost every waking hour to party politics are zealots by inclination, thus, by definition, intolerant of divergent opinions. Single issues dominate their lives. Those who are violently antiabortion and those who just as vehemently identify themselves as pro-choice are the ones who work in the precincts, go to the executive committee meetings, and do the nitty-gritty of their respective party organizations. They stuff envelopes, raise money, and volunteer for any and every chore. They hold the party offices, and party affairs dominate their lives. They are the people who, in both parties, are elected as delegates to the conventions that write the platforms. When the Republican Party was emerging, I was an activist. In those days our motivating issues were to oppose Democrats and establish a two-party state. I still believe it is as much a civic responsibility to attend precinct conventions as it is to vote.

Ray and I were in Taipei, Taiwan, just before the 1968 Nixon and Humphrey campaign, and there I heard an American woman at a nearby table ask her companions, "How in the world could two great parties come up with such terrible candidates?"

To my husband's consternation, I got up, went to her table, and asked, "Did you ever go to your precinct convention?"

She was bewildered. "What's that?" she asked.

"That's where the nomination process begins," I replied. She is not alone in her ignorance.

Those who call themselves affiliates of one or the other of the political parties just because they vote on election day never let the precinct convention interfere with their plans to attend the opera or symphony or a ball game. Then they generally complain about the results of their lack of participation—platforms with far-fetched pronouncements and delegates to state conventions who are zealous proponents of ever more extreme policies. In fact, fewer and fewer members of our increasingly disaffected electorate are hard-line, straight-ticket voters. That is why the growing middle is now determining general elections, although an actual national party of independents has not emerged—at least, not yet.

In the "us" vs. "them" division of the Republican Party, I, of course, am an "us," a designation some people mistakenly term "moderate." I strongly disagree with the accuracy of that label since it does not characterize me. I have very strong opinions on a variety of issues, but they just don't fit neatly into a left- or right-wing catechism.

In fact, the Republican Party today presents a problem for voters like me who are fiscally conservative but ask, "With the advent of amniocentesis, how can the state be empowered to dictate that a young couple bring to term a Down's syndrome or thalidomide fetus?" In my view, there are many more valid exceptions to a prohibition against abortion than just rape, incest, and the death of the mother. I once asked a woman what she would do if her thirteen-year-old daughter were impregnated by rape. She answered, "That little baby wouldn't know its mother was raped." One day I asked a man who repeatedly denounced homosexuals what he would do if amniocentesis could identity a homosexual fetus. He looked horror stricken, gazed up at the ceiling, and said, "Oh my God, I suppose we would have to bring the baby to term and then try to save its soul." There may be a place for those who hold inflexible opinions on belief-based issues, but there has to be room somewhere for those who, along with me, object to the rigidity of intolerance for other people's points of view.

Reflecting the depth of such divisions, in the 1990s, the Harris County Republican Party gained some national attention for its highly public "split," which appeared to produce two competing county chairmen, only one of whom—Betsy Lake, a "big tent" Republican—had been elected by the voters. Not surprisingly, in the

1950s and 1960s as well, factions existed in the county party, but since the party was small, the intraparty problems were manageable. My group had generally voted for Eisenhower, and we were lenient in our definition of a Republican. We respected differences of opinion within the framework of Republican principles. Our group also included many prominent Houston citizens. A few benefactors—the Albert Fays, the Dudley Sharps, and the Ted Laws—funded Republican headquarters. There is no doubt that it was an upper-class environment. Precinct chairmen were the peons. It was a top-down operation.

Perhaps more significantly, the divisions within the party were also based on those who could be counted as "old" Republicans and those who had recently changed parties. The converts to our party at that time were Democrats who were largely too conservative for the conservative wing of the Democrat Party and therefore had no real concept of Republican principles. While rejecting the label, these former Democrats were in fact unreconstructed segregationists. Together with members of the Birch Society, who were seeing communists under every bed, they constituted the "them" faction. At that time, there were more of "us" than of "them."

Following my experience as a candidate, I became a precinct chairman myself, having realized during my campaign that they were the people who did the work. As a believer in stronger grassroots participation, I wanted to change the party's structure as well as its image. I take credit, with another Republican, the late Craig Peper, for having started what came to be known as the neighbor-to-neighbor fund drive. This was an effort to encourage all Republicans to approach their neighbors and ask for contributions, however small. I calculated that if we could get a person to give even one dollar, we had a crack at that vote. No one paid much attention to this endeavor at first, but it marked the beginning of the elevation of the importance of the precinct chairmen.

As it turned out, I helped to create a monster. Today, the overblown importance of the county executive committee, whose membership consists of all Republican precinct chairmen, has emasculated the authority of the county chairman, who once served as the party's public image and controlled the local party's direction through appointment of party officers and committee chairmen. In the 1990s' split in the county party I mentioned earlier, it was the chairman of the executive committee who held himself up as chief Republican spokesperson and attempted to usurp the authority of county chairman Betsy Lake, who had been elected to the position by a majority of voters in the Republican primary.

I also mentioned earlier that involvement in the party structure was death to a prospective candidacy. Although generally true, there was one notable exception. In 1963, Jimmy Bertron, chairman of the Harris County party and one of "us," called me: "Marjorie, I don't want it generally known just now, but I'm moving to Florida. I think I've found a good replacement for us, so we could get a head start in warding off a takeover of the chairmanship in a special election. Would you get some of our precinct people together to meet him?"

"Who is it?"

"His name is George Bush. His wife's name is Barbara. They're newcomers to Houston, and you're going to love them."

Linda Dyson, my longtime friend, says that we had met George before the evening they walked into the Arsht home, but, honestly, I don't remember it. As far as I am concerned, that evening was the beginning of George's campaign for county chairman. It was also the beginning of a long and rewarding friendship. Since then I have repeatedly been asked, "Did you have any idea at that time that you were dealing with someone who would eventually become president of the United States?" My answer has always been the same: "The Bushes were charming. We were very pleased, but the fact is we were merely looking for a county chairman. And we were delighted that we felt we had a winner."

George and Barbara offered some big advantages. They were handsome and charismatic, but most of all they were strangers. For many years, George and Barbara had lived in Midland, Texas, where George had built a thriving oil business and where all but one of their six children were born. They hadn't had time to become controversial.

Even so, the "them" faction was not enthusiastic. They considered George a Yankee, one of the worst sins possible; a "Yalie," the second worst sin; and generally a rich kid, absolutely unforgivable. Nevertheless, George walked away with the election. With the exception of a few, like Nancy Palm, who was destined to become party chairman, those early reformed Democrats never lost their distrust of George Bush, regardless of his long and illustrious career and his many achievements. Today there exists no stronger supporter of all of the Bushes than Nancy.

Once ensconced at headquarters, George made moves to attract everyone to the Republican Party. There were pitfalls. Most of those who were interested in joining us were potential members of the "them" group: Democrats too conservative for their own party. In 1961, they had been "Democrats for Tower." In 1964, they were "Democrats for Goldwater," and they didn't want the word "Republican" printed anywhere. We tried to explain the situation: "George, these are not your friends."

"Why are you so suspicious? I've met with them, and they seemed very nice to me."

"They're going to do everything they can to undermine you."

"I just don't believe that. All they want is to come over en masse in some public ceremony. I don't see anything wrong with that."

Our general reception of his decision was "Oh, Lord!" We knew George didn't understand that this group wanted recognition that the Republican Party had adopted the old conservative Democrat postures, the ones with which they were comfortable. In particular, these people remained surreptitiously segregationist, still fighting the Civil War, and narrowly focused on a few hot issues. They had no intention of conforming to the tolerant Republican principles that George Bush represented. As requested, there was, however, a huge "come-over" at the Rice Hotel. The next day I got a call from Walter Sterling, chairman of the Harris County Democratic Party. "Congratulations!" he crowed. "Are we glad you've now got those inflexible so-and-sos!"

Although it is true that we did not at that time even think in terms of the presidency, certainly everyone around George Bush knew he was special. He was so attractive and smart, we knew he was destined for great things. It was not surprising that he should want to file for the Senate in 1964. I was unalterably opposed.

"George, your opponent will be Ralph Yarborough. He's the darling of the liberals. Republicans in Texas can win only when they're running against dyed-in-the wool conservative Democrats."

"But he has lost so many times, and he's so liberal. Texas is a conservative state."

"George, please listen. Texas Democrats are known as 'yellow dog' Democrats. This means they would vote for a yellow dog if it were running on the Democratic ticket. Their hands would fall off if they voted for a statewide Republican. And a Republican cannot win without Democratic votes. There are not enough Republicans in Texas to elect anyone statewide." He simply could not comprehend the fact that the only Democrats who would forsake their party for ideological reasons were the liberals, who, because they wanted to purge their party of conservatives, would vote for a Republican against a conservative Democrat any day of the week. Nonetheless, despite the fact that George Bush had been advised by more people than me that he would lose, he filed against Ralph Yarborough in 1964.

Once George made the decision, everyone rallied round in full support. One day he called me: "Marjorie, I've invited Grant Reynolds to come to Houston to help me with the black vote. He's general counsel for the national Republican Party and a highly respected black Republican. I'm having one event for him, but I need someone else to have a party for him and his Houston friends. Would you be willing to do that?" No one refused George, and it wasn't until I hung up that I wondered, *How am I going to tell Ray?* In that day and time in Houston, mixed-race social gatherings were unheard of.

When Ray came home that evening, I gulped hard and said, "George and Barbara are coming for dinner next Thursday evening." Any other words just stuck in my throat. He replied, "Good." Two nights later I tried again. "Barbara and George are coming to dinner next Thursday." Ray looked up curiously. "You already told me that. What's the problem?"

"Oh, nothing. I just didn't want you to forget and make another engagement. And oh, yes, they're bringing some friends." Nothing else came out. Again he said, "Good."

Try as I might, I couldn't picture him with African Americans as guests in our living room. Ray was a conformist when it came to the social mores of his time. Being the first to step forward and break new ground just wasn't in his nature.

I called several couples, good friends, explaining the unusual party I was having: the John Dysons, the Bill Spences, the Bailey Simmonses, the Bob Crouches—all Bush supporters. They promised to help make it easier for Ray. And then I called Craig Peper, my cohort in the neighbor-to-neighbor fund drive and one of our more liberal

Republicans. Craig, a forty-year-old confirmed bachelor, had migrated from the Northeast and considered Texas a bit backward, especially in race relations. Many people found him slightly strange because of his Eastern ways, but he liked me and I liked him. I explained about the party, and he let out a roaring laugh, especially when I asked him to come early and help me tell Ray about our guests.

Thursday night came. And right on time, thirty minutes before the other guests arrived, Craig appeared. I called up to Ray, "Come on down. Craig is here, and we'll have a drink before the guests come."

Down came Ray, delighted to see Craig. Once the pleasantries were exchanged, I said, "I want to tell you who is coming this evening" (a few years later I completely identified with the movie *Guess Who's Coming to Dinner*). I cleared my throat, and Craig came to my rescue.

"George Bush has invited a black lawyer from Washington and some of his professional black friends in Houston for dinner tonight. It should be an interesting evening."

Ray looked at Craig as though he were speaking in a foreign language, and then he turned to me, "Have you lost your mind?" Then he looked toward the front of the house. "Do you realize the front of this house is all glass?" Without waiting for me to answer, he moved to the front to draw the draperies, and then he realized that wouldn't really do any good since it was summer and still light outside. I hurried to explain to Ray who the other guests were so he would know there were others of our friends also involved.

"Do they know who's invited?" When I nodded, he said with a pained smile, "So I'm the only one surprised?" I nodded again.

Around that time, the doorbell rang, and the Bushes came in with their elegant, tall, handsome guest, Grant Reynolds. Ray's innate good manners prevented our guests from knowing he was in a state of shock. As the others entered, another unforeseen circumstance caused Ray to shed his bewilderment. Although I had decided on a buffet dinner, I had not anticipated the response of Harold Brown, my black chauffeur and bartender, and Annie Turner, my cook. They were totally baffled. They had never served a black person as a special guest in a white family's home before, and both suffered a kind of "brain paralysis." One guest asked for a Bloody Mary, and when Ray saw Harold reach for a small wine glass, he knew that he had to help behind the bar, which took his mind off the guests milling around in the lanai.

After some time I realized no food was coming from the kitchen. I went in to see what was happening and found Annie peeking out through the glass in the pass-through door. I had to get dinner on the table myself. Actually the party was a success. My friends visited with the black lawyers, doctors, and businesspeople who, in retrospect, I'm sure, were just as curious as we were about such a party. When all the other guests had left, George and Barbara and Grant Reynolds lingered. We had all relaxed by then, and the conversation turned to politics.

At that time, a man named Adam Clayton Powell was a congressman from New York. He was known for his outrageous behavior, and his constituents, loving the fact that he so arrogantly thumbed his nose at "whitey," kept returning him to office, term after term. As we sat around our circular sofa, I brought up the subject of Powell, saying that I considered him a disgrace, whereupon Grant quickly said, "*I* can criticize him, but *you* can't."

"The hell I can't" was my sharp retort. "I call down Jews when I think they elicit rebuke. I don't feel constrained to hold my tongue just for the niceties of race or religion." Out of the corner of my eye I saw that George and Barbara weren't all that happy, but I ploughed ahead, and in the end Grant relented and agreed that my position was valid. The most interesting outcome of the evening was that Grant Reynolds didn't just write me a wonderful thank-you letter. He also sent me a Christmas card every holiday season until he died.

Of course, that was just the first of countless parties of its ilk to take place in our home. And Ray hosted all of them most graciously. That party tore down the wall between the races at social events, but it had no appreciable effect on the black vote. In his book *All the Best: My Life in Letters and Other Writings* (New York: Scribner, 1999, p. 88), George refers to the issue of race as it came up in that campaign and to a letter he wrote me about it:

> Earlier that summer Congress had passed the controversial Civil Rights Bill of 1964—the Senate had debated a record-breaking eighty-three days before voting. It was a difficult issue for me. I opposed discrimination of any kind and abhorred racism. Changes obviously needed to be made, but I agreed with Barry Goldwater and others who supported the concept of civil rights

but felt strongly this bill was unconstitutional and threatened more rights than it protected. I decided I could not support the bill and said so in my campaign. Yarborough had voted for it, which would not help him in Texas. But I was not comfortable using that in the campaign because my reasons for not supporting the bill were very different from those who hated the bill for racist reasons. I wrote this letter to my friend and supporter Marjorie Arsht, who was a leader in Houston's Jewish community:

> *Dear Marjorie:*
>
> *. . . My heart is heavy—I have traveled the state for 2 weeks. The civil rights issue can bring Yarborough to sure defeat. I know this now for certain—but I am not sure that a fair and moderated debate on civil rights can do it. Goldwater's position is correct (and parenthetically so is mine.)—for Texas and for the USA. We must develop this position reasonably, prudently, sensitively—for we must be sure we don't inflame the passions of unthinking men to garner a vote; yet it is essential that the position I believe in be explained. I believe I am right—I know we must have restraint, yet I don't want this restraint to prevent right from prevailing—my heart aches for Tom D. [Tom Dixon, an African American friend and supporter] . . .*
>
> *What shall I do? How will I do it? I want to win but not at the expense of justice, not at the expense of the dignity of any man—not at the expense of hurting a friend nor teaching my children a prejudice which I do not feel . . .*
>
> *I want and need the advice of one who can perhaps understand what troubles me!*

A young man in my precinct, Joe Bailey, was a computer expert at a time when computer entries were made on punch cards. He worked for Shell Oil Company and had access to the necessary hardware. He was a smart young bachelor, slightly built, and a few years older than my children. He became a regular member of our household. My precinct, number 40, was one of the very first ones to be computerized. We lived then on North Boulevard near Rice University, but precinct 40 had a diverse population and was so balanced that, a number of years later, it became one of the "test" precincts that professionals used to predict the outcome of elections.

My neighbors and friends made telephone surveys, and Joe entered the responses. At the outset of the campaign, George Bush had 95 percent of the vote against Ralph Yarborough in our precinct, while Barry Goldwater had 80 percent against Lyndon Johnson. Because our newly acquired Democrat-Republicans insisted that only Goldwater's face and name be on every door-hanger, handout, and yard sign, George's percentage kept going down—first, 92 percent and then 90 percent. Goldwater held at 80 percent. We did a test every three weeks. By Election Day, Bush and Goldwater were dead even at 70 percent. Considering the makeup of my precinct at that time, those figures were disastrous. George Bush lost, as predicted.

Two years later, in 1966, George ran for Congress from the Seventh Congressional District. Finally, he had a conservative opponent, Frank Briscoe. George won, of course, and thereafter the Seventh Congressional District in Harris County became, by and large, sociologically Republican, a rock-solid seat. Today the most intense competition among candidates in that district takes place in the Republican primary, with the victor assured of election in November just as the Democrats had been in previous years. The 1966 election, however, did not remedy the division in the party. In fact, George's victory may have deepened the rift among Republicans in Harris County.

The "Bush Belles," first organized in 1964, when George ran for the Senate, expanded to full strength for his congressional candidacy. For the most part they were suburban housewives who worked day and night for George Bush, staffed his headquarters, and deeply resented the influence of the "new" Republicans, who, they felt, had not wholeheartedly supported George when he ran for the Senate in 1964. They were correct. The "new" Republicans never did really trust George Bush.

That same year, 1966, however, Sen. John Tower was up for reelection. John, under his still-lucky political star, was running against Waggoner Carr, a man almost as distasteful to liberal Democrats as Blakely had been in Tower's first election. Although the Bush volunteers approved of John, none of them darkened the door of the Tower headquarters. Instead, it was manned by "them"—the Goldwater people. And me.

Always a Bush advocate, I was still what some of my friends called "the great all-time Jewish Republican missionary." I continued trying to convert "them" to "us." Just as I had with my family, I was trying to play peacemaker because I felt that someone had to bridge the gap. And, of course, John Tower was my good friend.

Joe Bailey had moved back to Midland but still worked for Shell. It was decided that we would computerize Harris County for Tower. Joe prepared the sheets for listing every Republican anyone could identify by size of contribution, congressional and senatorial district, and precinct. It was a mammoth job. I was assigned the responsibility of coordinating the volunteers who would fill in the data for the keypunch people, and then everything was sent to Midland for processing.

My volunteers were all devoted members of the Goldwater faction, for the most part former Democrats. Iris Manes and Pat Skinner were my lieutenants. Although both were relatively new to the Republican Party, Iris, particularly, was a capable and indefatigable worker. She was an attractive blonde with a large following of formerly Democrat women, and she put them all to work. Iris and I made a good team, and we did a fantastic job. When all the data were in, Joe's prediction was a comfortable victory for Tower. We didn't dare tell anyone because it was so unbelievable. The actual results showed an even greater margin of victory than our data predicted: John won by two hundred thousand votes.

During the campaign I had gone back to my liberal friend, Billie Carr, and said, "Look, don't you still want to purge your party? Do you want Waggoner Carr for your senator?"

She was morose. "We expected to defeat your little professor this year."

"You don't have a candidate you can support."

"Well, I guess we'll have to wait for next time, but promise you won't talk about it! I'll tell my people, 'Vote for Tower, or if you just can't do it, go fishing.'" I kept my promise for many years, and so did she. Only John Tower and his assistant, Tom Cole, knew that John had been elected to two terms in the Senate by liberal Democrats. By the time he ran for a third term, he was unbeatable.

As Republican as the Seventh District is now, it should be remembered that the early years of George Bush's first term in Congress were anything but smooth sailing. In 1967, the then young and untested congressman from Texas was faced with a vote on open housing. The come-over conservatives, only newly labeled Republicans, didn't trust George much in the first place, and when they learned he had voted for the Open Housing Act, all hell broke loose. Still largely segregationist at heart, they considered that act almost treasonous. Accepting school integration, even in name only, was one thing, but open housing?

George received an avalanche of hate mail. I remember that one woman who had hosted one of his campaign coffees wrote him that she felt personally violated and assured him he would never again be welcome in her house. Volunteers at county headquarters fielded death threats. George decided to confront his critics at an open-forum town meeting. It was held in a high school auditorium in the Memorial and Spring Branch area of Houston, the heart of the Seventh District.

On the night of the event, the auditorium was filled to overflowing. Those of us who applauded George's courageous and correct stand held our breath. The audience was restive, but when George came to the microphone, an ominous silence greeted him. Nevertheless, he was forthright in his description of the response he had received from his district and described some of the messages, although I don't remember whether he identified any of the authors. He didn't have to. We all knew the source of almost every threat. And then he said simply, "I'm sorry if, by my actions, I have offended any one of my constituents, but I simply could not in good conscience deny the right to live wherever they choose [to] those courageous young men who have fought for their country." For a moment there was quiet—and then a burst of applause, almost raucous, with a standing ovation. To this day I feel a lump in my throat as I write about that evening since I firmly believe it was a defining moment for George Bush and a leap of faith for the Texas Republican Party.

One man and one woman represent each of the senatorial districts in Texas on the Republican state executive committee. They are elected in caucuses every four years at the state convention in nonpresidential election years. Nancy Thawley, smart and definitely old-line Republican, had represented the Fifteenth District for some time. As the "new" Republicans came along, she became more and more controversial. She hated the meetings and began sending me with her proxy. I attended so many state executive committee meetings that the members thought I had been duly elected.

During the Tower campaign, I announced that I was going to run for state committeewoman from the Fifteenth Senatorial District. My staunch friends geared up for action. Among them were Hilda Ruth, Bailey Simmons, Sarah and Kirby Gee, Linda and Johnny Dyson, Ruth and Hart Mankin, Bob and Nancy Crouch, and Bill and Nancy Spence. Later as volunteers, Linda and Sarah, along with a few others, managed George Bush's Houston congressional office.

After my announcement, I kept waiting for an opponent to surface. Pat Skinner badly wanted the job but couldn't decide whether she could win. She was on again, off again. Then word circulated that Imalee Barry, wife of Desmond Barry, a popular but unsuccessful candidate for Congress, would run. Imalee was a nice, sweet, congenial person. No one ever took her very seriously in the political world, however. She was mainly decorative. I didn't spend any time worrying about the possibility of her opposition because I had to put together my own election strategy.

It was essential that I have important people nominate me and certainly not anyone closely associated with me in the public eye. My first choice was John Cater, an outstanding young banking executive who was very active in all of the Bush campaigns. His square jaw and general demeanor showed the strength of a natural leader. I also needed a woman to second my nomination, and I wanted Kitty Elliott, a lovely, dignified brunette who was a good friend. An added advantage, in my view, was that she had run Dez Barry's campaign. When I asked John to nominate me, I told him of the possibility of Imalee's entry. He, too, had been closely associated with the Barry campaign. A week before the convention he came to my house on a Sunday morning and said, "We're going to find out once and for all about Imalee." He picked up the telephone. "Dez, John Cater here. I want a straight answer. Is Imalee a candidate for state committeewoman or not?"

"She is absolutely, positively not," Dez replied. "She doesn't want to do it, and I don't want her to do it."

"Is that final?"

"It is. You have my word on it."

Armed with that assurance, I went to Kitty, who was delighted to accept.

No one could understand why I didn't have an opponent. Sidney Buchanan, the "golden" boy, was opposed in his race for state committeeman by Fred Weston, an important Republican who had been tremendously helpful in my campaign for the legislature. Obviously, the "thems" were delighted to have a person of Fred's stature interested in running for party office.

The Republican Party held its convention that year in San Antonio. Bailey and Hilda Ruth shared a suite with Raymond and me, and our living room served as a meeting place for strategic planning.

Hal DeMoss and Bill Cassin were Sidney's principal lieutenants. Both were my friends, but both considered me a liability to Sidney's candidacy. Bill and Hal kept assuring us that it was in my best interests for Sidney and me to campaign separately. Their intent was transparently the opposite. However able, I was just too controversial. I often wondered whether that was because I was so outspoken or because I was Jewish.

Both Hal and Bill were outstanding young leaders in the party. Although both of them were lawyers in prestigious firms—Hal with Bracewell Patterson, Bill with Baker Botts—they differed greatly in temperament. Hal was calm and judicious. To the annoyance of many, he managed to convey the impression that he was "above the fray." We couldn't depend upon him to be on one side or the other of any issue. Because of this, he was more often than not chosen by out-of-town politicos to head important efforts on the party's behalf. He was, however, a staunch supporter of Sidney, whom he considered a sure winner. Bill, on the other hand, was emotional, high strung, and imperious—the executive type.

Ray, who remained through everything my strongest supporter in all public activities, was an alternate to the convention in San Antonio. As such, he had not been seated at the same time as the delegates. Therefore he was privy to all of the chatter in the back of the room while the alternates' credentials were being verified. When he finally sat down beside me, I looked at him with alarm. He was clearly upset, greenish pale, and muttering that he was going to kill somebody. This usually quiet man had totally unraveled. I was actually afraid he would have a stroke. And I had no clue as to the reason. I was afraid to ask.

Soon the caucus began. It was a rule that the committeeman would speak first, and then a vote would be taken but not announced. Then, after a brief intermission, the committeewoman would speak. Sidney and Fred were nominated and seconded and made their ten-minute speeches. After their vote was taken, it was time for the intermission. Hal, always the arbitrator, came and told me that I did indeed have an opponent: Imalee Barry. I glanced over at John Cater's face. He was both dumbfounded and furious. I knew then what Ray had heard in the back of the room. It seems that—overnight—little badges had been handwritten with "I'm for Imalee and Dez is too." Suddenly they popped up everywhere.

Hal continued, "John Cater and I tossed a coin, and Imalee will speak first."

Dez Barry came to the podium to introduce his wife. Loud cheering and applause. I found myself trying to hold Ray in his seat. Poor Imalee. Even I felt sorry for her. She rambled on about some trip she had taken to Washington State, what fun it had been, and other unrelated, equally irrelevant topics. She was finally stopped by the timekeeper.

I had no speech prepared. Originally believing I had no opponent, I had decided to speak extemporaneously of hearts and flowers, sweetness and light, and the joy of the campaigns ahead. As an experienced public speaker, I had a beginning and an ending prepared, but whatever I had thought I would say was now out the window. I didn't have a note in my hand. Somewhere between my seat and the podium I decided, *Okay, you've asked for it. No holds barred. I'll give you something to remember!* I stood at the podium using the old unfailing ploy: I just stood there silently until I was sure I had their undivided attention. And then, slowly enunciating each syllable, I said, "my . . . name . . . is . . . Marjorie Arsht. I am a candidate for state committeewoman from the Fifteenth District of Texas." I paused. "My . . . husband . . . is . . . not . . . running." If a pin had dropped at that instant, it would have sounded like a clap of thunder.

Later, one of my friends, Alliene Smith, longtime secretary to George Bush, told me that her heart had almost stopped. She was convinced I had lost the election at that moment. Since there was no recording and no written draft, I don't really remember just what I said after that opening. There are those who say it was one of the best performances I ever gave. I do know that I didn't mince any words. I didn't pretend we were all friends. I do remember saying we had a job to do and it was their responsibility to decide who could do it best.

Sidney and I both knew it would be a vote along factional lines, so that if one won, the other would be likely to win as well. That was, of course, before my speech. Sidney had arranged for some code from a vote counter to let him know whether he had won or lost, so he knew quickly that he had won but couldn't find a way to tell me.

To the delight of John Cater and to the ecstatic, enthusiastic cheering of my husband, I received two more votes than Sidney. I made no attempt to disguise my triumph to Hal DeMoss and Bill Cassin, who had considered me a handicap to Sidney. I also knew where those two extra votes came from. Two neighbors, one a former Rice classmate and the other a Rice professor, both members of "them," lived in my neighborhood, were often at my house, and were my friends. When we emerged from the caucus, they came running. They were delighted that their votes had stood out and wanted me to be sure I knew the source.

Sidney and I served our terms gallantly. In those days, Republicans from around the state all knew each other. Under Peter O'Donnell, the aristocratic, wealthy, and distinguished state party chairman, Dallas was always ahead of Houston in unity. Both in Dallas and at the state level, Peter managed to avoid the many squabbles we had experienced in Houston. He was a strong leader.

Coming home to Harris County was something else. The executive committee had changed hands as well as character. Recognizing that they needed to have a "name" as county chairman—both for prestige and for fundraising—they saw to it that the dignified, illustrious Dudley Sharp got the position. But the real operation of the party fell to Vice Chairman Nancy Palm. A woman with strong opinions, she made a good executive. People like Dudley and Albert Fay simply didn't understand, however, that Nancy—their friend and neighbor in Memorial—didn't really share their vision for the Republican Party. She was the "queen" of the new Republicans and a staunch conservative Democrat even at the time that George Bush had opposed Frank Briscoe. As her nickname, "Napalm," indicates, Nancy was tough. She gave no quarter and ran the party with unmatched efficiency under Dudley's titular position. She could count on the total loyalty of the former Democrats, to the dismay of the old-line Republicans, who kept leading their lives as they had in the old days, going to the ballet and the opera and leaving the nitty-gritty of politics to subordinates.

Since the summer of 1966, our family had lived at 2016 Main in a precinct that boasted twenty-one primary voters—hardly a power precinct. Inasmuch as I was now state committeewoman representing the whole district, I didn't want to serve as precinct chairman, in which capacity I would have to vote on contested issues. (I was, I am proud to say, still adhering to my principles of political propriety.) Therefore, my daughter Leslye, then a student at the University of Houston, applied for the position and was accepted. Everyone seemed to be delighted. They knew that although she had been active as a teenage volunteer, particularly in the Bush campaigns, they correctly assumed that she wasn't experienced enough to detect all the ins and outs of intrigue that were under way in the executive committee.

By early 1968, realizing that Leslye would be graduating and leaving for Washington, D.C., I called on Dudley. "Dudley, I need a favor."

"Anything you want."

"Leslye will soon graduate and therefore vacate the precinct chairmanship of our little insignificant precinct. My term as committeewoman will soon expire. I would like to replace her."

"Marjorie, surely you want something more important than to be a precinct chairman after all you've been to this party."

"Dudley, there is no more important position in the party than that of precinct chairman."

"What's the problem then, if that's what you want?"

"Don't you realize that your vacancy committee will not look upon me with favor?"

"Don't be silly."

That's how out of touch Dudley Sharp was with the goings-on of the Harris County Republican Party. I couldn't make him understand that it wasn't my precinct, with its twenty-one primary votes, that was a problem. They didn't want my voice on the committee. By that time, most of the precinct chairmen were just recruits who knew nothing and simply followed instructions without question. I therefore wasn't surprised when the vacancy committee turned me down. Still, they had to do a lot of research to find a replacement because most of the twenty-one Republican voters in that precinct lived at 2016 Main. They finally found and appointed a dressmaker on Smith Street who said she was a Republican. I don't remember her name, and I doubt that any records would reflect it.

Of course, at the next primary, I filed for precinct chairman. The election was a joke because there was no question as to whether I'd win (I did). I even had to conduct the precinct convention that elected me because my opponent, that poor woman, had never attended one. But I then did something I had never done before (and have never done since) in politics. I abdicated the field. I never went to an executive committee meeting, and I never raised or gave a dime. Some might have called it a Pyrrhic victory, but it really was more than that. I truly had other things on my mind.

Eventually, however, even Dudley came to understand the "problem." The executive committee subscribed to the theory of "winner take all," and they shared no authority. When the committee moved to deprive Dudley of certain appointive powers and to further diminish his role as chairman, he simply walked out of the meeting. And that was when Nancy Palm, his vice chairman, became the first female county chairman of the Republican Party in Harris County. Undoubtedly Nancy was one of the strongest and best chairmen our county has ever had, though I doubt that we, the defeated ones, acknowledged that fact at the time. In reality, the indefatigable and around-the-clock dedication of the new Republicans under her leadership paid off. Under her tutelage, the Republican Party grew steadily, although it would not reach its present dominant position for another twenty-five years. I'm happy to say that today Nancy and I are very good friends and both Presidents Bush do not have a more loyal or vocal supporter.

As for the executive committee, to my knowledge they have never relinquished their control, even though they were partially held in check during the chairmanship of Betsy Lake. Because the recent executive committees have stripped the county chairmen of authority, the Republican Party organization as such has lost its prestige in Harris County. This is in contrast to the early days, when our county chairmen were recognized leaders in the community.

Politics notwithstanding, the sixties were a difficult decade for us. When Aunt Adeline, Uncle Lep's wife, inherited the old Levy home on the corner lot of Main and Gray in the 1930s, the will stipulated that if nobody lived in the house, it should be torn down. This was to prevent its becoming a funeral home, as had happened to so many of Houston's fine old houses.

After Aunt Adeline's death, various enterprises, from drive-in eateries to parking lots, had occupied the property. Eventually Bill Ladin—a very successful attorney who had known the Meyer family his whole life—came up with a different idea. He persuaded Uncle Lep that rapidly growing Houston needed a downtown luxury apartment house. Uncle Lep agreed and approached Ray to join the venture, although it was far removed from Ray's area of expertise in the oil industry. Uncle Lep would provide the land, and Ray would provide access to construction funds, using contacts he had in the financial industry.

It was a terrible decision. Not only did Ray have neither the experience nor the kind of resources needed to participate in such an enterprise, but there was also the matter of his health. In my view and that of many others, Raymond inspired confidence. Slightly under six feet and with a mop of hair so dark brown it was almost black, he wore his Hickey-Freeman suits with the demeanor of a man who felt as good as he looked. For years, Ray shrugged off my occasional suggestion that he have a physical checkup with "Why should I go to a doctor when nothing hurts me?"— that is, until the sudden death of Eddie Pulaski, a friend who was Ray's age.

I said, "That does it. You haven't had a checkup in all the years we've been married. I'm going to make an appointment for you tomorrow morning, and don't you even think about canceling it."

At ten o'clock on the morning of his exam, I heard Ray's car in the driveway. Why had he come home instead of going on to his office? He walked slowly into our bedroom with a sheepish expression on his face and said, "I suppose I should really thank you for making me go see Julian this morning. He gave me some medicine and told me to go to bed for the rest of the week. My blood pressure is really high. Two hundred over one hundred ten. I never told you why I was so reluctant to go to a doctor. When I was twenty-one, my father bought an insurance policy for me that required a medical examination. The doctor told me my blood pressure was high and to come back in a week. I never went. I figured if nothing hurt me . . . I didn't want to fall into the trap of living with doctors the way my father did." A potential time bomb just walking around. Ray stayed home the rest of that week. Afterward he went diligently once a month to Julian's office to have his blood pressure monitored.

The medication prescribed after that first visit caused his blood pressure to drop so sharply that he would fall asleep sitting in a chair. During the next six months, although he acted perfectly normally, he was so relaxed that his business judgment and memory were affected, although we didn't realize it at the time. And then it got worse.

Ray and I both were avid football fans. On an October weekend in 1964, we drove to Austin for a game between the University of Arkansas, Ray's alma mater, and Texas University, where Alan was enrolled. Ray seemed edgy, an unusual state for my usually calm, laid-back husband. We had some difficulty with a lamp in our room at the Driscoll Hotel. From the bathroom I heard Ray's uncharacteristically strident voice. He was engaged in a loud, violent argument with the repairman over Barry Goldwater, whose campaign was then at a fever pitch. I quickly intervened.

"What's the matter with you? Do you know how ridiculous you sound?"

"It's just a disgrace that people are so dumb," he murmured. "How can anyone in his right mind oppose Barry Goldwater?"

"Lots of people, but that's not the point. Why are you so overwrought?"

He didn't answer except to mumble, "I'm going to take a walk."

At the game, Ray was overly excited. Unlike his usual exuberance at sporting events, this exhilaration seemed strained and artificial. Driving back to Houston, Ray started sobbing. Out of nowhere. Just sobbing. I didn't know what to do. He kept saying he was worried about Alan, who was unhappy at school. Instinctively I knew that couldn't account for such a collapse. At eleven o'clock that night, as soon as we reached our home on North Boulevard, I went to a telephone in the children's playroom at the other end of the house from our bedroom. I closed the door and called Julian.

"I don't know how to describe Ray's emotional state. I've never seen him like this. He seems distraught. He doesn't know I'm calling you, but I think something's wrong."

Julian didn't even pause. "I'm going to tell him it's time for his biannual cardiogram. I suspect we're in serious trouble."

I didn't close my eyes that night as I watched Ray's restlessness, even as he slept. The next morning he came home again directly from the doctor's office, but this time I knew what to expect because Julian had called me.

"Marjorie, Ray is in the throes of what we call a silent heart attack. After a brief glance at his cardiogram, I told him he wasn't going anywhere but down the hall with me to a cardiologist. Dr. Struthers took one look at the graph and said to Ray, 'Do you have any pain at all? Hand, arm, shoulder, chest?' Ray shook his head and lit a cigarette, whereupon Dr. Struthers said, 'Put that cigarette down. You can't smoke any more. You're having a heart attack, and, although you don't have any pain, you're in mortal danger. If you don't go home, go to bed, lose thirty pounds, and quit smoking, you're going to have a stroke or drop dead or both.'"

Our lives changed that day. That old adage about marrying "for better or worse but not for lunch" well describes Ray's convalescence. Ray was beside himself. He worried about business. He was on the telephone constantly. And I lost more weight than he did. Our food was tasteless since we started cooking without salt and butter. Ray was cross and almost unmanageable. He had never been sick except for an occasional cold, and he wasn't accustomed to this imposed inactivity. After about six weeks I telephoned Julian.

"I don't know how long we can continue this regimen. I can't keep Ray off the telephone. He's losing weight and as far as I can tell hasn't sneaked any cigarettes. But our lives are almost intolerable. He can't accommodate to this restraint."

"I think it's time to add another component," Julian said. "About five o'clock every afternoon I think Ray should have a couple of shots of whiskey. It should stimulate his weak heart muscles. If he tolerates that, then perhaps in the late afternoon he can have someone from his office come to visit for an hour."

We developed a cocktail hour, and Ray began watching the clock about three in the afternoon. Not just office personnel but also friends came for brief visits. For people who drank alcohol only at Christmas or on New Year's eve or some other special occasion, it was a radical departure from our normal lifestyle.

After almost three months Ray's physical condition stabilized, and he gradually moved back into his former life. Even so, everything about his business seemed to go downhill from then on. Venture after venture failed. After so many years spent in depleting the resources of his established production by chasing pot-of-gold-at-the-end-of-the-rainbow adventures, even Ray realized he had to face the fact that he would probably never succeed in developing another Spindletop. A bit of the spark went out of his life.

During this time my Uncle Lep persuaded Ray to join him and Bill Ladin in the development of 2016 Main. I argued against it. What did any of them know about running an apartment building? With the decline in Ray's oil business, I suspect he thought the apartment project might be a bright new endeavor, but I also believe that the medicine he was taking affected his judgment. Whatever the reason, I was overruled, and we became embroiled in that doomed enterprise, a burden that I am convinced shortened Ray's life.

We eventually realized that the due diligence required for a project as large as 2016 Main simply hadn't been fully carried out. Although a demographic study had concluded that people were moving out of their large homes into high-rise apartments, the report did not indicate the reality, which was that they would be moving to high-rise buildings in their own neighborhoods, not downtown. And it definitely didn't indicate that the people who did want to live downtown were principally secretaries who couldn't afford a luxury establishment such as 2016 Main. As a result, rents had to be lowered beyond the projected revenues in order to attract occupants. By 1965, 2016 Main was in serious trouble.

Because Ray's involvement in this project was predominantly financial, his share of the problem increased each month as revenues failed to meet the building's obligations. In 1966, we were required to sell our wonderful house on North Boulevard quickly and at a sacrifice. We moved to the apartment that had been prepared for us at 2016, hoping both Ray and I could help the building.

Manager after manager either quit or were terminated. In 1969, I was asked to take over the position until someone experienced and effective could be found. It was a thankless and awful job. I had undertaken responsibilities for which I had never been trained: supervising the upkeep of the establishment while trying to rent apartments and attempting tactfully to cajole rent from those who were late with their payments. I worked in that office ten and twelve hours a day, while Bill and Ray sought a manager who could handle the job's many problems. Fortunately, my tenure in this position lasted less than a year, but I found everything about the 2016 Main building distasteful even though the penthouse built especially for us was spacious and luxurious.

Those were also the years when I wrote long diatribes on my prized electric typewriter. I wrote to manufacturers about faulty products, to friends arguing politics, and many, many letters to the editor about whatever happened to be the controversial topic of the day. My machine had no correcting key, so if I made a mistake I had to type the entire page again. However, it did have a selection of fonts. To my present dismay and embarrassment, when I review those old onionskin copies in heavy script font, legal-size page upon legal-size page, single spaced, I wonder where I found the time to do all that writing. I pity those unfortunate souls who had to read such lengthy arguments in hard-to-read script. But a lot of people did.

The principal controversy in which I involved myself was the issue of school prayer, which had erupted like a volcano when well-inten tioned people in New York State attempted to fashion a prayer amenable to all elements of their polyglot public school constituency. Some of us understood, even then, that, in attempting to correct that mistake, the Supreme Court opened a Pandora's box. Instead of sending the issue back to New York and saying, "You can't do that," the Court issued a still largely misunderstood opinion ostensibly outlawing prayer in schools. The effects of that opinion have lingered long beyond that decade.

In 1963, when an article appeared in the *Houston Chronicle* headlined "Jews Oppose Prayer in the Public Schools," quoting Mr. Goldstein, a staff member of an organization called the Jewish Community Council, I exploded. The council's only duty was coordinating the calendars of the various temples and synagogues in Houston so that their various public programs would not conflict. Certainly it had no authority to issue statements on policy. I wrote a response to the prayer article and took it to Everett Collier at the *Chronicle,* who gave it a prominent place on the editorial page. The newspaper provided the headline for my remarks: "Jewish Council Can't Speak for All."

My position on this issue was—and still is—founded on my belief that extremism elicits extremism. To outlaw prayer is just as intolerant as to require it. No one knows how the dilemma this subject continues to present will be resolved. I believe it had a better chance of being settled by reasonable people outside the precise verbiage of a legal document. In my opinion there is no substitute for good judgment—or plain old common sense—on a case-by-case basis.

As usual, the Jewish response to my piece was mixed. Most reactions were favorable, although many people deplored "airing our problems in public." As usual, I responded that every opinion I had was open to public scrutiny.

Chapter 5

The Later Years

My daughter Margot was living in California, where she settled following her elopement some years earlier with Don Lane, an airman stationed at Ellington Field in Houston. Because we had known very little about Don or his family, our anxiety at the time had been considerable. After her difficult childhood, Margot had matured into a very charming young woman. She had weathered one early disastrous marriage, and we had been concerned for her when she jumped so quickly into another.

Margot and Don, both lacking in maturity, were fun loving. They moved from one small town to another in the string of communities between Oakland and Hayward as Don changed jobs, working at an airport, then a filling station, and then a grocery store. Along the way they had five little boys—one now just a newborn. Four of them were being cared for by Don's mother. Tragedy had intervened only months before, during Margot's pregnancy, when the sports car Don was working on slipped from its blocks and crushed him.

Then came the phone call on April 9, 1970. "Mrs. Arsht, this is Dr. Arnold Gilmore at the hospital in Las Gatos, California." I had trouble focusing on the words. I squinted at the luminous dial by my bed, my eyes barely open. Two o'clock in the morning. The voice continued, "Your daughter Margot is mortally ill. At most she has a few hours to live."

My cries awakened Raymond, who, when he saw me on the telephone, jumped out of bed and ran to another room to pick up an extension. "What in the world? Was there an accident? I just talked to her. What's the matter?" My words tumbled out one over the other. I asked more questions than the doctor could answer, and Ray was questioning, too.

The doctor himself began to shout and finally prevailed on us to listen. "I do not know the immediate, exact cause of her trauma. And that is why I need your permission to perform an autopsy when the time comes."

I caught my breath and thought, *An autopsy? Was death that certain?* I said, "Can't it wait until we get there?"

"Mrs. Arsht," he said quietly, "you can't get here in time."

And we didn't. My thoughts that night ran the gamut of emotions. Fury that I hadn't been informed earlier of her illness, shock at the suddenness of the facts, all mixed with profound grief. I had spoken to Margot on her thirtieth birthday, less than two weeks earlier. Since she really hadn't sounded very well, I told her I would come to California as soon as I could, but she assured me it wasn't necessary. I remembered turning to Ray after that conversation and saying, "I think something is wrong with Margot. I wonder if she's sick. She said she just had a cold, but she didn't sound like her old self."

Ray had answered offhandedly, "Whatever problems Margot has ever had, it's not her health. She's as strong as an ox." And she had been, after early childhood. I attributed it to the enormous amounts of cod liver oil I had poured down her throat.

I roused myself. We were booked on the first flight out in the morning, but I had so much to do before then. I wrote instructions and made lists of whom to call. Ray's mother. Marie. My cousins. Ray arranged plane tickets. Responsibilities crowded in.

Ray was distraught. He held his head in his hands during the entire trip to California. We flew to San Francisco, rented a car, and drove to Las Gatos, a small town south of San Francisco.

A tall, lanky man with a gaunt look, Dr. Gilmore was waiting for us at the hospital. When I saw him, I knew his prediction had been correct. We were not in time. I asked about Margot's six-month-old baby, and he said it was his understanding that the baby was with a friend, but he didn't know the friend's name. He sat with us in a small waiting room and discussed Margot's case.

"Two months after childbirth, Margot came to me complaining of an inability to lift one arm. Because she had had a respiratory infection I suspected polio and took a muscle biopsy. Nothing. I suggested therapy, but that didn't seem to produce results. I didn't hear from Margot again for some time until she complained of an inability to swallow. I tested her for multiple sclerosis or muscular dystrophy, but tests for both were negative. I was called late yesterday to see her in the hospital and found her beyond any possibility of survival." He concluded with, "I don't know what caused her death. I only know positively that she didn't have either muscular dystrophy or multiple sclerosis."

Ray and I were devastated. It was so sudden, so hard to comprehend. But reality prevailed, and my attention quickly turned to Bruce, the baby. Ellen Lane, the other grandmother who lived in Livermore, California, didn't have a clue as to his whereabouts. I had called her from Houston, but she didn't drive and had no means of transportation. Ellen was a complex woman. Just under five feet in height and weighing less than one hundred pounds, she was a bundle of energy. Born into a farm family in northern California, the eldest of twenty-one children of the same mother and father, she had begun taking care of babies when she was a small child herself. By the strangest twist of fate, she and her husband, Louis, were never able to have any children of their own. They adopted two boys, both nephews, one of whom became Margot's husband.

Babies were what Ellen knew, however, and, as soon as Margot had one, Ellen had insisted on caring for him. In view of Don and Margot's unstable household, it was wonderful that Ellen was there to take care of the babies as they came along. They were her life. Our principal role with them would be to help in their support, and we did.

When Ellen didn't know the whereabouts of baby Bruce, I had to look elsewhere. Finally, a staff person told me that, in California, hospitals are required to call a state agency when a child is orphaned and no family members are present. The social worker had seen Margot when she arrived at the hospital and knew where the baby was. The hospital called the social worker. We waited three hours for her to come to the hospital.

When she finally appeared, she seemed a nice enough woman in her midforties. She apologized for her delay, saying that she had to pick up her child at school. She sympathized with us. Yes, she knew where the baby was, and he was just fine. He was staying with the mother of one of Margot's friends. Why didn't we take care of all the things needed after such an unexpected death and just leave the baby where he was for a few days? We talked of many things. Of Margot and her last hours. Another hour passed. Was it my imagination, or did she seem reluctant to disclose Bruce's whereabouts? I explained I wasn't leaving Las Gatos without seeing the baby. Finally, she gave us the telephone number and the name of Mrs. Barker, who did indeed seem gracious and helpful. She answered my questions.

"Mrs. Arsht, Bruce is just fine. I know you have so many things to do. You have to go to Livermore and make all the arrangements. I'm delighted to take care of the baby until everything is settled."

It was late in the evening. Suddenly it seemed the practical thing to do. Ray and I were exhausted. We had been on an emotional roller coaster for hours. I assured Mrs. Barker we would come for the baby in the morning. Then Ray and I checked into a Livermore motel and collapsed into a troubled, restless sleep.

The next morning Ray was still paralyzed with grief. I called Mrs. Barker to ask her about Bruce. Assured that he was fine, I decided we would come the following morning since we had so much to do. It was my first experience in trying to arrange a funeral far from home.

Ellen and I went to the mortuary, picked out a casket, and arranged for a burial plot next to Don's. We looked through the catalogue to choose an emblem for the flat stone markers required in that cemetery. We chose a Star of David to be placed next to Don's cross. Ellen called her minister, who had known Margot. He was out of town that day but would return the next.

The second day after our arrival, Ray and I drove to Las Gatos to see Bruce. Mrs. Barker's home was lovely, the baby in a sturdy crib, and Mrs. Barker herself seemed completely responsible. She assured us that it was no trouble to keep Bruce. Why didn't we wait until after the funeral to take him? In my mind's eye I saw Ellen's crowded little house. We needed time to prepare for a new baby and to buy a crib, supplies, and clothes. I had to admit it was practical to wait until after the funeral. I spoke to Mrs. Barker each day and promised to compensate her for Bruce's care.

Reverend Carlson was a warm, caring man who wore a "Shalom" pin in his lapel. He called on us at Ellen's house, and, although I knew we could have located a rabbi, it seemed perfectly natural for someone who knew Margot personally to give her eulogy. And a beautiful tribute it was. He took his text from the Old Testament, the story of Ruth and the biblical exaltation of a good woman. No rabbi could have honored Margot and us more than that Baptist minister.

The day after the funeral, as Ellen and I were making lists of things a new baby needed, Mrs. Barker called. She was crying so hard we had trouble understanding her. I thought something had happened to the baby. We finally comprehended that the State of California had informed her Bruce was now a ward of the state. A California law stipulated that if an orphaned baby was not in the custody of a family member within three days of the last parent's death, then that child belonged to the state. It was the fourth day since Margot died. He was still with Mrs. Barker. The State of California had legally "kidnapped" my grandson.

Now I understood that social worker's insistence that Bruce remain with Mrs. Barker. It was a carefully planned strategy. I made inquiries and discovered that California had passed a law legalizing abortions and that, as a result, there was a serious shortage of adoptable babies. State agencies were especially interested in increasing the supply of babies by "babynapping" orphans.

I found a lawyer in Livermore, David Harris, who prepared an appeal. We received a stay. The courts allowed Bruce to remain with Mrs. Barker—but not with his family—until we resolved the matter. I called Tom Cole, Sen. John Tower's executive assistant in Washington, D.C. Ronald Reagan was then governor of California. Tom promised me they would arrange an entrée to the governor's office if need be.

Ray and I went back to Houston with the understanding that I would return for the hearing, scheduled thirty days later. One day I spent eight continuous hours on the telephone with government agencies in California. They realized I wasn't going to let them take away my grandson without a determined fight. Two days before I was to leave for California, I received a call from the head of the California Children's Services Department.

"Mrs. Arsht, we have decided to drop our claim to Bruce Lane. We have reviewed all the data and agree with you that the baby can go to Mrs. Lane in Livermore. There won't be any need for you to come to the hearing. It will be just a formality."

I was greatly relieved. Traveling back and forth was costly. It was a time of financial strain for us, but I was determined nothing would stand in the way of securing the safety of my grandchild. When Ray came home, I related the events of the day. He was not convinced. "You know, Marjorie, I think it might be a good idea for you to go anyway. Considering that department's past performance, I don't trust those people." And he was correct. When I arrived in Livermore, the night before the hearing, I called the lawyer and said, "Mr. Harris, even though I know tomorrow is just a formality, my husband thought I ought to be here anyway, so I'll be going along with you tomorrow."

He was an unexcitable young man, much too lethargic for my taste, but he knew how to draw up legal papers, and that is all I really needed. In a drawl more characteristic of the South than of California he said without emotion, "Mizz Arsht, ah just received a ten-page document stating California's full intention of pursuing the guardianship of Bruce. They must have changed their minds." I felt faint. I called Ray, who insisted that if the hearing went against us we would appeal to the governor.

Another snag presented itself just outside the courtroom. I had insisted that Bruce's four brothers accompany us in order to demonstrate that the baby had a family. Ellen had dressed them with care. With trim haircuts and shiny faces, the four little boys were picture perfect. But suddenly Ellen got cold feet. She didn't want to go into the courtroom or let the boys go in. She decided that she had no formal adoption papers for the other four, and the judge could take them all away. I thought I would lose all self-control. It took all the persuasion Louis and I could muster to finally convince her to join us.

In the courtroom, the state contingent was at full strength. The heads of every department of Children's Services attended—ten impressive men and women defending the state's right to Bruce. And there I was, with that miserably inadequate young lawyer, Louis, and Ellen, trembling with fear, actually willing to sacrifice one child for the benefit of the other four children. And of course, Mrs. Barker was there with Bruce.

The judge entered. The state presented its case. Eloquently. The grandparents weren't young, and their small house was already overflowing. California stipulated that so many square feet were required for every child cared for in a private home. The Lane home didn't meet the specifications required for five children The baby's future would be best served in a loving household eager for a child and capable of giving that child every advantage.

Our lawyer began to mumble our case. I squirmed so much I thought I might wear out the chair. Finally I couldn't stand it and asked the judge whether I could speak. "Your Honor, I am Bruce's maternal grandmother. I have served for many years on the board of an adoptive agency in Houston, and I have participated in the placement of hundreds of babies in wonderful homes. However, without fail, when those well-cared-for and beloved children reached puberty, sometimes earlier, sometimes later, they want to know where they came from and where their relatives are. Bruce Lane has four brothers. He is entitled to them and they to him. More important, the state has called attention to the fact that the Lanes and my husband and I are old. May I remind the court that the Lanes have another son, John, and I have two other children, Alan and Leslye, all young adults who could and would see to the well-being of these children. There is another generation standing in the wings."

I went on to point out the fact that the only reason Bruce was in Mrs. Barker's care for more than California's three-day requirement is that the state's own representative had encouraged me to leave Bruce there while we made arrangements for my daughter's funeral. I had no way to know about that law, and even though ignorance may be no defense, it was an arranged and deliberate deception unworthy of the spirit of justice. In conclusion I said, "It should also interest the court that I was called in Texas a few days before this hearing and informed that the state would drop its claim and that it would be unnecessary for me to come. It's a good thing I did come, isn't it? Is that the kind of strategy of which the State of California and its courts approve?"

Complete silence. Finally the judge asked about the housing facilities. I answered that we would make arrangements to purchase the larger house across the street from Ellen and Louis. The state regrouped and appealed to the judge. "Nowhere in Mrs. Arsht's eloquent plea is there any mention of love. We want a loving home for this little boy."

I was on my feet, but the judge held up his hand, as much as to say, "Enough!" After only a brief period of deliberation, the judge gave us Bruce with the caveat that there be a year of probation, after which the court would review the case. And every day, an observer for the state parked from midmorning until dark one block from Ellen's house. The same observer called on her once every week for an interview in order to prepare a report on Bruce's status. For one whole year. I don't know how Ellen stood it. After the final review, however, Bruce was ours.

Three months had passed since the funeral, and I still hadn't had a report on Margot's autopsy. I called Dr. Gilmore. He demurred but said he would check. Two weeks later I had a letter stating the diagnosis: muscular dystrophy. I called Dr. Gilmore.

"Mrs. Arsht, I confess that the reason the report was delayed is that I kept sending it back. It is incorrect. Margot did not have muscular dystrophy. Neither I nor they know what she had."

We did not learn the real cause of Margot's death until five years later, when Billy, Margot's thirteen-year-old son, began stumbling. The Livermore, California, physician sent him to San Francisco General, a teaching hospital, for examination, and the doctors there, after examining Margot's autopsy slides, diagnosed both Margot and Billy as having amytropic lateral sclerosis (ALS), the incurable Lou Gehrig disease. Billy died fourteen heartbreaking months later. Eventually we discovered that there are two forms of ALS. One affects people after middle age; the other, more virulent type strikes teenagers and young adults.

Many years afterward, in 1999, Ellen called me with terrible news. Bruce—then thirty—had developed a weakness in his left arm, and John, his older brother, had taken him to the ALS clinic in San Francisco. She hadn't called until they were sure. There was no doubt that Bruce, like his mother and brother Billy before him, had ALS. He lived fourteen months from the onset of the disease and died on February 22, 2000.

There is a special kind of grief, a sharp, piercing heartache that comes when a child or grandchild dies. Those deaths seem to contravene the laws of nature. Now I was having to struggle through another one, the third. At the time, it seemed almost too much to bear.

After Margot's death, I knew, for emotional and financial reasons, that I had to go to work. I had been a "professional volunteer" for most of my life, but now I faced a whole new ball game. The only paid employment I had ever had was as a schoolteacher before I married, and, although I had a lifetime teacher's certificate, there were new rules. You had to teach your major. By this time, there weren't many openings for French teachers, and besides, if I had to teach, what I wanted to teach was history or government.

In the late summer of 1970, I went to see my friend Alfred Neuman, president of the University of Houston, to discuss my returning to school in order to enhance my certification. No problem. He sent me to administration. I had thought enrollment in the graduate school would be a breeze, but entering the University of Houston wasn't easy at all. I called on the dean of the graduate school, Arthur Weiman, a young, dark-haired, diminutive professor sitting behind a desk that seemed too large for him. I introduced myself, explained my purpose, and asked for his suggestions as to which courses I should take.

"Mrs. Arsht, do you have your GRE score?"

"What is that?"

"That refers to the Graduate Records Examination, without which no one can enter graduate classes." He added quickly, "If you decide to take the test, you won't have to make a very high score. And you can take it over and over again as many times as you wish." His condescension was humiliating.

"What score are you talking about?"

"Well, we require a score of only 1,000, but in some cases we make allowances." He was trying to be nice, yet he was aggravating me more by the minute.

"What does the University of Texas require?"

"I believe they may demand 1,100."

"What does Rice require?"

"Oh, Mrs. Arsht, you don't have to worry about that. Rice requires at least 1,200, but that's not necessary for your purposes."

"When are these tests given?"

"Generally in October or November."

"It's now August. I want to start classes in September, when the term begins. What classes may I take before having a GRE score?"

"Well, we don't recommend anyone taking more than two courses after they have been out of school as long as five years. And of course, your courses would have to be undergraduate."

"Would you be kind enough to suggest two that would be helpful after I've passed the GRE? And would you please see to it that I am signed up for the test?"

"Actually, you can take any two undergraduate courses you like."

His attitude infuriated me. The little snip. But in my heart of hearts I thought, *If I don't make better than 1,200, I'm never going to see that little bastard again.*

October came and, along with it, the notice for the GRE. Honestly, I do not think I was ever that frightened in my life. My particular test room was monitored by a high school principal, who was determined to display unquestioned authority and impose strict rules. When he called "time," we had to shut our books. There would be no bathroom breaks—sorry. Anyone failing to observe any rule would be out of there. We had empty chairs between us. I never knew whether the girl next to me knew everything or nothing. When I was halfway through my answers, she shut her book. I came home completely drained and said to my husband, "This is just no good. I'm going to be humiliated." He tried to reassure me, telling me to please remember that my life did not depend on that silly score.

I concentrated on the two undergraduate classes I had been allowed to take, including one with Richard Murray, a respected political analyst. One day when he was talking about pressure groups and political action committees, he named all of the Republican ones. The Manufacturers Association and the National Rifle Association were just a few of a long list. When he finished, I asked politely, "Professor, what about COPE, the labor group?" At the time I didn't quite understand his enigmatic smile or why he chuckled as he acknowledged that it was indeed a political pressure group.

That whole semester I tried to be sure my past political activities were never discussed. Most of the students were youngsters and had no idea who I was. At the end of the term, when I approached Dr. Murray to thank him for his course, he said, "You know, Mrs. Arsht, I have followed your political activities for many years with great interest." I was dumbfounded. I thought I had been completely anonymous. Suddenly I understood his amusement at my question about the labor unions.

In December, my husband came upstairs to our apartment with the mail in his hand. He said, "There's something here from some testing service. Do you know what it is?" I sat down hard in a chair. He asked what in the world was the matter with me.

I said, "That's my GRE score."

"Do you want me to open it?"

I nodded. As he opened the envelope I held my breath. Slowly scanning the paper, he said, "It says here something about 690."

I gasped, "I knew it. I just blew it." Then he added, "There's another column that says 540."

I grabbed the paper. I had made 690 on the verbal and 540 on the math. That made 1,230! Ray got me a Scotch.

Chafing at the bit, I couldn't wait to get to the university, knowing that the testing service always sent a copy to the school where the test was taken. Nonchalantly I entered Dean Weiman's office. "By the way," I said, "I received my test scores. I was very disappointed in the verbal results. I should have done better than that."

With a frozen look on his face he said, "You did just fine, Mrs. Arsht." He didn't smile, but I did.

"Will you please sit down?" I asked politely as I walked into my first classroom at Booker T. Washington High School on a hot steamy day late in September of 1972, three weeks after school had started. The students, seventeen- and eighteen-year-old African Americans, most of them towering over me, were milling around and talking to each other as though no teacher were present. The classroom was stark: a blackboard behind the teacher's desk, a bank of windows on one side, bookcases at the back, and writing arm chairs, but no maps or exhibits anywhere. Still polite, I asked again, "Will you please take your seats?" No one paid the least attention. I took off my shoe and banged it as hard as I could on the desk, at the same time pulling myself up to my full height of five feet and shouting at the top of my voice, "Sit down!"

That got their attention. I wrote my name on the board, on second thought erasing my first name, lest in their apparent lack of respect they should start calling me "Marjorie." As I turned to face the now-seated but fidgeting students, one young man called out, "Where's her car?" The class tittered. Every eye was trained on me.

"Everyone come to the window," I said, my voice having returned to a normal pitch. They left their seats and moved to the window wall, obviously curious. "See that blue car with the black top? That's my car. If something happens to it, I'll get a new one, and whoever damages it will go to jail. Now take your seats."

From the back of the room came a muttered "Where'd she come from?" A student from across the room called out, "I think she comes from Gatesville," a well-known juvenile detention center. I had to face the blackboard to keep them from seeing my struggle not to laugh. Moreover, I didn't want them to know I hadn't taught anywhere in many years. After composing myself, I answered the student, "No, I don't come from Gatesville, but when I get through with the lot of you, I'll be experienced enough to teach there." Silence.

I recalled my first meeting with Franklin Wesley, the dignified, slightly built, soft-spoken African American principal of Booker T. Washington High School. He had asked, "Are you a soul-saver, Mrs. Arsht?"

"A soul-saver? I don't understand what you mean. I'm a teacher."

"Never mind." He quickly changed the subject. "You'll be replacing a very nice young woman who simply could not handle these students. It'll be a challenge. Are you prepared for that?"

I was assigned to tenth-grade students in a European history class. After previewing their textbook, I had decided I'd find their level of competence by having each of them read something from their next assignment. "Open your textbooks to chapter three. We'll read some paragraphs, beginning on my left." Sandra, a pretty, bright-eyed girl, read about four words and stopped. The next word was "revolution," and she couldn't read it. I prompted her, but before the next sentence was finished, I knew I was in real trouble. Instead of progressing down the aisle, I asked if anyone would volunteer to read the next lines. Not a hand was raised. These six-foot-tall boys and blossoming girls couldn't read.

Forget the textbooks, I thought. For the rest of the term, I mimeographed material I prepared over weekends that I knew they *could* read. I put a set of dictionaries in the room. Every day, one disappeared. Although teachers were responsible for any books checked out to them, I considered even the losses a good investment.

My fourth day in class, with the weather still very hot, one boy walked in wearing an Eisenhower jacket, the back of which bore a large patch that taunted, "Fuck you." The students were giggling and calling out "See Frank's jacket!" On a small piece of paper I sent a note to the vice principal, Herman Mabrie; it said, "I don't know what the dress code in this school is, but there's a kid in my class with 'Fuck you' on his back. If it's all right with you, it's all right with me." Herman, stocky and tough, was there in a flash, and that boy was out of the room.

At that time, George Bush was ambassador to the United Nations, and I wrote him about that classroom episode. In his own hand he wrote me back the following: "There are some days in this place when I would like to borrow that kid's jacket!"

Occasionally I made a mistake. Speaking to one of the students, I asked, "What's that boy's name?" An immediate uproar in the class.

"Did you call Jim a *boy?* His name is *Jim!"* I never made that mistake again.

Realizing these students knew nothing about the library, I decided to assign each one a country in Africa and have them find out everything about its population, industry, and government. I went down the aisles and reached Eddie. "Eddie, I want you to take Ghana." He muttered, "Aw, I don't want Ghana. I don't even know how to spell it." From across the room came a voice, "Shucks, Eddie, go on and take it. It's Ghana like in 'gonorrhea.' "

One of the unforeseen, unfortunate consequences of integration was the assignment of experienced black teachers to white schools and white novices to black schools. In addition, many of the young white teachers felt sorry for the students who didn't have their own rooms or good reading lights or caring parents, so they didn't demand anything. The old-fashioned discipline got lost. They let the standards slide. They were "soul-savers." They cared, but they didn't teach. Achievement went by the board, and the students developed no pride in learning. (At the time I taught, the teachers may have been integrated, but the students weren't. In all of Booker T. Washington High School, there were only two or three white students.) Now I knew what Mr. Wesley had meant, and I realized then and there that I surely wasn't a soul-saver. I was determined that the students learn something, even if they didn't learn tenth-grade material.

My greatest reward came on the last day of school. One of the students who had given me no end of trouble came to me and said,

"Mrs. Arsht, you and I have had our problems, but, you know what, I learned something this year!" That one remark by that one student made the sometimes hilarious, sometimes brutally frustrating year worthwhile.

Unfortunately, that was my last day at Booker T. Washington because I needed to make more money. When an opportunity with Time Equity, a real estate firm, presented itself, I first obtained a salesperson's real estate license and then a broker's license and undertook a new career in my late fifties, selling limited partnerships in raw land. For about five months I was very successful. Among other things, I managed to broker an almost impossible sale of one property that gave the only access possible to land intended for a major planned community development twenty miles north of Houston, later known as the Woodlands. Raw property sales, however, came to a dead stop with the oil embargo in 1973, when any property outside the Houston city limits became as unsaleable as a dead potted plant at a garage sale.

Buster Dobbs and Earl Martin, who headed the real estate office that brokered the Woodlands tract, were so impressed with my efforts that they offered me a job overseeing their new residential department, so I left Time Equity. At the same time, I accepted an appointment teaching real estate at the University of Houston, preparing men and women for their license examinations as salespersons and brokers. From those classes I staffed newly licensed agents for the new division I headed.

May 25, 1979, started out like any other Friday morning. Ray left the house about eight o'clock for his office in the Main Building. By nine I was almost ready to go to my real estate office just a few blocks away from our townhouse on Post Oak Park Drive. I heard Marie Murray, our longtime housekeeper, moving about in the kitchen. She came to the stairs and called up to me, "Mrs. Arsht, I need a favor. Would you mind fixing the hem of my new dress so I can wear it tomorrow night?"

I looked at the clock. I had an eleven-thirty meeting across town for which I would have to leave at least by eleven. Nothing at the office was really pressing. "All right, Marie, I'll do it now before I go to a meeting." I called my office, told them I would be in after lunch, and then sat down at the sewing machine with Marie's pinned-up red linen dress in my lap.

While I sewed I thought of the delightful party we had attended the evening before. My cousin Gina Stern and Nina Kamin and her husband, Jake, had entertained at the Sugar Creek Country Club. It had been a gracious affair, and we had had a good time. Everyone said Ray never looked better in his life. On the way to the party, Ray had mused, "We should have gone to see the children over this Memorial weekend." I was cutting the thread of the last stitch on Marie's dress when the phone rang. I looked at the clock thinking, *I have to leave in a few minutes. I hope this call isn't some long-winded client.*

"Marjorie, this is Al Dugan. Is anyone at home with you?"

"Marie's here. Why?" I asked Raymond's former business associate, who had an office in the same building as Raymond.

"I hate to be the bearer of such terrible news, but Ray had a heart attack."

I started screaming into the telephone. "Where is he? I'm leaving right away."

Somehow he broke through my shouts and said, "Marjorie, please, listen to me. It's over. He's gone. And I need to know the name of a funeral home and your doctor."

It was as though a screen, normally full of light, had suddenly gone black. I stared unbelievingly into space and mumbled some answers like an automaton. Marie came running when she heard my cries. With an outward calm that belied my inner turmoil, I looked at her standing in the doorway and said, "Mr. Arsht is dead."

It was Friday morning before Memorial Day weekend. The children! Were they going away somewhere—Alan in New York and Leslye in Washington, D.C.? I couldn't remember. I had to think. I called Alan, but he wasn't in his office, so I left word. I called Leslye, who was at lunch. I left word for her to call home. Poor Alan. Some girl whom he had never seen before caught him in the hall. "Are you Alan Arsht? Your father just died." Poor Leslye. She returned what she thought to be a routine call from home. Marie answered and delivered the message. These children who worshipped their father had lost him.

I called my friend Carolyn and my cousins Pauline and Gina, who were playing bridge somewhere. And Linda Dyson. And the rabbi. "Hy, would you please tell Ray's mother?"

A few years before, Lou, the husband of my friend Carolyn Roberts, had died. When she insisted we go immediately to the bank's lockbox, I didn't question her. I needed to do something just to move around. I felt like a robot. There wasn't much in the lockbox—some papers and a few stock certificates. I think Carolyn thought there might be money that should be retrieved before the court forbade access until the probate of a will. But nothing of any use to me was in it.

Our rabbi, Hy Schachtel, was waiting when we returned from the bank. He went with me to George Lewis's funeral home to pick out a casket and help with the newspapers. I had to choose pallbearers. There is much to do when someone dies. The time and date of the funeral were set—Sunday morning, May 27, 1979, at 11:00 A.M. at the funeral home chapel.

By Friday evening, when Leslye, Alan, and Audrey, his bride of three months, arrived, bringing with them Jocelyn, Alan's five-year-old daughter from his first marriage, everything had been arranged. Pauline, Gina, and others manned the telephones, which rang constantly. People came and went. Virginia Battlestein brought a tray of cold meats and cheeses. Others brought cakes. Alex Katz, Audrey's father in Massachusetts, wouldn't fly in an airplane. He called every hour on the hour and insisted on talking only to me. Alan's first wife's family, the Freedmans, telephoned. Flowers began to arrive.

I might have been on a railroad train, looking out the window and watching the scenery. I didn't shed a tear. I felt numb. Occasionally I thought I was dreaming, having a nightmare and then, shaking myself, realized I was awake.

Suddenly it was Sunday morning. We were there, sitting in the family area of George Lewis's chapel, to the right of the podium where the rabbis stood in front of Ray's casket. Although Hy Schachtel was by then emeritus and Rabbi Karff was the new senior rabbi, I didn't know Sam Karff very well and insisted that Hy give the principal eulogy. I heard the beautiful words, but I don't remember a single one. I wish they had been recorded. Everyone said that even though Hy was known for his eloquence, he really outdid himself that day.

Rabbi Karff read from Scripture and recited the Twenty-third Psalm. Ray's mother was helped in her wheelchair to view her son in his casket one more time. She cried out in pain. I didn't know why I couldn't cry.

And then the service was over. People began coming to the family enclave. George and Barbara Bush were there, along with so many others. The large auditorium was full, even on a holiday weekend when people generally left town. My sister, Elène, her husband, Leon, and their children came to greet us. She introduced herself to Leslye and Alan. Even in my semicomatose state I was surprised to see her. For a split second I didn't recognize her. It had been so long since I'd seen her. I remember parroting to her as I did everyone else, "Thank you for coming."

My mother didn't come. She told me later that she had a sore foot. She didn't explain why she sent no flowers or memorial remembrance. I thought she really liked Ray, and she probably did. It's possible she just didn't feel like going, or maybe her hair wasn't fixed.

That whole weekend I felt divided into two separate people. One was talking to guests, eating, sleeping, and moving arms and legs, and the other was just out there somewhere, disembodied, emotionally treading water.

Alan stayed a week; Leslye, two. Then they left. They had to go on with their lives. Linda Dyson, who had worked for me in my 1962 campaign for state representative and who had been my friend for the ensuing seventeen years, came with me to Ray's office that Monday morning. She worked for and with me throughout the next twenty years.

I didn't know anything about Ray's business, except what I had absorbed over the years through a kind of wifely osmosis, but Linda and I pored over files. When I found myself repeating the same thing to each of Ray's three sets of attorneys, who charged a large fee by the hour, I dismissed them all. Instead, I went to see Tom Moore, the lawyer who had worked with me in real estate. "Tom, do you know anything about the oil business?"

"Yes, I do."

"Can you probate a will?"

"Yes, I can."

"You're hired."

As scrupulously neat as Ray had been in his personal life—his suits hung a certain few inches from each other—he was anything but organized when it came to business records. Furthermore, he hadn't used a personal secretary for some time. Tom engaged a young accountant who came to the office and set up a new set of books and organized the files. Even so, I called either Alan or Leslye every day with some kind of problem until one day I heard Leslye sigh. I realized then I had to quit depending on them. From that day on, I made my own decisions, good and bad.

Six months after Ray died, I still hadn't cried. Every evening at six o'clock, watching the news with a scotch and water in my hand, I found myself looking at the door to the garage and expecting Ray to walk through it. Then Marie's mother died. I didn't know her, but I felt that I owed it to Marie to go to the funeral. I really didn't want to go—there was a football game on television that Sunday, and normally on Sunday I rested. Still, I just had to go.

With a map in hand I found my way to the small white wood-framed church in far northeast Houston and waited for the service. The music began—music that one hears only from a black choir in a black church—soulful, heartfelt, throaty, throbbing spirituals. It touched a chord and I began to cry—and then to sob. When the light blue casket trimmed with roses and vines came in, I fell apart. I couldn't stop the waterfall. I couldn't control the outburst. After a while Harold Brown, our former chauffeur and old friend, came to my side. "Mrs. Arsht, I think I need to take you home."

The emotional tsunami in Marie's little church left me drained and exhausted. For several days I went to bed as soon as I came home from the office. I couldn't seem to get enough sleep, but with the relaxation of taut nerves came a new kind of clarity. I finally faced the stark cold reality of Ray's death.

Memories became my therapy. I began to wonder why I had been so shocked at Ray's death even though it was sudden. There had been many clues along the way. Each evening, instead of watching the door, waiting for Ray to enter, I reminisced about the forty-two years we had spent together, remembering the good times and the bad. Gradually I began to see him once again as the dashing young man he had been.

In April, six weeks before Ray died unexpectedly, a friend of many years, Linda Underwood, had called from the office of Gov. Bill Clements. "Marjorie, we want you to serve as a regent on the board of Texas Southern University."

I demurred. "My plate is full," I said. "I'm busy at the real estate office, I'm teaching, and you know I'm really burdened with worry over our finances. I don't know what the responsibilities of a regent are. Moreover, I can't afford to be a donor."

"Do me a favor," Linda insisted. "Just come for an interview. We don't want any money."

Ray insisted I go. "You're perfect for such a position. At least see what's involved."

In Austin, I plied Tobin Armstrong with questions. Tobin, whose wife, Anne Armstrong, would later become ambassador to Great Britain, screened all of Bill Clements's appointees. After the interview, the staff relayed to me his comments. "You know, we were supposed to interview Marjorie, but she interviewed us!" The Texas Senate confirmed me even before any written personal vitae were recorded. I had attended only one meeting of the regents before Ray died. With Ray's death, I wanted to resign. The other regents, however, insisted I stay. "Take as long as you need, and then come back to us," they said.

Nine regents serve on the board of Texas Southern University (TSU), a historically black, urban university located in Houston. Their six-year terms are staggered, three new regents coming on as three leave. When the group of three to which I belonged began our term, we converted one sitting Democrat to our side, and the governor filled a vacancy created when a regent resigned, so almost immediately we had a Republican majority. During my term, six regents were African American, and three, white. In order to demonstrate that our concern for the university was paramount, we retained as chair a cordial, elderly gentleman, former regent, and a Democrat, Ernest Sterling from Beaumont.

When we began, the situation at TSU was at a point of crisis, particularly in the area of finances. No certified audit had been approved for seven years, and the university was at the verge of losing its law school accreditation. Immediate measures were required. Governor Clements gave us a task force to identify and remedy the financial morass we found. He sent a team of experts drawn from Rice University, Texas

University, and Texas A&M University to overhaul the bookkeeping system. Within a year, we had a certified audit.

We met with the accreditation people and persuaded them that TSU was under new management and that the state of Texas, under the leadership of Governor Clements, would do whatever it took to bring the university and its various disciplines into compliance with required standards. We got a stay and eventually brought into line reluctant professors who had been running the law school as though it were a private fiefdom.

It is important to note that, to accomplish all of this, Governor Clements had made substantive appointments to TSU's regents, eschewing the previous custom of filling slots with political paybacks or as an honorary award. Appointments to the board had long been treated as political plums, handed out to very nice people—ministers, teachers, community leaders, and such—without regard to their qualifications for running a university. Governor Clements threw those precedents out the window. He chose professionals with experience in business or education, people who would be able to contribute to the well-being of the university, without any consideration of personal aggrandizement. Many of the appointees were Republican African Americans.

One day the governor called Ben Love, president of Texas Commerce Bank. "Ben, I need a banker on the TSU board." Ben Love sent Lee Straus, one of the bank's rising stars, a young man who proved invaluable. Lee arranged for much-needed supplemental financial assistance in order to install new computer hardware. Although Lee was certainly not a Republican, he was a major asset to the board. When we fired a long-standing, ineffective university president, Granville Sawyer, Lee arranged with a group of bankers to subsidize the president's salary in order to make it a desirable post.

In removing the president, we had to overcome serious objections from the alumni community. In general, the alumni resented a Republican board of regents taking such a drastic step even though our actions might have been justified. In any case, they viewed with alarm anything that disturbed the status quo at TSU. Board chair Sterling threatened to resign until, at a TSU dinner, Mack Hanna leaned over, put his arm around me, and said within earshot of Sterling, "You keep on doing what you're doing." After that, Sterling was mollified and, in fact, took—and deserved—great credit for moving the university ahead. Hanna was the richest and most influential black man in Houston. His approval was all that Sterling needed to legitimize the removal of TSU's president.

A search committee made up of representatives from Rice, TSU alumni, and the board of regents was created to find a new president. Among the applicants was Leonard Spearman, then in Washington, D.C. Because I was going to Washington on another matter—my daughter lived there—I offered to do a preliminary interview. Spearman said later that if he hadn't been a hardy soul, he never would have come to TSU because I was so tough in outlining what we expected of a TSU president. When he did come for the formal interview with the full board, he was prepared, and he met with their approval. We, on the other hand, gave him full authority in the matter of student admissions and faculty personnel. Heretofore, the board had regularly interfered by promoting friends or affiliates.

Those were exciting and rewarding years. Our tenure was remarkable in that we all took our responsibilities seriously. Governor Clements threw partisan politics out the window, and we restored fiscal and financial stability to a worthy institution. But then Mark White defeated Bill Clements for governor, and the situation changed accordingly. The young banker, Lee Straus, who had filled an unexpired term, came up for reappointment after Mark White, a Democrat, succeeded Clements as governor. I told Lee to forget it—that he didn't have a chance. He argued that all of his Democrat friends at Commerce Bank were pressing Governor White on his behalf—that he really wasn't a Republican and so on. I bet him a dinner. Sometime thereafter, I received a call from Lee. Not only had he not been reappointed, but he had also learned about his replacement in the newspaper. We made a date for the dinner I had bet him.

One of Governor Clements's outstanding appointees to fill a TSU board vacancy was Maurice Barksdale from Ft. Worth, Texas. He and I became fast friends. A man of medium height, Maurice was trim and vigorous at forty-six. He had a cheerful, upbeat, optimistic personality and quickly became everyone's favorite. I have never heard him speak unkindly of anyone. And he is *very* smart. Maurice had become an authority on public housing. As a self-made millionaire in Ft. Worth and a prominent black Republican, it was not surprising that he would be invited to serve in the Reagan administration. His appointment as deputy assistant secretary for multifamily housing at the Department of Housing and Urban Development (HUD) received immediate approval. He and his wife, Faye, moved to Washington in October of 1982. We were distressed to see him leave the board of TSU.

At first I thought Maurice was joking when he called me in January of 1983 from Washington, D.C., to say, "I absolutely need you up here!" When I realized he was serious, I tried to explain to him that the idea of my going to Washington was absurd because I was running Ray's small oil company. (Ray's death had marked the end of my real estate career.) Surely there were thousands of young people who could help him better than a sixty-nine-year-old grandmother. He insisted he desperately needed my speech-writing skills and that he had to have someone who was tough enough to guard the door to his office. He thought no one else could fill that bill and urged me to make a trip to Washington to take a look. He suggested, further, that I might, after all, have a ball.

My children thought the idea fantastic. "Grandma is going to Washington," they gleefully told their children, and since they all lived on the East Coast, they immediately began making plans before I could catch my breath. *Well,* I told myself, *it wouldn't hurt to take a look.*

As soon as I arrived in Washington and visited Maurice's office, he didn't seem at all helpless. "I'm in charge of this whole floor," he boasted. "Together, you and I are going to make a difference in the national housing programs. We're going to cut out the waste and enforce the laws. There is so much to do." His enthusiasm was infectious. I forgot his original sense of desperation and decided it might just be a lark after all. I took the job.

My daughter Leslye, who had once lived in Washington, came from Boston to help me. We found a comfortable apartment at the Buchanan House, a high-rise complex in Crystal City, Virginia, just across the Fourteenth Street Bridge from HUD. Still skeptical and thinking I might be there only a few months, I signed a six-month lease and shopped for bare essentials at discount stores like the Door Store and Pier I. It never occurred to me that my appointment would be anything but routine. After all, I was doing the government a favor. They saw it differently, however.

Marjorie with former secretary of state James A. Baker Jr.

With the assistance of one secretary, I managed what was left of Ray's small energy investment business. Who would have believed that it would take endless telephone calls and much exchange of paper among my accountant, my attorney, and the powers that be in Washington to be certain that my involvement in the oil business presented no conflict of interest with public housing? Common sense apparently plays no part in decisions of that kind. It finally took the intervention of my friend Jimmy Baker, President Reagan's chief of staff, to move my approval papers off dead center. It wasn't as though I was up for a Cabinet post. In fact, I had no idea at the time just how insignificant my official position would be.

Finally having arranged with Washington to skip Friday once a month in order to return to Houston to attend TSU board meetings and see to my business affairs, I was ready to pack. I would need my car and prudently arranged for someone to drive me from Texas to D.C. Unfortunately, the driver had a last-minute family crisis and canceled, but I didn't tell anyone about that.

My daughter Leslye planned to come to Houston for her high school reunion the weekend I intended to leave. I always gave a party for her and her friends as well as some of mine whenever she came to town. That particular year, she chose a brunch, which provided a good time for me to say my farewells and still have a half day to drive before making my first stop. When Leslye arrived the day before her party, I told her I planned to drive myself to Washington. She immediately called her brother in New York. "Alan, you won't believe it, but Mother plans to drive herself to Washington. You have to do something." Leslye handed me the telephone.

"Mother, why don't you wait a few days and make other arrangements?"

"I don't want to do that," I explained to my son. "The car is packed, I have found out how to operate the CB in the car, and I've had a full briefing by AAA." I assured him I had the necessary maps, the car had been thoroughly checked and tuned, the tires were new, and I expected to start early and stop early, perhaps taking a half day longer than I needed. I added that as soon as Leslye's party was under way, I would say my goodbyes and leave.

"There's nothing I can say to change your mind?" he persisted.

"That's right."

"Will you at least call every evening?"

"Yes, I'll do that."

My children and I have a healthy relationship. I tell them what I think, and they do as they please. They tell me what I should or should not do. I listen politely and do as I please. It's a fine system. After that conversation, Leslye gave up, too. Further, she promised she wouldn't tell anyone.

Twenty people were milling around the house, drinking Bloody Marys, mimosas, and screwdrivers or eating breakfast from the buffet. When I saw that the guests had been taken care of and were enjoying themselves, I started making the rounds saying, "I want to tell all of you 'goodbye.'"

At first there was a startled silence. With a frown on her face, my friend Carolyn Roberts asked, "Where are you going?"

"To Washington."

"When are you leaving?"

"Now."

"Who's driving you?"

"I'm driving myself."

Everyone began talking at once as I made my way to the back door leading to the garage. They all began crowding around the car, and Carolyn's face, in particular, as she stood in the doorway to the garage, will forever be etched in my mind's eye. It showed a combination of shock, exasperation, and disbelief. She honestly thought I had lost my mind.

My journey began. As I drove out of the driveway, I felt enormously relieved. After so many days of bustle and hassle, I was actually looking forward to the quiet and solitude. My housekeeper, Marie, had only one fear. "Packed up cars like that, covered with a tarpaulin, are the cars people steal or at least break into. You have to unpack that car every night." Among the things stuffed into the car were a large television, my heavy typewriter, and suitcases of clothes. I had no intention of unloading all that at motels, although I assured her that I would take some precautions. And I did.

Every evening when I stopped, I chose a motel that had a drive-through entry. Then I would locate the night manager, who, for ten dollars, would let me park the car in front of his door, where he could watch it. The arrangement worked like a charm.

In Alabama I got a speeding ticket and, not surprisingly, was able to settle the fine by paying it to the arresting officer. The next morning, a huge eighteen-wheeler pulled up beside me. The driver was a giant black man, gesturing frantically. I reached for the CB and asked, "What's the matter?"

"Oh, you have a radio. What's your handle?"

"Handle? What's that?"

"What you call yourself. Your name!"

When I hesitated, he must have understood that I was wary. He quickly said, "I'm going to call you 'Yellow Canary' because your car is yellow. You're going much too fast, and there's a speed trap ahead. I'm going to give you some words like 'bear' and 'forest' and when you hear them, you slow down." He guided me all that day until we were approaching Roanoke, Virginia, when he said, "I have to leave you here, but I've radioed ahead, and my trucking buddies are going to take care of the Yellow Canary. They'll guide you all the way into Crystal City." And they did.

With every passing mile of my trip from Houston to Crystal City, Virginia, my anticipation of my new assignment at HUD grew more enthusiastic. I saw myself making important decisions, writing memorable speeches for Maurice, and actually making a serious contribution to my government and my country. Since Maurice was such an important official at HUD, who knew where all this would lead?

Tired but happy, I drove into the parking garage of the Buchanan House. The underground mall housed an assortment of businesses: a beauty parlor, a florist, two restaurants, and some variety and specialty clothing shops. They were not very good but were wonderfully convenient during inclement weather and when one was as exhausted and hungry as I was, late that balmy June afternoon in 1983.

The Buchanan House was ideal for my purposes. Aside from being close to HUD, it had a twenty-four-hour attended desk, which took care of receiving papers for my signature and messages regularly sent from Linda in my Houston office. Moreover, it had porters when I needed one for heavy lifting as well as roving maids available by the hour.

The sunny, cheerful, two-bedroom, two-bath apartment I had leased on my preview visit had parquet floors pretty enough not to require rugs. The second bedroom was actually a den with bookshelves and double French doors opening onto the living-dining room area. For such a temporary and hastily assembled domicile, it turned out to be a very nice place to live. I took a few days to get settled. Because I felt no sense of permanence about anything I was doing, I had brought virtually nothing but clothes from home and only those for summer.

For my first day at the office I dressed with extreme care. I wore a dignified, tailored, yellow linen suit, white sensible shoes with medium heels, and small gold earrings. I had gone to the hairdresser. Maurice arranged for one of his special assistants, Bob Davidson, to show me the ropes. Bob was a retired military man and a stickler for obedience to rules. Around sixty, he had a round ruddy face and despite his erect bearing showed signs of thickening at the waist. When he learned I was picked up for lunch that first day in a government car by a friend, an official in the Agriculture Department, he was frantic. I had no idea that it was a breach of government protocol for low-level government employees to ride in official automobiles. With utmost concern, he made me promise I would never ever ride in a government car again unless I was with Maurice.

Bob acted as though he had failed in his duty on that very first day. In light of some of the egregious sins that would subsequently come to light at HUD by people who *did* have the right to ride in government cars, it seems even sillier now than it did at the time. Still, he was a sweet, kind man who wanted only the best for me, and we became good friends.

HUD is a grim edifice, depressingly gray both inside and out. The dimly lit, dingy halls are bare; the cubicle offices, utilitarian. Hordes of people are constantly moving from place to place, shuffling innumerable files and papers. At first I was intrigued by all the activity—until I realized that most of what they did was irrelevant.

The admonition against riding in government cars was the first lesson I learned. The second one was the following: Where you sit is who you are. Under Bob's supervision and working several offices away from Maurice, I was totally oblivious to the fact that the placement of my desk indicated I was of no importance whatsoever. Hearing that Maurice was bringing someone from Houston, everyone expected a person of stature, but suddenly they all concluded that must be a mistake. If I had been important, he would have placed me in an office next to his. He must just be doing some friend a favor, they thought, and dismissed me outright. That was, of course, their mistake.

It is impossible for the average person to imagine the quantity of paper that goes in and out of a federal agency. Aside from my principal occupation, which was writing speeches for Maurice, I was directed to review and approve with my signature all correspondence before it reached Maurice's desk. This consisted of all of the very long letters replying to questions to, or complaints about, HUD. The letters were prepared by professional civil servants and then approved by political appointees like Maurice and me.

I grew very sorry for the staff, whom I had routinely denigrated as bureaucrats before I worked with them. I sympathized with their having to break in a new set of political neophytes every four years.

I honestly believe that most of them, though Democrats, voted for President Reagan's second term just to have a breather.

In the letters I received, I immediately spotted grammatical errors. Dangling participles and split infinitives drove me up a wall. So in the beginning I sent the letters back all marked up. I didn't realize how many "sign offs" went before me. A letter, started over, took weeks to go through the chain of approvals. Finally, after giving the initiating writers a few basic lessons in grammar, I gave up. If the letter was even fairly readable, I passed it along. That was my first compromise but not my last.

In our section, we had at least one meeting a day, sometimes more. Before Maurice received his subsequent promotion, Phil Abrams had been the assistant secretary and Maurice's immediate superior. He didn't like me at the outset, and the feeling was mutual. Originally from Boston, Phil was a tall, portly, bespectacled man who reveled in his authority. He loved long meetings every morning, so half the day was wasted while he listened to the department heads report everything they and everyone under them had done since the day before—*everything* except how many times they had gone to the bathroom.

Although I was eager to learn, I couldn't seem to follow what anyone was saying at Phil's meetings. Secretly I worried that I might be losing my hearing, so I went to a specialist and bought a hearing aid. When that didn't help, I became truly alarmed until I discovered there was nothing wrong with my hearing. I just didn't understand their language. They were speaking in acronyms. The "Gang of Four" and the "Gang of Five" referred to members of various committees. "POTUS" stood for "president of the United States."

I had been truly impressed with Maurice's title and not a little proud of my own until I learned the third lesson of Washington: The longer your title, the more insignificant you are. The most important person has a very brief title: Mr. Secretary. Then comes the undersecretary. After that there are several assistant secretaries, who are followed by even more deputy assistant secretaries, modified by the name of the section of HUD of which they are in charge. When you get down to what I was, a special assistant to the deputy assistant secretary for multifamily housing, you aren't even as important as a fly on the wall. I didn't know that in the beginning, which was just as well. A few months after I arrived, Maurice was promoted to

Marjorie with former senator Phil Gramm.

assistant secretary for housing, which dropped one word from my title as well as his, thereby increasing my importance to everyone but me.

Ironically, the assistant secretary for housing originally had a longer title. He was called the assistant secretary for housing/federal housing commissioner because he set the interest rates for federal mortgages. By the time Maurice received his promotion to that position, the responsibility for setting rates had moved to the Labor Department. That is probably the only time in government history that shortening a title meant less importance to the position.

On the job I encountered a few problems, of course. Take fingerprinting. All government employees must have a set of fingerprints attached to their file. In HUD's basement, a small woman with very black, obviously dyed hair, dedicated her life to producing perfect sets of prints. After the third try with mine she became distraught and called in a specialist from the FBI. My prints still weren't up to standard but were reluctantly accepted for the file. With all of my degrees and honors, I failed fingerprinting. No one heeded my suggestion that perhaps because of my age, mine had just worn off.

The fourth lesson: the importance of a parking place. HUD has two parking lots. One—for medium-rated personnel—is in the bowels of the building, and then there is street-level space for about forty cars. Everyone else has to ride the subway, which had a convenient station at L'Enfant Plaza, a hotel and shopping mall complex adjacent to HUD. I rode it, too, until I obtained the blessing of all blessings: my own parking space. When Maurice obtained one for me on the upper level, my stock went through the roof. I was finally *somebody,* erasing the calumny of sitting in the wrong place.

Then there were the forms. Government thrives on forms: applications, personal information, employment status, and periodic updates of them all. The average age of people filling out those forms is twenty-five, so there is one line each for questions such as "Name all the places you have lived" or "List all the countries you have visited." Every form I filled out had to be accompanied by pages of addenda. There were also age-group charts for insurance. Of course, I was off the graph, which caused great consternation to those accustomed to routine processing.

However, not everything was routine business. Almost every day, a party was held in someone's office. Usually a voice came over the intercom saying, "This afternoon in 408!" Someone was always being promoted, leaving, or coming. Occasionally something fancier than wine and snacks appeared. If a rule against alcohol or partying existed, no one paid attention to it. One appointee took an assignment on Capitol Hill, so his friends arranged for a belly dancer to provide going-away entertainment.

Marjorie and former first lady Barbara Bush.

I should have been prepared for what happened to me, but I wasn't. There were no personal secrets at HUD. Rumors, both fact and fiction, spread through the building like wildfire. Everyone knew who was sleeping with whom, who was in trouble "upstairs," and who was getting a divorce. I didn't realize that everyone's records provided fodder for the gossip mill. Nonetheless, I wasn't publicizing the fact that I was about to have a seventieth birthday. Hurrying to meet my children for a celebration in Montreal, Canada, I was frantically putting the finishing touches to a speech for Maurice before leaving, when I was summoned to a meeting in the conference room.

I explained to Maurice's secretary, Mattie Cuffie, that I was rushing, had a deadline, and couldn't go. She informed me that it was urgent and wouldn't take more than a minute. The meeting turned out to be a surprise birthday party for me, with a male stripper who was served up along with a cake loaded down with seventy candles. The stripper's fig leaf was in the shape of an elephant's head, trunk flapping as he gyrated his hips. Everyone had a marvelous time except me. After my first startled glance at the weird creature without clothes, I never looked at him again. I don't think I looked at anyone. I can't remember ever being so uncomfortable or so embarrassed, and I hated myself for showing it. The more I squirmed, the louder everyone laughed. Later on, I had to come back to HUD from Canada and face those still-grinning faces in meetings, which are the principal business of government.

Fortunately, not many months later, Maurice took Phil's place as assistant secretary. We then moved from the sixth to the ninth floor, only one floor below the secretary, whose office was for some inexplicable reason protected by guards. The change in location automatically raised everyone in Maurice's entourage three levels more in importance.

The departmental meetings became meaningful and abbreviated, and they weren't scheduled every single day, which everyone appreciated. And I became busier. Maurice's duties increased, and therefore mine did as well. We worked long hours and sometimes weekends. On occasion, when Leslye called me I actually had to tell her I didn't have time to talk. "Aha," she would say gleefully, "now you know what it's like." The tables had turned. After Ray died, I had trouble understanding that when I called Leslye or Alan, their lives were so busy that sometimes they didn't have time for me. They both took great delight in the reversed situation.

At Christmas time, I almost quit. At one of the innumerable cocktail parties I had criticized a member of the department. Before I went to bed that night, I received a call from Maurice's wife, Faye, my best friend and confidante in Washington. She let me know in no uncertain terms that I had committed the sin of sins. I suppose I had. I had forgotten political protocol, however hypocritical it might be. Being critical of a fellow worker was just not "done" in Washington. I was upset because I certainly didn't want to embarrass Maurice, and yet I knew I simply could not be the automaton I was supposed to be. I decided to make up my mind about leaving during the holiday break. Maurice and Faye knew nothing about my travail.

I had promised my daughter Leslye, who lived in Boston, and my nine-year-old granddaughter, Jocelyn, who lived in Maryland, that I would go with them to Disney World in Florida for Christmas week. I was miserable the whole time. They thought I was cross because Florida had an unusual blizzard and I had to stand out in the cold while they rode ridiculous roller coasters. But I am stubborn. I finally decided not to let some dimwit bureaucrat deter me from my appointed course. HUD would just have to put up with my independence. And so I returned to my office, wiser and much more cynical about my contribution to the general welfare of humanity. I was also more cautious. I grew to appreciate President Truman's famous remark: "If you want a friend in Washington, get a dog."

One young man in his early thirties, Steve Bollinger, assistant secretary for Community Development (CD), died suddenly one Sunday while traveling for the department. By Monday morning, people who had never given me the time of day were suddenly in my office, solicitous and suggesting we have lunch. By that time, even though I had originally sat in the wrong place and had too long a title, word had gotten around that I was well connected at the White House. Vice President Bush was a personal friend, and so was President Reagan's chief of staff, Jimmy Baker, both of whom I had known for years. I also had other friends from Houston in important government positions scattered around Washington, especially in Congress. Poor Steve had not even been buried when the vultures in the department began circling in hopes of being appointed as his successor.

Some people pulled no punches. They asked outright for my support in getting the appointment. I had an answer for them: "It would be unseemly as Maurice's subordinate for me to lobby for any one person to fill Steve's post." I had become diplomatic since I did not say to them, "I wouldn't recommend you for dogcatcher." In the end, the appointment went to Al Moran, the highly respected regional director of HUD's Chicago area and a prominent black Republican. When there is a logjam for a vacancy, it is not unusual for the department and the White House to look elsewhere. Governor Thompson of Illinois was close to the White House and recommended Al for the position. Maurice was delighted with the choice.

As it turned out, I had made more friends with the professional staff than with the political notables at HUD. In particular, a woman named Maddie Hastings became my mentor. She was a true specialist

Marjorie with former president George H. W. Bush at his home in Kennebunkport.

in HUD's labyrinthine rules and regulations, especially concerning the complexities known as Section 8. This is a body of rules governing, among other things, subsidies for multifamily housing, particularly the type known as "mod rehab units," which are dedicated to improving the condition of existing public housing stock.

Most people think the laws we live under are made by Congress, but Congress makes laws that are primarily appropriations to agencies. The agencies in turn make the rules that determine the application of those laws. It is those rules that determine who gets how much money, when they get it, and where it is disbursed. HUD publishes the rules it develops in the *Congressional Register* and asks for comments during a thirty-day period. However, only interested parties such as contractors, developers, consultants, and especially Congress know what it's all about. Representatives have a vested interest in directing rehab dollars to their own districts. Sometimes the agencies accommodate the comments they receive, and sometimes not. Once the thirty-day period has expired, published rules become law. None of this would be too bad if, on occasion, new rules replaced old ones or if any were ever repealed, but none are. So Section 8 is layered, like an onion with a multitude of skins.

Because I was writing speeches for Maurice, it was important that I understand the rules and procedures and know the pertinent facts. Every time I thought I finally understood a regulation, Maddie would explain that I had the 1975 rule correct, but the regulation had been amended in 1976. And so it went. I'm not sure I ever did learn it all, but I tried. I made sure Maddie checked every speech that involved technicalities. Fortunately, most of the speeches I wrote dealt with Maurice's goals and ambitions for HUD as well as its successes, problems, and failures. I knew a lot about the failures.

During the second year, I was given another major assignment. I was charged with calculating the money attached to mod rehab units, once they had been awarded. Developers and contractors eagerly sought these government subsidies and drew on the expertise of consultants to obtain them. Just plain old ordinary folk can't navigate the maze of forms required for getting money from the government. As a result, consultants got rich because they understood the paperwork.

I confess to being shocked when I learned that a budget request from HUD had actually been *increased* by Congress. Representatives wanted to be sure that enough funds, otherwise known as "pork," found a home in their districts. Every single member of Congress understood the rules concerning Section 8.

A different index existed for each community, depending upon its cost of living, which was determined by some guru somewhere. For instance, Albany, New York, received less money per unit than Cleveland, Ohio. Only then did I realize the staggering amount of money that flowed through HUD, and I began to see a pattern. More units (meaning more dollars) were going to some states than to others. I took my concerns to Maurice, who seemed strangely noncommittal. Only then did I realize that many of the large decisions involving millions and millions of dollars were made "upstairs."

The secretary of HUD, Sam Pierce, a tall, distinguished-looking black man from New York, was a remote person whom President Reagan is alleged to have confused with the mayor of Washington, D.C., when he first appeared at a Cabinet meeting. No one ever saw Sam Pierce in the building, the halls, or the cafeteria. I sometimes wondered whether a helicopter pad on the roof of the HUD building provided him with access and egress. One day I had an appointment away from HUD and didn't arrive at my office until ten o'clock in the morning instead of the usual eight o'clock. I had entered the elevator when Secretary Pierce walked in. I recognized him from his pictures. He immediately withdrew without even saying "Good morning." But I had discovered his secret. He didn't arrive until late, used a control key to be sure he rose to his guarded tenth floor alone, and left before anyone else.

I saw his office only once, when he summoned me to ask, my file in his hand, "What are you doing here at HUD?" I knew he had looked at my financial statement and my references, all highly placed people at the White House and in Congress. I explained that I had come to help Maurice Barksdale. He was puzzled, as were many around me, about why I had come there to accept such an obscure position with no personal gain in mind. He and his staff very definitely had "gain" in mind and later brought disgrace to themselves and to the department.

The HUD scandals became public four years later—in 1989. I was back in Houston by then and read in the newspapers that an independent prosecutor, Arlin Adams, had been appointed to probe the abuses of the awarding of mod rehab units. Not surprisingly, his investigations took him to other departments such as the Community Development division, which controlled the Urban Development Action Grants, otherwise known as UDAGs. Ironically, as far as I know, the only person who has actually gone to jail in the wake of the indictments is Dubois Gilliam, a deputy assistant secretary for CD who wasn't the original target of the investigation. Gilliam has served his term, and it is rumored that he is once again doing business with HUD. Deborah Dean, Secretary Pierce's assistant, was also convicted; however, her penalty was very light—six months' house arrest. Debbie was a very good-looking young woman, a member of the prominent Gore family, albeit the Republican branch. Lance Wilson, at Secretary Pierce's right hand, was a tall, handsome, charming, and intelligent black man from New York. Both were as visible in the department as Sam Pierce was invisible. The influence they both exerted over the secretary was common knowledge. However, strange as it may seem, Lance was completely exonerated.

Secretary Pierce accepted responsibility for mismanagement and for having tolerated a climate of corruption in his offices. The government exempted him from punishment. Many others, such as Thomas Demery, assistant secretary; Phillip Wynn, former assistant secretary and former ambassador to Switzerland; Silvio DeBartolomeis, acting secretary; and Joseph Strauss, special assistant to Secretary Pierce, received suspended sentences. They were convicted of giving money to their friends, their families, and themselves without regard to the actual housing needs of low-income families.

Maurice testified before the Senate. Not surprisingly, he was among the few high-ranking officials at HUD who were recognized as being beyond reproach. And, although federal agents visited me on several occasions at my home in Texas, my title was much too long for me to have been considered a part of any important decision making.

Just before the 1984 election, Maurice began reminding everyone that he had promised to stay only for the president's first term. In addition, he told everyone his mother was ill. In the early morning hours after President Reagan's second inauguration, in January of 1985, he and Faye were packed and out of there. I had to stay another few weeks to clear out all our possessions from the office. I had promised my children I would have my Houston housekeeper, Marie, come to drive me home. Two days before she was to fly to Washington, however, she broke her foot. I didn't tell anyone about her accident. I drove myself back to Houston the way I had come—by myself.

One day, while I was still in Washington, my secretary interrupted a group of us. "Mrs. Arsht, sorry, but you have a call from Houston on your private line." Secretaries never entered the sacrosanct meetings that, however meaningless, characterize all bureaucracies unless there were an identifiable emergency. HUD was no exception. No one had the Washington phone number to my private office line except my mother's household, my children, and my secretary in Houston. I reserved that line for my personal use and for the internal use of HUD personnel. I took the call in my office, wondering what problem could be presenting itself.

"Marjorie, this is Ross Davis." He was Elène's second son. My heart skipped a beat. My only acquaintance with my nephew had been an occasional glimpse across a crowded room. I knew he was a grown man, but I didn't have any idea how old he was.

"Has something happened to Mama?" I asked before he could continue.

"Oh no, I just wanted to discuss the Tannery stock with you. Are you familiar with it?" He was referring to the stock in that old Yoakum tannery that Daddy had helped to develop into Tex-Tan so long ago.

"Yes, I am. What has happened to it?"

"The heirs of the Welhausen family, which represent the majority stockholders, have decided to liquidate their holdings, so there is a cash disbursement to Mome—a lot of money, over two million dollars." All of Elène's children called Mama, their grandmother, Mome.

"I knew that stock was valuable, but what's the problem?"

"Marjorie, I'm sure you have noticed that Mome is failing. Nothing acute, but the handling of her affairs—the checks and bills and deposits—are just too much for her."

"What happened to the last bookkeeper?"

There was a pause. Ross cleared his throat. "Mome fired her. She told me the woman was stealing." Poor woman. I could imagine what had transpired. I remembered a time, not too long before, when Mama had begged me to help with her books. I found a drawer full of checks needing to be deposited, bills to be paid, and bank statements to be balanced. And then, after I worked on them for a few weeks, she accused me of having written a check to myself. I asked her to show me the check, and she said she had torn it up. I got out the checkbook and showed her the uninterrupted sequence of checks, but she couldn't be mollified. I remember leaving her apartment shaking with fury from head to foot. Her intransigence matched her paranoia. And, of course within a week or two she had forgotten all about it.

"I know she needs help," I said. "What are you proposing?"

"I suggest that I be given a power of attorney. I will, of course, discuss any major investments with you and keep you informed of everything I'm doing. But the weekly handling of routine matters is just easier if I do it myself."

I couldn't think of a valid argument although I knew I was stepping into a quagmire. I was far away, and he was on the scene. I also realized he didn't really have to ask me, so I said, "Ross, go ahead. I think that's a practical solution." Two days later I had another unexpected call.

"Marjorie, this is Elène." She didn't have to tell me. I remembered that voice, almost identical to my own.

"I wanted to tell you that I have rearranged Mama's household. She needs someone around the clock and on weekends, so I'm getting a third shift. I just wanted you to know."

It was ridiculous. Elène had been managing Mama's nurses for a long time without asking me anything. All I could think of to say was, "Well, thank you for telling me. Is there anything I can do to help?"

"Oh no," she added quickly. "I think just one authority is best."

"Whatever you say."

The conversation ended with perfunctory "good-byes." I hung up the telephone and stared at the walls, aware that my heart was pounding. The sequence of conversations, first with Ross and then with Elène, was too artificial not to make me suspicious. Was it unreasonable to assume that they were doing something that their lawyers insisted be prefaced with friendly gestures to me? I called the children to report this odd circumstance. Two calls out of nowhere and really for nothing they couldn't have done by themselves. The children discounted the whole matter, as they usually did where my worries about Mama and Elène were concerned. Alan said, "Maybe they're just trying to be friendly."

Leslye commented, "Mother, don't be so skeptical. I think it was nice of them to call."

Suddenly I remembered that they were going to discover that the tannery stock was no longer in a dedicated trust with Elène as the sole beneficiary. It had been returned to Mama's name and would now be a part of her divisible estate. I knew that some kind of brouhaha lay ahead. My suspicions were not ill founded.

Then a third call came. The voice of Elène's daughter, her eldest child, came through on my private line. "Marjorie, this is Lynn Lasher. It is very important that you get my grandmother's papers back from that lawyer you took her to see." A clipped voice, unfriendly. No superficial pleasantries. My heart skipped a beat. What was she talking about? The only attorney I'd taken her to see was long ago. I decided to be sure.

"Lynn, I took Mama to see Robert Piro a long time ago, and all the papers that he prepared were returned to her when she requested them."

"I don't know anything about Piro. I'm talking about Al Diamond."

"I don't know any Al Diamond."

"That's funny. He knows you, and my grandmother says you took her to see him."

"Lots of people know me that I don't know. I have never seen or heard of Al Diamond, so I surely didn't take Mama to his office." I heard a sarcastic chuckle.

"I surely hope you will search your memory. My grandmother is furious." This meant, of course, that Elène was furious.

"I'm sorry about that, but I simply can't help you. Good-bye."

The conversation ended as abruptly as it began. Memories of how this had all begun came flooding back. One day while I was still working in real estate, the phone rang in the town house where Raymond and I were living.

"Marjorie, I've done something terrible, and I need your help."

Mama's voice was uncharacteristically subdued, even humble. I could hardly hear her. "What have you done?" I asked quickly.

"I need to come see you about it. Three o'clock?"

"Fine." I worried all day long. At two-thirty I began to walk the floor of our town house. Because of its size, I couldn't take many steps either way, but I was too nervous to sit down. Promptly at three o'clock, the doorbell rang. There stood Mama, neat and prim in a white-collared, navy blue dress, dark circles under her eyes. As she settled into a chair in our small den off the kitchen, nervously twisting the handkerchief in her hands, she refused my offer of iced tea or anything stronger. I waited. She swallowed and cleared her throat several times before any words came out. Even when she spoke I had to strain to hear her. Her head bowed, she seemed to be talking to her hands. She looked up suddenly.

"I'd like a glass of water."

While she drank I racked my brain. What had she done? What could be *this* bad? Then the words spilled out.

"When I was so angry with you that time in Tulsa, I deeded all the Bendel property to Elène, and now she won't give it back to me. And there's more. I'm not sure, but I think she has taken everything else, too." I couldn't suppress the gasping sound that escaped my throat. Suddenly she was herself again, belligerent but a bit defensive. "You did say you were going to sue me, you know. Leon Jaworski told me you went to see him."

"I did no such thing, Mama. Listen to me carefully." I paused between each word. "I said I didn't think the Louisiana courts would allow you to disinherit me. I don't know Leon Jaworski. Naturally I've heard of him, he's famous, but I have never met him, much less entered his office."

Looking directly into my eyes, she said with conviction, "He told me you did."

It would do no good to argue. All she had to do was wonder whether I *might* go to see Leon Jaworski, and that thought became fact—like with Gina at Christmas, when she insisted Gina had called her a bitch, and all Gina said was "Merry Christmas, Aunt Myrtle." Taking a deep breath, I faced the current dilemma. "What do you want me to do about it? If you can't persuade my sister to listen to you, how can I? She won't even speak to me."

"I think you know the lawyer Uncle George used. I want to go see him. And I want you to go with me. I'm not strong enough to go alone."

Mama not strong enough? What a joke. I called Jim Brelsford at the prominent Houston firm of Vinson and Elkins, a longtime friend of mine. He informed me he no longer did estate work and began recommending others in his firm. I knew who they were, and I was sure she wouldn't accept them. He thought for a minute and recommended Robert Piro. "He's at Baker and Botts, in his early forties, and a competent, understanding man. I'll call him and make an appointment for your mother." Mama would be satisfied with someone from another important firm in Houston.

When the time came for Mama's appointment with Piro, she insisted I go with her, despite my protests. I was extremely uncomfortable and kept suggesting I leave, assuring her I would return to pick her up. Mama, of course, wouldn't hear of my leaving her at the lawyer's office. She wanted me to stay. She liked Robert Piro and gave him her voluminous stack of legal papers. He listened to her long story. I refrained from interrupting while she cloaked her own role in innocence. Finally, after some time spent examining the papers, Piro spoke.

"Mrs. Meyer, the outright deed is irrevocable so long as your daughter will not willingly return the property to you. However, these documents reveal that you have sizeable holdings of equities that are in a revocable trust. You have every right to cancel that instrument. How would you value the portion of your estate outside the Louisiana property?"

Mama was listening carefully. "Oh, maybe half and half." Then she added, "You mean I can cancel that trust? I just can't change the Bendel property?"

"That's correct. You could leave all the other assets to Marjorie to equalize the inheritance."

"Why, that's wonderful. What a relief! Let's do it." Mama was ecstatic.

I held up my hand. "I can't sit here and let Mama do that. If the trust is revocable, why don't you put all the assets back in Mama's name?" The idea of taking Mama to a lawyer and ending up with some of her assets was intolerable to me. I'm not sure now whether Mama really understood the difference, but Piro agreed that he could prepare the necessary papers for the brokerage house and for the transfer agents in order to effect the conversion. And it was so ordered. One half of the assets that were returned to Mama's name eventually constituted my children's and grandchildren's inheritance.

"However," Piro continued, "there are a few other things we have to do. I always recommend that when people reach a certain age, they execute a power of attorney to be used only in case of incapacity, by someone in whom they have total confidence. You know we all face the possibility of dependency. What about Marjorie? Do you have confidence in her?"

I was horrified. I protested, remembering the check-writing episode. "Mama, pick a bank or something. I do not want that responsibility."

But that day, Mama was on a high and in charge. "Mr. Piro, I have every confidence in Marjorie. She will be perfect. I know I can trust her. Execute that paper." My persistent protests hit a stone wall.

Piro continued, "We have another policy in this firm. Whenever there is an incipient family conflict, our client must be interviewed by at least four members, separately and individually with no one else present, in order to be sure the client clearly understands what he or she is doing and why. I would like to make an appointment two days from now, so that four of our lawyers will be available for private interviews with you." Mama glowed. She thanked him effusively and said she would return whenever he wanted. She insisted on taking Ray and me to dinner at Maxim's that evening to "celebrate."

A few days afterward, I dropped Mama off at Robert Piro's office for her interviews, praying she would change her mind about the power of attorney. Three hours later, she called that she was ready for me to come get her. Piro met me at the elevator.

"Your mother knows exactly what she's doing and why. Our attorneys grilled her thoroughly, and she passed every test they could devise." Mama was signing documents when I walked in the office.

"Here is the power of attorney," a secretary said as she handed me a paper. I accepted it as gingerly as if it were a hot potato and turned to Mama, handing her the paper. "I don't want this, Mama. Please."

"Don't be silly. Just put it away."

Six weeks later Mama's voice on the telephone expressed her fury. With no salutation, she exploded. "What have you been doing with my affairs? You bring the original of that power of attorney to me right this minute. You have a nerve. I'm perfectly able to take care of myself."

"Mama, you insisted I take that paper. I haven't done one thing with it. I didn't want any part of it. Have you forgotten your meeting with Mr. Piro?"

"I don't know what you're talking about. I accidentally found this copy while I was looking through some papers, and I want it destroyed—now!"

After a few weeks of strained encounters, when neither Mama nor I even mentioned Robert Piro or my returned power of attorney, I had a call from him. "Mrs. Arsht, your mother has called us every day for the past several weeks. As you know, we retained a copy of her will in our vault. She insists on having it returned and, although we hesitated, thinking she might change her mind again, we are obliged to return it to her. I felt I should inform you."

I was embarrassed but said to him, "How do you explain this behavior?"

"It appears that your mother has a serious mental problem. Our tests are intensive and thorough, but she must have had a window of lucidity. I suggest you get a lawyer to represent you—and quickly."

That's easy to say, I thought. I remembered my father instructing me long ago that "the strong must always take care of the weak. You will always have to take care of your mother and sister." But they weren't weak, either one. That night when I related Robert Piro's call to Raymond, he said, "Look, Marjorie, there are no surprises here. That lawyer is correct. Your mother has these periods when she is perfectly charming and normal, even fun to be around, and others when she is paranoid and impossible. I don't believe this is the end of it." And, of course, it wasn't.

Several years after the Piro episode I had a call from Mama. Whether livid or penitent, Mama never equivocated. "Marjorie, who is your lawyer?" she asked.

"Why?"

"I need to talk to him."

"What's the problem?"

"Just give me his name and number." She had begun the conversation in a placid mood, but as I continued to question her, she was becoming more and more agitated.

"I'm not going to give you his name or number until you tell me the reason you want to contact him." A long pause. And I just waited.

Finally, with a sigh she said, "Look, I need to talk to him about a will, and I don't want anyone to know anything about it."

"Anyone" meant the Davis family. "Mama, do you remember what happened with Bob Piro?"

She didn't answer for a while, and I just held the telephone. In resignation, she broke the silence. "This has nothing to do with that or any other lawyer. I just want something simple, and you don't have to have anything to do with it."

"All right, so long as you mean that." I gave her Tom Moore's number and hoped she would forget about it. But she didn't. She called him and naturally he called me. Just like everyone else, Tom was enthralled with her common-sense approach. She had asked him what he would charge, and Tom, knowing something of the relationship because he had handled all of Raymond's affairs for me, gave her a ridiculously low figure of a couple of hundred dollars, feeling he would be doing a good deed. When the time came for him to make his final visit to Mama's apartment, he called me.

"Marjorie, I know you want no part of any of this, but it's important that you meet us at your mother's apartment and bring Marie. We have worked out a very simple document, just a few pages, but a clear and equitable division of her property. She is absolutely paranoid about anyone knowing what she is doing. I told her I could bring my wife, Veda, but there had to be another witness also. She wanted no one from her household, and when I suggested Marie, she was ecstatic. And then she insisted that you come, too, in order that you know what she's doing."

"Tom, haven't I told you how much I detest this? It always ends miserably. Mama is volatile, and tomorrow she may not remember one thing you have done, or she may have decided she doesn't want what she did the day before."

"Marjorie, you don't have to do or sign anything. Just bring Marie."

And so, like every other time, despite my reluctance, I went. Tom had done what he promised her, and she was pleased. A short document, directed that her total property, including what had been deeded to Elène, be appraised by an impartial professional and the total be divided in half, the deeded property being subtracted from the cash amount of personal, liquid assets due Elène. Besides a few personal bequests, that was it. I had to admit that it was fair. The will was signed, and Tom sent Mama his bill. I didn't know until after Mama died that she never paid it.

After Lynn's call, I wondered whether they knew about Tom's will. Had Mama been to the lawyer Lynn was asking about before or after Tom?

During the time I'd been in Washington, Marie had been going to see Mama every week. She would clean her hearing aid, put in a new battery, or perhaps just talk. In the past, when Mama traveled, Marie helped her pack or unpack. Marie is a lively, outgoing, loquacious human being, and they enjoyed each other.

Not long after Lynn's call, Linda Dyson reported to me that the doorman at Inwood Manor, where Mama lived, had stopped Marie at the door and told her she couldn't go upstairs to see Mama. Alan happened to be visiting me in Washington at the time. He couldn't believe that Elène would do such a thing, and he thought I should call her to be sure there wasn't a mistake.

I called, with Alan listening on the extension. It wasn't really a conversation. Elène just yelled at me. After a brief diatribe about Marie spying and upsetting Mama, she hung up in my ear. Alan walked into my bedroom and, with his usual dry sense of humor, said, "I don't think she likes you very much."

Two weeks later it was time for my usual monthly trip home to sign checks for my small company, attend the TSU regents' meetings, and see Mama. When I arrived at her apartment, I saw that she had really deteriorated. She was totally preoccupied with the fact that Elène insisted on giving her a ninetieth birthday party, and she didn't want to go. When I asked her why she didn't refuse, she looked pitiful, and I felt sorry for her. She didn't seem to want to talk about Marie, but when I mentioned the incident with the doorman, she roused herself enough to say, without her usual fire, that if I didn't produce the papers that both the lawyer and I had, I wouldn't be welcome in her house any more.

It was obviously a programmed speech. I had to assume that the Diamond will had been very unsatisfactory to the Davises. My insistence that I didn't know Al Diamond didn't even register. She just kept repeating what she had been instructed to say—without much feeling, but firmly. I knew I had to contact Al Diamond, so I stayed in Houston an extra day and called on him at his office. "How in the world did my mother get to you?" I asked him.

"Why, Martin Stoger, her accountant, sent her to me. And boy, does your mother despise her son-in-law Leon Davis!"

Martin Stoger? Who was he? And then I remembered. One afternoon, while Linda Underwood and I were visiting Mama, Mama complained bitterly about her accountant of many years. She said Leon controlled him. Linda suggested Mama use her own accountant, Martin Stoger. Accustomed to Mama's on and off moods, I paid no attention at the time. I had never heard of Stoger. Obviously Mama had sought his services and, through him, gotten to Diamond. In her way, Mama was both ingenious and resolute.

For most of twenty years, my contact with my mother had been cursory and, with my sister—except for Ray's funeral—nonexistent. Into her late eighties, Mama's physical health had remained good. She was a vain woman. She worried about her appearance, and she dreaded the party Elène planned for her ninetieth birthday. I am convinced the anxiety and stress over it made her sick. Shortly after the event, she began to have some ministrokes, not physically paralyzing, just causing slightly slurred speech and an air of distraction. In the ensuing months, Mama declined more and more rapidly in mental acuity and physical agility. She required twenty-four-hour nursing care seven days a week.

Elène took complete charge of Mama's household, including the hiring and firing of nurses, who were scared to death of her. They poured out their sad stories to me, who, of course, was helpless to check any of their tales for validity or to correct the inequities, if true. They also told me that Mama had made a new will. I had surmised by this time that Elène didn't know about the Moore will, but, knowing Mama's penchant for making wills, she probably wasn't taking any chances.

The nurses reported: "Mrs. Arsht, a lot of people crowded around Mrs. Meyer's dining room table, a lawyer and Mr. Gillis, you know, the accountant, and Miss Elène. They had Mrs. Meyer sign a bunch of papers. Someone named Paul Martin was here." Paul Martin! He was the lawyer who had presided over deeding the Bendel property to Elène.

One winter day I was visiting Mama and found her in great distress. She was having trouble breathing. I called Elène, who summoned an ambulance. We followed in our separate cars to Methodist Hospital. Mama was taken to a small suite on the twelfth floor of Fondren Tower. I never failed to be impressed with the ambience of that area. Mama's accommodations consisted of a pleasant living room with a couch and chairs for visitors and a section curtained off for her bed. This special wing had a separate parking garage and its own elevator. When visitors reached the proper floor, they entered a luxuriously furnished foyer over which the portraits of the donors held sway.

There was never a sound. People felt compelled to whisper. No footsteps sounded on the carpeted halls. I often wondered whether rich people didn't cry out or make the noises so characteristic of normal hospital wards. There were no clangs or rattles or rushing orderlies or nurses pushing gurneys. Elegance and dignity prevailed. Mama's doctor, Kim Bloom, had been contacted and had issued orders. Mama's nurses were in attendance. Elène and I began what can best be described as an arm's-length truce.

During the ensuing days we said hello and good-bye and exchanged whatever necessary reports or information had to be conveyed to one or the other. No chitchat except that, one afternoon, Elène asked me about Margot's death. Had she really died of ALS or something else? It seems she needed the information for the medical background checks of one of her daughters. In the evenings Leon came and ofttimes Elène's children. Leon was always the soul of congeniality, and if they went out for something to eat, he always offered to bring me a sandwich.

Mama's heart was strong, and she lingered while her kidneys gradually weakened. She became less and less alert, but one morning, when I entered the screened area where she lay, she smiled a broad smile, and I knew from her eyes that she knew who I was. That was her last day—the morning of January 21, 1987—one month short of her ninety-fourth birthday.

A few hours after my arrival, she began the raspy rattle that I remembered from my father's deathbed in 1948. There is nothing pretty about death. And no matter what the relationship with a parent, to watch that parent die is a wrenching experience. As I watched Mama reflexively struggling to breathe, I knew she wasn't suffering, but I was. My chest hurt. I don't cry easily, so there were no tears, just a deep, crushing sadness. Maybe it was because I looked so much like her that I was facing my own mortality. Or maybe because when a close relationship has been unsatisfactory, there is always regret that it couldn't have been otherwise.

The will that was probated following Mama's death overturned the one that Mama had Tom Moore, my lawyer, draft for her. Thus, the governing will became the one Mama had signed during the period of her deterioration, after she suffered from a string of ministrokes. At first glance, Mama's will seemed straightforward enough, that is, for anyone not familiar with the history. Mama was dividing everything she had a legal right to bequeath, namely the Texas assets. Basically this meant that half of those went to my children and Margot's children with me as trustee. The other half went to Elène, also acting as trustee. In addition, I personally received half of the proceeds from the sale of her apartment and half of what was left of her personal effects. What wasn't mentioned in the will was the Louisiana property, the Bendel estate that Mama had inherited from her bachelor uncle, Isaac Bendel. This was the property she had deeded to Elène following my trip to Tulsa. Although originally the Bendel property had consisted of real estate, primarily farmlands, once oil was discovered, its value greatly increased. At the time of the deed transfer, it represented a value approximately equal to the Texas assets. By the time she died, it was worth considerably more. Securing disbursement of her estate became one of the most trying and disturbing experiences of my life.

Shortly before Mama died, one of the oil properties in the Bendel estate developed a payment problem requiring a title search in which my name appeared. While the problem was being resolved, oil production monies accumulated. The Davises would not release the divisible Texas assets, covered in Mama's will, until they received from me a release of the claim that the title search had revealed. Attorneys were involved, and there was much contention. In the end, after great misery, we were able to reach a modest settlement, but the actual release of the Texas assets didn't take place until March of 1992—five years and two months after Mama had died. I have never known whether Elène knew about the Moore will before Mama died. Mama made wills the way most people make grocery lists. I heard after she died that she had filed at least thirteen.

In retrospect, I do not understand why I never considered Mama mentally ill. There were surely enough signposts along the way. I knew that her unpredictable nature had occasioned periodic treatments by psychiatrists over the years, although I am relatively unclear on details since Elène supervised these episodes. Even back in the 1940s, Elène had taken her "to Galveston"—meaning to the facility there for shock treatments. In the 1960s, a period of acute memory loss suggested that she must have been given them again. Still, she could be so normal, sometimes even fun, that I never accepted that her mercurial moods could be attributed to anything but a bad disposition.

And nothing could have made me declare Mama incompetent before the world, no matter how questionable I might regard the conditions under which she signed her governing will. Bob Piro had actually urged me to do so when Mama revoked the will he drafted. But I couldn't do it then any more than I could do it after Mama died. I didn't have the stamina to fight before the world for material goods at Mama's expense. I really never seriously considered it.

More recently, however, I have wondered whether there could have been a genetic base for her instability. As a child, I remember hearing my father, when he was really aggravated, say to Mama, "You're what people get when first cousins marry!" In fact, Grandmother Lena and Grandfather Armand had been required to go to Orange, Texas, to get married, since marriage between first cousins was against the law in Louisiana. I don't know whether modern genetics would confirm that relationship as a possible cause of Mama's problems, but I am certain that serious problems did exist, even if I do not have a medical name for the condition. And I can discuss it now since it all happened so long ago.

The late eighties and nineties provided some absorbing opportunities, most of which I enjoyed very much. In 1988, when I learned George Bush would be nominated for president at the national convention to be held in New Orleans, I decided I really wanted to be a delegate. In the past, delegates had been chosen by the proposed nominee, but now, with the populist movement in power, an election was demanded. A committee appointed by George chose me, along with two others, and I went to my senatorial district caucus well prepared to address that body.

Everyone expected Beverly Kaufman—then very active in Republican women's clubs and now Harris County Clerk—to win outright, but I surprised them by making the runoff with her. At that time, there were a considerable number of new delegates to the senatorial district conventions, many of them evangelical Christians who had never before been active in politics. I was largely unknown to them, and I tailored my presentation for their benefit, ending my speech with a prayer, which was grist for their mill. I won. After the election, a man came up to me and said, "Mrs. Arsht, we never even knew your position on abortion."

I answered, "I support George Bush."

"That's no answer," he said.

"That's *my* answer," I replied. I'm sure he was sorry he voted for me.

Beverly became my alternate delegate, and we had a wonderful time in New Orleans. Bob Schieffer of CBS News interviewed me as the oldest delegate. I heard later that another woman was really older than I but had not given her correct age on the form. *Houston Post* reporter Bill Coulter approached me after George had announced his choice for vice president. "Marjorie, you have to get to George Bush and have him withdraw that name. Dan Quayle is a disaster!"

I replied, "I don't know anything about the man, but if I know George Bush, he's loyal to the end, and you had just better get used to Dan Quayle."

In 1992, I was elected by congressional district caucus to be a presidential elector pledged to George Bush. It is an unwritten rule that electors be chosen on the basis of their past support for the nominee, inasmuch as the position is today largely honorary. I doubt that my opponent had ever walked into a Bush headquarters, and I did beat him, albeit by only one vote.

The electoral college is in many ways an anachronism. It used to be the mechanism for the actual election of the president, when electors traveled to their state capitals and cast their votes according to their preference, although even then, the way the state went, so went the electors. Now the college serves both as a brake on whatever the passing fancy of a populist nationwide plebiscite might be and as a reinforcement of the structure of our country as a republic.

In Texas, electors meet in the senate chamber of the capitol in Austin after the election and cast their vote for the state's winning presidential candidate. It is rare that an elector departs from the state's election results although that person has the right to do so and on rare occasion has done just that. Although an interesting experience, I found the meeting of the electors a sad occasion that year because we knew by then that, even though George had won Texas, he had lost nationwide to Bill Clinton.

In 1990, an opportunity arose that was considerably more fun. Governor Clements's office called and asked me to serve on the Licensing and Regulations Commission in Austin. This commission regulates diverse activities such as boxing and manufactured housing. It seems that the commission had previously been an agency, a creature of the legislature, managed by a director. A squabble resulted in the change from agency to commission, with the governor appointing members to fill some vacancies. The terms of the six commissioners were staggered, with three vacancies filled every six years. In that way, it was ensured that one group would carry over from the previous gubernatorial administration.

After I had accepted the post, I heard that Governor Clements had learned the past director had left many problems behind and that he had to make three appointments. He is alleged to have said, "Get Marjorie Arsht. She knows how to fire people." I suppose he was thinking of my stint as a TSU regent, when I had led the charge to dismiss the longtime president. Nevertheless, being a boxing commissioner was one of the more enjoyable positions I have ever held. Among other duties, I attended all of the boxing matches in this area.

In 1994, the year of my eightieth birthday, I began a whole series of celebrations. Over the long Columbus Day weekend in October, my daughter-in-law, Audrey, arranged for an en famille gathering in La Jolla, California. Everyone came: Jocelyn, Alan's older daughter, came from the University of Pennsylvania; Leslye from Washington, D.C.; Alan, Audrey, and Alexandra from New York; as well as the California Lane grandchildren, John, Pete, and Bruce; and Jim, his wife, Merrilee, and their two little girls, Ashlee and Samantha. It was the only time that all of us had come together just for fun.

Audrey had everything arranged—dinner reservations at the best places, a trip to the famous San Diego Zoo, and a commercial photographer who took a marvelous picture of the whole family that we all cherish to this day. One of my best birthday presents was Merrilee's announcement that she and Jim were going to have another baby.

Pres. George W. Bush with Marjorie and family in the Oval Office. Left to right: Merrilee Lane, wife of grandson Jim Lane; Samantha, great-granddaughter; Marjorie; President Bush; Rebecca and Ashlee, great-granddaughters; and grandson Jim Lane.

On my return from California, my friend Dee Coats called. "Al and I are thinking of putting our house on the market, and we wanted to have a party before we do it. You travel so much, and we can have the party any time, so I want to be sure we schedule it when you're in town." It occurred to me that it was very thoughtful of her to plan a party to suit my convenience. When a friend, Jack Burton, picked me up and drove nonchalantly to Dee's house in Memorial, I had a no idea of the real surprise in store for me. We walked in to the cheers of a crowd and saw a huge banner across the living room that said, "Happy Birthday, Marjorie." Someone caught a picture of me with my mouth open. It was truly the most complete surprise of my life. Ordinarily someone leaks a hint, but not that time. It was a compliment that I cherish to this day.

My actual birthday on November 1, 1994, was a treat in itself, albeit a bittersweet one. My cousin Pauline, who had never been to Strasbourg, where our fathers' family originated, joined me in going there a few days before a Rice trip we were both taking through Provence. So I was able to spend my eightieth birthday with the same people with whom I had spent my nineteenth, André and Paulette Dreyfus. They were the only survivors of that once large Meyer family. André was in the hospital and practiced his fractured English while I used my rusty French. I was so glad to have seen him. He died soon afterward.

When, in 2001, my friend and attorney, Morris Hamm, gave up his law practice, he decided to move to California with his devoted friend, Kathleen Johnson. Shortly before the move, Kathy came from California to help Morris pack, and I invited them to lunch on a Thursday. My dependable housekeeper and friend of many years, Marie Murray, took ill and didn't come Tuesday or Wednesday, but she assured me she would come on Thursday.

With our guests due at 12:30, Marie and I went to Eatzi's, a store renowned for its excellent prepared foods. We bought vegetable quesadillas for the first course, cold salmon with dill sauce, spicy Southwestern shrimp and pasta, and asparagus vinaigrette for the main course, to be followed by exquisitely decorated fruit tarts and coffee for dessert.

While Marie tidied the house, I set the table with my finest monogrammed pink linen placemats trimmed with lace and their matching napkins, my Lenox plates, bordered in pink, my sterling silver utensils, and my best crystal, including flutes for the vintage champagne, "J," which was Morris's favorite. I opened our packages from the store and arranged the food on the plates, which went into the refrigerator to be kept cold. From my miniature garden I picked some mint, which, with tiny cherry tomatoes I had purchased, would give the presentation color. In the freezer were some of our Junior League's famous orange rolls.

As the doorbell rang, I thought of my beloved grandmother Lena, who believed that everything served from her table should be homemade and preferably homegrown. I know that my feet are firmly planted in the twenty-first century because the only thing homegrown for that elegant champagne lunch was the mint.

When you are older, of course, the years have a way of passing more rapidly, like leaves swept along a sidewalk by a brisk November wind. In May of 2003, we celebrated Alan's sixtieth birthday with a family trip to Montego Bay, Jamaica. In 2005, Leslye turned sixty. I have a hard time believing that so many years have passed, but my head, if not my heart, tells me that they have. Some aches and pains here and there remind me that I, at ninety, am after all not immortal. Nevertheless, I am well aware that my life is different from that of most people my age.

Only a few of my contemporaries are still living. Some, of course, are not in good health. But others really don't seem to care about current issues and certainly not at all about the future. Many people years younger than I have nothing to do with computers and, strangely, aren't even very curious about them. I can't understand that. For me, email has become an essential tool for communicating with my children and friends. I can't imagine having written this book on my old Selectric typewriter, having to redo any page that had an error.

I still regularly attend the monthly meetings of the Magic Circle Republican Women's Club. When I can, I volunteer one morning a week at the George H. W. Bush office, indexing his correspondence into their computers. When the speaker interests me, I go to meetings of Pachyderm, a Republican civic club. In addition, I have season tickets to the Texans' football games and go to see the Astros whenever I can. When I can't, I watch the games on television. I cannot imagine life without interest in the present or concern for the future.

I know I am lucky to be able still to take part in so many activities. That isn't to say that every week or so I don't add another item to the list of things I can no longer do. I can't walk distances, so I make use of a wheelchair in airports, a fact that would have dismayed me not too many years ago. I avoid steps and fast escalators and find myself searching out even freight elevators when public ones are not available. Every so often, when faced with uneven terrain and I don't have an arm to lean on, I make use of a cane. I am unashamed that my car boasts a handicapped license plate. However, behind the wheel of a car and at my computer—all seated occupations—I manage very well.

I don't dwell on the past. What I do instead is make the most of each day since, when I think about it, I know they are numbered. I just try not to think about that fact very often. I am so proud of my children. My son, Alan, with his wife Audrey, who is like another daughter to me, have established a warm, hospitable, and loving home. Alan has turned out to be a very successful contributor to society, a devoted, responsible husband and father, along with being a thoughtful, caring son to me. My daughter Leslye is the kind of daughter parents dream of having. She is successful in a challenging career in education and in her busy life always has time for me if and when I need her. I cherish my grandchildren—Alan's daughters, Jocelyn and Alexandra, and Margot's three surviving sons, John, Raymond, and Jim Lane. My grandson Jim and his charming wife, Merrilee, have given me Ashlee, Samantha, and Rebecca, who I know are the three loveliest great-granddaughters in the world, bias acknowledged.

I hope there is a lot more living for me in the overall plan of things. I think what I will hate most about dying is knowing I'll miss so many things. Will Houston's football team, the Texans, win a Super Bowl? Will the Israelis and Palestinians ever live side by side in harmony? Will people have helipads on their roofs instead of garages? I'll even miss the *Lehrer News Hour* every weekday afternoon and the *Wall Street Journal*'s crossword puzzle on Friday.

In celebration of my ninetieth birthday, Alan, Audrey, and Leslye arranged a memorable party at Houston's elegant Petroleum Club, where they spared no extravagant detail. A five-piece ensemble provided music for dancing and a show-stopping centerpiece—topped with a silver hat in keeping with the party's theme of "Hats Off to Marjorie!"—decorated each of the eleven tables. There were cocktails, hors d'oeuvres, a beautiful buffet, wines, and champagne. I expected the usual birthday cake, but that's not what arrived. Instead, the staff rolled out an arrangement of what appeared to be presents—several large boxlike rectangles swathed in candy-colored icing, surmounted by confectionary bows—together with a plaque containing birthday greetings and nine small candles to blow out. I didn't think I would dance, but I did.

The toasts were many and varied. Former president George H. W. Bush sent a greeting. Beverly Wooley, a state representative and

Marjorie's ninetieth birthday party, with children and some grandchildren. Left to right: Alan, Audrey, Jocelyn, Marjorie, Alexandra, and Leslye.

longtime associate, presented a proclamation from Texas governor Rick Perry. State representative Martha Wong read a commemorative resolution passed by the Texas House. Linda Poepsel read one of the four cards sent by Pres. George W. Bush. And my friends all gave papers, each of which will appear in an album the children are preparing. The eighty-eight guests reflected all of the various facets of my life. My cousin Pauline, age ninety-one, and Kathrine Stokes were there, too.

The forty-year friendships were represented by Nancy Crouch, Linda Dyson, Liz Ghrist, and Barbara Patton, all of whom helped build the early Republican Party and stood behind George H. W. Bush in his early years. The youngest set were my writing group, all the age of my children or younger. Both of my children made toasts. My daughter-in-law, Audrey, recounted a letter I wrote her more than twenty-five years ago. My granddaughters told stories about me. Alexandra said that, while other grandmothers were lolling about in Florida, hers was either cruising down the Amazon or observing penguins in Antarctica. Included among the guests were Marie Murray, my longtime housekeeper, and her husband, Sylvester. Marie has been with my family for almost forty years. Also present was Harold Brown and his wife. Harold came to us more than fifty years ago, and although he is not a part of our daily lives today, he visits whenever the children come home. He helped to rear them.

My daughter-in-law, Audrey, says that for my one-hundredth birthday we'll have a quiet dinner at home.

I suppose that if I had to draw some kind of a lesson from my life it would have to be an appreciation of having lived it. Life is a challenge and a blessing. Every day is worth cherishing.

During our Yom Kippur service we recite this poem, which with each passing year becomes more meaningful:

Birth is a beginning
And death a destination.
And life is a journey:
From childhood to maturity
And youth to age;
From innocence to knowing:
From foolishness to discretion
And then, perhaps, to wisdom;
From weakness to strength
Or strength to weakness—
And often back again;
From health to sickness
And back, we pray, to health again;
From offense to forgiveness,
From loneliness to love,
From joy to gratitude,
From pain to compassion,
And grief to understanding—
From fear to faith;
From defeat to defeat to defeat—
Until, looking backward or ahead,

We see victory lies
Not at some high place along the way,
But in having made the journey, stage by stage,
A sacred pilgrimage.
Birth is a beginning
And death a destination.
And life is a journey,
A sacred pilgrimage—
To life everlasting.

Acknowledgments

There are so many without whom I would never have finished this book.

My friend, Morris Hamm really started it all.

After hearing so many of my Yoakum stories, he insisted I write a book. He directed me to the late, great Rice professor, Venkatesh Kulkarni, who convinced me I should write a memoir using the techniques of fiction.

After the professor's untimely death, a group of his students were reluctant to forsake the writing environment so they have met for years every other Saturday in a classroom on the campus of Rice University. Kathryn Brown, Judith Finkel, Madeline Westbrook, Bob Hargrove, Elizabeth Hueben, Linda Jacobs, Karen Meinardus, and the late Joan Romans have been my friends, my mentors and in a way my inspiration.

They have critiqued my chapters with equal portions of praise and condemnation.

Friends have read a chapter here or two. Dee Coats read major portions early on.

Mention must be made of the invaluable assistance in researching oil and gas prices given me by Mr. James L. Williams of London, Arkansas.

And then, of course, my valiant editor, Babette Fraser Hale, who with infinite patience has reduced this story to its publishable length. Surely without her this endeavor would never have been brought to fruition.

Index

The initials MMA and RA are used for Marjorie Meyer Arsht and Raymond Arsht. Photos are indicated with *italic* type.

ISBN 1-58544-476-6
9 781585 444762 52995